RESTORATIVE JUSTICE: FROM THEORY TO PRACTICE

SOCIOLOGY OF CRIME, LAW AND DEVIANCE

Series Editors: Mathieu Deflem (Volumes 6–10)
Jeffrey T. Ulmer (Volumes 1–5)

Recent Volumes:

Volume 1:   Edited by Jeffrey T. Ulmer, 1998

Volume 2:   Edited by Jeffrey T. Ulmer, 2000

Volume 3:   Legal Professions: Work, Structure and
             Organization – Edited by Jerry Van Hoy, 2001

Volume 4:   Violent Acts and Violentization: Assessing,
             Applying and Developing Lonnie Athens' Theory
             and Research – Edited by Lonnie Athens and
             Jeffrey T. Ulmer, 2002

Volume 5:   Terrorism and Counter-Terrorism:
             Criminological Perspectives – Edited by Mathieu
             Deflem, 2004

Volume 6:   Ethnographies of Law and Social Control –
             Edited by Stacey Lee Burns, 2005

Volume 7:   Sociological Theory and Criminological
             Research, Views from Europe and
             United States – Edited by Mathieu Deflem, 2006

Volume 8:   Police Occupational Culture: New Debates
             and Directions – Edited by Megan O'Neill,
             Monique Marks and Anne-Marie Singh, 2007

Volume 9:   Crime and Human Rights – Edited by Stephan
             Parmentier and Elmar Weitekamp, 2007

Volume 10:   Surveillance and Governance: Crime Control and
             Beyond – Edited by Mathieu Deflem, 2008

SOCIOLOGY OF CRIME, LAW AND DEVIANCE   VOLUME 11

RESTORATIVE JUSTICE: FROM THEORY TO PRACTICE

EDITED BY

HOLLY VENTURA MILLER

University of Texas, San Antonio, USA

Emerald

JAI

United Kingdom – North America – Japan
India – Malaysia – China

JAI Press is an imprint of Emerald Group Publishing Limited
Howard House, Wagon Lane, Bingley BD16 1WA, UK

First edition 2008

British Library Cataloguing in Publication Data
A catalogue record for this book is available from the British Library

ISBN: 978-0-7623-1455-3
ISSN: 1521-6136 (Series)

Printed and bound by MPG Books Ltd, Bodmin, Cornwall

Awarded in recognition of
Emerald's production
department's adherence to
quality systems and processes
when preparing scholarly
journals for print

INVESTOR IN PEOPLE

CONTENTS

LIST OF CONTRIBUTORS   *vii*

INTRODUCTION   *ix*

PART I: CURRENT CONTEXTS IN RESTORATIVE JUSTICE

SEEKING JUSTICE IN THE 21ST CENTURY:
TOWARDS AN INTERSECTIONAL POLITICS
OF JUSTICE
  Kathleen Daly   *3*

FROM WAR TO PEACE: INFORMALISM,
RESTORATIVE JUSTICE AND CONFLICT
TRANSFORMATION IN NORTHERN IRELAND
  Graham Ellison and Peter Shirlow   *31*

THE AGENDAS OF THE RESTORATIVE JUSTICE
MOVEMENT
  Gerry Johnstone   *59*

CROSSING CULTURAL BOUNDARIES:
IMPLEMENTING RESTORATIVE JUSTICE IN
INTERNATIONAL AND INDIGENOUS CONTEXTS
  Gabrielle Maxwell   *81*

PART II: EVALUATING RESTORATIVE PROGRAMMING

EVALUATION OF A RESTORATIVE MILIEU:
RESTORATIVE PRACTICES IN CONTEXT
  Paul McCold   *99*

FAITH-BASED MENTORING AND RESTORATIVE
JUSTICE: OVERLAPPING THEORETICAL,
EMPIRICAL, AND PHILOSOPHICAL BACKGROUND
    Ronald L. Akers, Jodi Lane and Lonn Lanza-Kaduce   *139*

LOCALIZING RESTORATIVE JUSTICE: AN IN-DEPTH
LOOK AT A DENVER PUBLIC SCHOOL PROGRAM
    Wesley G. Jennings, Angela R. Gover and   *167*
    Diane M. Hitchcock

RESTORATIVE JUSTICE AND YOUTH COURTS: A
NEW APPROACH TO DELINQUENCY PREVENTION
    Holly Ventura Miller   *189*

PART III: NEW DIRECTIONS FOR RESTORATIVE JUSTICE

POWER, PROFIT, AND PLURALISM: NEW AVENUES
FOR RESEARCH ON RESTORATIVE JUSTICE AND
WHITE-COLLAR CRIME
    Nicole Leeper Piquero, Stephen K. Rice and   *209*
    Alex R. Piquero

CHALLENGING CULTURES OF VIOLENCE
THROUGH COMMUNITY RESTORATIVE JUSTICE
IN NORTHERN IRELAND
    Anna Eriksson   *231*

GETTING BEYOND THE LIBERAL FEEL-GOOD:
TOWARD AN ACCOUNTABILITY-BASED
THEORETICAL RESEARCH PROGRAM FOR
RESTORATIVE JUSTICE
    J. Mitchell Miller, Christopher L. Gibson and John Byrd   *261*

SUBJECT INDEX   *279*

LIST OF CONTRIBUTORS

Ronald L. Akers

Department of Criminology, Law and Society, University of Florida, Gainesville, FL, USA

John Byrd

Department of Criminal Justice, University of Texas, San Antonio, TX, USA

Kathleen Daly

School of Criminology & Criminal Justice, Griffith University, Brisbane, Queensland, Australia

Graham Ellison

Queen's University, School of Law, Belfast, UK

Anna Eriksson

Department of Criminology, School of Political and Social Inquiry, Monash University, Melbourne, Victoria, Australia

Christopher L. Gibson

Department of Criminology, Law and Society, University of Florida, Gainesville, FL, USA

Angela R. Gover

School of Public Affairs, University of Colorado at Denver, Denver, Colorado, USA

Diane M. Hitchcock

School of Public Affairs, University of Colorado at Denver, Denver, Colorado, USA

Wesley G. Jennings

Department of Justice Administration, University of Louisville, Louisville, Kentucky, USA

Gerry Johnstone   School of Law, University of Hull, Hull,
                               UK

Jodi Lane   Department of Criminology, Law and
                               Society, University of Florida,
                               Gainesville, FL, USA

Lonn Lanza-Kaduce   Department of Criminology, Law and
                               Society, University of Florida,
                               Gainesville, FL, USA

Gabrielle Maxwell   Institute of Criminology, Victoria
                               University of Wellington, Wellington,
                               New Zealand

Paul McCold   International Institute for Restorative
                               Practices, Bethlehem, PA, USA

Holly Ventura Miller   Department of Criminal Justice,
                               University of Texas, San Antonio, TX,
                               USA

J. Mitchell Miller   Department of Criminal Justice,
                               University of Texas, San Antonio, TX,
                               USA

Alex R. Piquero   Department of Criminology & Criminal
                               Justice, University of Maryland,
                               College Park, MD, USA

Nicole Leeper Piquero   L. Douglas Wilder School of
                               Government and Public Affairs,
                               Virginia Commonwealth University,
                               Richmond, VA, USA

Stephen K. Rice   Department of Criminal Justice, Seattle
                               University, Seattle, WA, USA

Peter Shirlow   Queen's University, School of Law,
                               Belfast, UK

INTRODUCTION

Restorative justice has transitioned from a peripheral theory of social control to a staple of mainstream sociological criminology in recent years. With an emphasis on reparation and reintegration, restorative programs and practices have become attractive alternatives to a criminal justice system characterized by punitiveness and marred by ineffectiveness. While typically discussed in the context of real-life criminal justice practice, the sociological roots of this movement are robust. Though the idea of restoration as justice is not particularly new, nor is it necessarily sociological, the theoretical basis is solidly grounded in both classical and contemporary sociology. Restorative justice draws heavily from both functionalist and symbolic interactionist paradigms and relies on the conceptual fusion of several leading criminological theories.

Currently one of the most popular alternatives to traditional adjudication, restorative justice is traceable to ancient approaches to indigenous forms of justice (Zehr, 1990). The restorative approach to crime and justice gained impetus in the 1970s and 1980s from the victims' rights movement, experiences with reparative sanctioning and processes, and the rise of informal neighborhood justice and dispute resolution programs (Galaway & Hudson, 1990; Schneider, 1985). The attraction of a restorative-based approach today is due in large part to the overwhelming empirical evidence produced by criminologists in recent decades suggesting that traditional criminal and juvenile justice methods are ineffective at best, and counterproductive at worst.

Restorative justice, as opposed to traditional criminal justice, is based on several values and assumptions, the foremost of which is that all concerned parties should be included in the response to crime – offenders, victims, and the community. This is based on the belief that crime is fundamentally an offense against another person or the community and secondly an act in violation of the law (Braithwaite, 1999; Crawford & Newburn, 2003; Johnstone, 2002). Crime is the result of severed or damaged social bonds between individuals or between offenders and the larger community. These bonds must be repaired in order for victim reparation and offender reintegration. Consequently, crime control lies primarily in the hands of the community, not the criminal justice system. This proposition remains consistent with the greater effectiveness of informal social control mechanisms in general as compared to formal methods.

A second proposition of the restorative approach, which differs significantly from criminal justice, is offender accountability. Whereas accountability is generally conceptualized as the mere receiving of punishment in the traditional system, the restorative philosophy defines it as assuming responsibility and taking action to repair harm (Bazemore & Schiff, 2005; Dingan, 1990; Galaway & Hudson, 1990; Roche, 2004). Other than appearing before court and either pleading guilty (typically arrived at through plea bargaining) or being found guilty at trial, offenders are not required to take actual responsibility for their actions. Restorative justice, conversely, mandates such responsibility and requires reparation, monetary or symbolic, on the part of offenders. To fully restore bonds severed by criminal offending, interaction between offenders and victims is necessary.

Traditional and restorative approaches also differ on the worthiness of punishment. Classical deterrence theory suggests that punishment can both deter crime and change offenders' behavior if applied with certainty and celerity. Although research has been inconclusive as to the viability of a deterrence-based approach, generally speaking, recidivism rates between 60 and 70 percent fail to offer overwhelming support for the success of criminal justice in its present form. Restorative justice proponents contend punishment alone is not effective in changing behavior and, moreover, is disruptive to community harmony and relationships. For restorative programming, the purpose of punishment is not to deliver "just deserts" but rather presents an opportunity to instill offender accountability, offer victims reparation and reconciliation, and rehabilitate offenders through treatment and competency development (Schneider, 1985; Umbreit, 1999; Zehr, 1990).

The focus of response also varies between criminal and restorative justice, specifically in terms of what is temporally emphasized. In a retributive model of justice, responses focus on offenders' past behavior while restorative models focus on the harmful consequences of offenders' behavior while placing emphasis on the future. In particular, restorative approaches ask what can be done in the future to repair current harm and prevent further victimization? By separating the behavior from the offender, the process becomes less antagonistic and adversarial thereby allowing offenders to recognize the consequences of their behavior without a sense of being attacked by the system. Additionally, by focusing on consequences of behavior as compared to the behavior itself, victims necessarily become a focal concern in case disposition (Strang & Braithwaite, 2001; Umbreit & Coates, 1992).

Contrary to traditional criminal justice, victims' rights are embraced within the restorative framework. Whereas "victims' rights" are little more than an abstraction in criminal justice, victims are central actors in programs rooted in a restorative philosophy (Crawford, 1996; Johnstone, 2002; Umbreit, 1999). Despite the efforts of the victims' rights movement over the past three decades, victims still remain on the periphery of mainstream criminal justice. Conversely, restorative practices are committed to victim participation in addressing crime and delinquency. Because the emphasis centers on dialogue and reparation it is impossible to effectively deal with offending without the participation of victims. For this reason, many victims report greater satisfaction with case resolution in restorative program than in traditional adjudication (Braithwaite, 1999).

Ultimately, the restorative justice model provides the basis for reconciling the interests of victims, offenders, and the community through common programs and supervision practices that meet the mutual needs of all concerned stakeholders. However, while representing a clear alternative to retributive justice, the question remains as to its ability to consistently produce more favorable outcomes. Specifically, does restorative justice effect lower recidivism, greater offender accountability, greater victim and offender satisfaction, increased public safety, and offender reintegration?

THE CURRENT VOLUME

This volume, "Restorative Justice: From Theory to Practice", pays homage to the sociological foundations of the movement and explores the practical side of theoretical application. Contributions are from a range of leading theorists and methodologists whose primary interests lie in the development and advancement of restorative justice. These scholars offer diverse, cross-cultural perspectives which are particularly important given the major contributions to this area from outside of the United States. The popularity and implementation of restorative justice practices abroad necessitates the participation of such scholars and adds to the diversity and quality of the volume. The following chapters focus on theoretical advancement, methodological refinements, practical issues, or combinations of such.

The volume is comprised of three parts: Part I explores current contexts in restorative justice; Part II contains chapters examining the practical side of restorative justice with evaluation research as the primary focus; and

Part III looks to the future of the movement and details new directions for restorative justice. Contributions are diverse and topics are wide-ranging; from reconciliation in Northern Ireland to faith-based mentoring in Florida, this volume covers a multitude of issues both in the United States and abroad. Restorative justice researchers will find this volume to be a rich source of current theoretical and methodological advances within the restorative framework.

The volume begins with a chapter written by renowned scholar Kathleen Daly who examines the "politics of justice" within the restorative framework; Part I also includes contributions from key figures in the restorative justice movement including Graham Ellison (chapter "From War to Peace: Informalism, Restorative Justice and Conflict Transformation in Northern Ireland"), Gerry Johnstone (chapter "The Agendas of the Restorative Justice Movement"), and Gabrielle Maxwell (chapter "Crossing Cultural Boundaries: Implementing Restorative Justice in International and Indigenous Contexts"). Part II focuses on the application of restorative justice with chapters authored by one of the leading American restorative justice researchers Paul McCold (chapter "Evaluation of a Restorative Milieu: Restorative Practices in Context"), and prominent sociologist Ronald Akers (chapter "Faith-Based Mentoring and Restorative Justice: Overlapping Theoretical, Empirical, and Philosophical Background"), among others. Topics range from faith-based mentoring (chapter "Faith-Based Mentoring and Restorative Justice: Overlapping Theoretical, Empirical, and Philosophical Background") to school-based restorative justice initiatives (chapter "Localizing Restorative Justice: An In-Depth Look at a Denver Public School Program") to youth courts (chapter "The South Carolina Youth Court Initiative for Delinquency Reduction: Findings from a Statewide Evaluation").

Part III concludes with new directions for the restorative justice movement including a chapter authored by Nicole Leeper Piquero, Stephen Rice, and Alex Piquero who examine the viability of restorative justice in the context of white-collar crime (chapter "Power, Profit and Pluralism: New Avenues for Research on Restorative Justice and White-Collar Crime"). Chapter "Challenging Cultures of Violence Through Community Restorative Justice in Northern Ireland" takes us to the United Kingdom as Anna Eriksson analyzes the ability of community-based restorative justice to challenge cultures of violence in Northern Ireland. The volume concludes with a contribution from J. Mitchell Miller who challenges the rapid spread of restorative programming *sans* an accountability-based framework and draws attention to the danger of implementation without intensity.

REFERENCES

Bazemore, G., & Schiff, M. (2005). *Juvenile justice reform and restorative justice: Building theory and policy from practice.* Portland, OR: Willan Publishing.

Braithwaite, J. (1999). Restorative justice: Assessing optimistic and pessimistic accounts. In: M. Tonry (Ed.), *Crime and justice, a review of research* (Vol. 25, pp. 1–127). Chicago: University of Chicago Press.

Crawford, A. (1996). Victim/offender Mediation and Reparation in Comparative European Cultures: France, England and Wales. Paper presented at the Australian and New Zealand Society of Criminology Conference, Wellington, January/February.

Crawford, A., & Newburn, T. (2003). *Youth offending and restorative justice: Implementing reform in youth justice.* Portland, OR: Willan Publishing.

Dingan, J. (1990). Repairing the damage: Can reparation work in the service of diversion? *British Journal of Criminology, 32,* 453–472.

Galaway, B., & Hudson, J. (Eds). (1990). *Criminal justice, restitution and reconciliation.* Massey, NY: Criminal Justice Press.

Johnstone, G. (2002). *Restorative justice: Ideas, values, debates.* Portland, OR: Willan Publishing.

Roche, D. (2004). *Accountability in restorative justice.* Oxford, UK: Oxford University Press.

Schneider, A. (1985). *Deterrence and juvenile crime: Results from a national policy experiment.* New York: Springer-Verlag.

Strang, H., & Braithwaite, J. (Eds). (2001). *Restorative justice and civil society.* Cambridge, UK: Cambridge University Press.

Umbreit, M. (1999). Restorative justice through juvenile victim-offender mediation. In: G. Bazemore & L. Walgrave (Eds), *Restorative juvenile justice: Repairing the harm of youth crime.* Monsey, NY: Criminal Justice Press.

Umbreit, M., & Coates, R. B. (1992). *Victim-offender mediation: An analysis of programs in four states of the US.* Minneapolis: Citizens Council Mediation Services.

Zehr, H. (1990). *Changing lenses: A new focus for criminal justice.* Scottsdale, PA: Herald Press.

Holly Ventura Miller
Editor

PART I:
CURRENT CONTEXTS IN
RESTORATIVE JUSTICE

SEEKING JUSTICE IN THE 21ST CENTURY: TOWARDS AN INTERSECTIONAL POLITICS OF JUSTICE

Kathleen Daly

ABSTRACT

After setting the political and personal contexts, defining key terms, and comparing Indigenous and restorative justice, I clarify three interrelated sites of contestation between and among feminist and anti-racist groups as these relate to alternative justice practices. They are the inequality caused by crime (victims and offenders), social divisions (race and gender politics), and individuals and collectivities (rights of offenders and victims). I outline an intersectional politics of justice, which seeks to address the conflicts at each site. My intersectional framework attempts to align victims' and offenders' interests in ways that are not a zero sum game, and to find common ground between feminist and anti-racist justice claims by identifying the negotiating moves each must make. It proposes that victims and offenders have positive rights that are not compromised by collectivities.

Restorative Justice: From Theory to Practice
Sociology of Crime, Law and Deviance, Volume 11, 3–30
ISSN: 1521-6136/doi:10.1016/S1521-6136(08)00401-6

Since 1978, as a student and academic, I have been interested in the relationship of inequalities to crime and justice, and in alternative ways of doing justice. My research began with studies of gender, crime, and sentencing; and in the mid-1980s, I started to read and write on the race and gender politics of crime and justice. In the mid-1990s, I moved from the United States to Australia to see and understand the emerging idea of restorative justice. In 2001, I began to study new forms of Indigenous justice. In this chapter, I discuss what I have learned, and I attempt to mediate conflicts that have emerged between feminist and anti-racist groups in seeking justice.[1] My chapter has three parts. After setting the context and defining key terms, I present and compare two innovative justice practices: restorative justice and Indigenous justice. Next, I clarify three interrelated sites of contestation between and among feminist and anti-racist groups as they relate to restorative and Indigenous justice. Finally, I outline a way forward by sketching an intersectional politics of justice.

For simplicity, my essay characterizes justice practices and their politics in simple terms, and often by using dichotomies. These are analytical short cuts, which may help us to make sense of complexity and difference; but when we scratch the surface, the dichotomies often fail us. One such dichotomy is victim and offender. We know that among offenders, there are many indications of victimization and trauma. Likewise, among victims, there are also offenders. These blurred boundaries of victimization and offending are well documented in research on males' and females' pathways to crime; in profiles of prisoners; and in reports on violence in educational and social welfare institutions. An intersectional politics of justice should be actively engaged in breaking down dichotomies and crossing boundaries. At the same time, I suggest that the inequality between a victim and offender that is caused by crime is a dichotomy that must be explicitly recognized and redressed in some way.[2]

SETTING THE POLITICAL CONTEXT

Over the past two decades in nations such as the United States, Canada, Great Britain, Australia, New Zealand, and many European countries, the response to crime is moving in different directions. One tack is innovative: it promises to break out of established forms of criminal justice, to do justice differently. The other tack is repetitive: it promises to intensify established forms of criminal justice, to do justice more efficiently (the neo-liberal strand), and often, more punitively (the neo-conservative strand)

(O'Malley, 1999). As many have observed (e.g., Garland, 1996, 2001; O'Malley, 1999), a major problem for government is managing these contrary and volatile trends. My essay focuses on developments in the innovative strand.

Starting in the 1960s, a variety of social movements called for the transformation of criminal justice. One set of critiques came from victims, and a second, from offenders. Victims said they were forgotten in the criminal process. They felt that they, not the defendants, were on trial. They wanted vindication and validation, but this did not occur. For some, this translated into demands for new criminal laws and procedures that made it easier to prosecute and punish crime, and for others, into more services and support for victims. Offenders said too many people were arrested and incarcerated, often on trivial matters. For certain groups, especially racialized groups, the criminal justice system was harmful and oppressive. This translated into demands for less criminalization, less use of custody, and for more alternatives to established criminal justice (Daly & Immarigeon, 1998).

In the late 1970s and early 1980s, and partly in response to these critiques, established criminal justice began to devolve and fragment, with the introduction of informal justice, neighborhood dispute centers, and mediation (e.g., Abel, 1982; Harrington, 1985). This activity intensified in the early to mid-1990s, with the rise of restorative justice (Daly & Immarigeon, 1998) and a variety of Indigenous justice practices in Canada (Green, 1998), the United States (Yazzie & Zion, 1996), and Australia (Marchetti & Daly, 2004, 2007). During the 1990s, specialist and problem-oriented courts (such as the drug court and the domestic violence court), often, but not always, guided by therapeutic jurisprudence, were introduced in the United States (Wexler, 1990). These courts evolved and spread rapidly to other countries (Freiberg, 2001, 2005; Winnick & Wexler, 2003). New forms of international criminal justice have been and are being created (Charlesworth & Chinkin, 2000; Roberts, 2003), including new forms of transitional justice (Bell & Campbell, 2004; Chinkin & Charlesworth, 2006; Hesse & Post, 1999; Rubio-Marin, 2006).

Justice has exploded: it is operating under many new guises than ever before. Although it is tempting to suggest that these diverse developments are guided by overarching principles of restorative justice (Sullivan & Tifft, 2006) or therapeutic jurisprudence (Winnick & Wexler, 2003), my view is that we should recognize the specific contexts and politics of justice aspirations and practices. At the same time and despite particularity, there are shared elements and affinities across diverse practices (Marchetti &

Daly, 2007). This theme is developed when comparing restorative justice and Indigenous justice.

THE PERSONAL CONTEXT

My research interests in race and gender politics and in innovative justice practices are intertwined. During the mid-1980s, I became troubled by my feminist colleagues' focus on victims in the criminal process, to the exclusion of offenders (Daly, 1989). This came to a head, when in May 1992, I was invited to speak at a plenary panel at the Law & Society Annual Conference in Philadelphia on the Clarence Thomas confirmation hearings. Recall that Clarence Thomas, a black man, was nominated to the United States Supreme Court in 1991. During the Senate's hearings in October, a University of Oklahoma law professor and black woman, Anita Hill, testified that Thomas sexually harassed her over a period of time in the 1980s when he was Chair of the Equal Employment and Opportunities Commission, and she worked in his office. The exchanges between Thomas, Hill, and the senators were one of the most extraordinary events of our time: they dramatized the political cleavages and historical scars of race, gender, and sexual politics in the United States (Morrison, 1992). Thomas denied Hill's allegations as groundless. Critics accused Hill of being disloyal to her race, of trying to bring down a black man. In my plenary address, I asked: "If Thomas admitted he harassed Hill, and if he admitted this in ways you found sincere, and if he apologized for what he did and said he would make amends, what would have been your response? Would his admissions, apology, and efforts to make amends have been sufficient, ... or would you want more of a sanction" (Daly, 1992). My remarks caused some controversy. I appeared to have broken with feminist convention, which at the time was concerned with strengthening formal legal approaches to violence against women, not with alternative justice forms.

My Australian colleague John Braithwaite heard the paper, and some months later, in February 1993, he sent me a manuscript for comment. It was on the topic of family group conferencing in a place called Wagga Wagga, New South Wales. He said that conferencing (which would later be branded restorative justice) had benefits for both victims and offenders in cases of sexual and family violence. Sitting at my dining room table in Ann Arbor, Michigan, I vividly remember reading about conferencing practices with interest and excitement. We went on to co-author the paper (Braithwaite & Daly, 1994), and it was the start of my journey to Australia in 1995.

RACE AND GENDER POLITICS OF JUSTICE

The term "race and gender politics of justice," as I use it, encapsulates the different emphases that Indigenous (or racialized political minority groups) and feminist groups take in seeking justice. In general, Indigenous groups emphasize offenders' interests; feminist groups, victims' interests. This dichotomy shows the fault lines in Indigenous and feminist politics; and as one would expect, the politics are not that simple. There is growing interest in intersectional race and gender politics, which aim to negotiate differing Indigenous and feminist interests in seeking justice.

Intersectional thinking is recent, evolving, and applied in varied ways. It is used *empirically* to represent the multiple and shifting identities of people (e.g., Maher, 1997; see also McCall, 2005) and *politically* and *analytically* to critique categorical thinking in law, social theory, and social movement groups (Crenshaw, 1989, 1991; Marchetti, 2008). I use the term in the latter sense to address the conflicting interests of victims and offenders, social movement groups, and individuals and collectivities in responding to crime.

Intersections of race and gender was introduced by Kimberle Crenshaw to challenge the ways in which race and gender were used in law, and in feminist and anti-racist theories and social movements. For example, in law, when filing an anti-discrimination legal claim, one could lodge a complaint as a female or as a black person, but not as a black female. A female was presumptively white; a black, presumptively male. For theory, Crenshaw (1991, p. 1243) said that "feminist and anti-racist discourses failed to consider intersectional identities such as women of color." At the time, feminist theories were principally about gender; and anti-racist theories were about colonialization, culture, and race-ethnicity. Moreover, neither feminist nor anti-racist social movements represented the interests of racialized women (Huggins, 1994; Moreton-Robinson, 2000).

Like other racialized women, Crenshaw pointed out that "black women are marginalized in feminist politics as a consequence of race, and they are marginalized in anti-racist politics as a consequence of gender." However, she added a new dimension by saying that "black women do not share the burdens of these elisions alone:"

> When feminism does not explicitly oppose racism, and when antiracism does not [oppose] patriarchy, race and gender politics often end up being antagonistic to each other and both interests lose. (Crenshaw, 1992, p. 405)

Crenshaw's point is crucial to my thinking. If we want to do justice differently, we must find ways to align race and gender justice politics, and not permit the antagonisms to stall a more constructive and progressive agenda. An intersectional politics of justice may be a way to achieve this goal.

Currently, and depending on the jurisdiction, race and gender politics are often antagonistic. The negative effect is most deeply felt on racialized women, for whom seeking justice poses major dilemmas. For example, critics of Indigenous women's organizations say they are too closely aligned with feminist interests (or what is termed women's or *individual rights*), not with the *collective interests* or rights of Aboriginal people. In response, Indigenous women say they are being asked (unfairly) to put community interests ahead of their interests as women. Relating this to criminal justice, Emma LaRocque (1997, p. 81), a Canadian Indigenous woman, says "it remains a puzzle how offenders, more often than victims, have come to represent 'collective rights'." She argues that in the interests of "social harmony, ... the pendulum has swung way too far to the advantage of [offenders] within Native communities."

A related concern is that reputedly "cultural" arguments are used against Indigenous women (Razack, 1994, 1998).[3] More than 15 years ago, Audrey Bolger (1991, p. 50) and Sharon Payne (1992, pp. 37–38) called attention to "bullshit traditional violence" and "bullshit law," respectively, in Australia. Described by an Aboriginal woman in the Northern Territory as one of three kinds of violence in Aboriginal society (the others were alcoholic violence and traditional violence), "bullshit traditional violence" refers to men's assaults of women, usually when they are drunk, which are justified as a "traditional right." Payne noted a similar phenomenon, but used different categories:

> Aboriginal women are saying that they are being subjected to three types of laws. ... white man's law, traditional law, and bullshit law. The latter [is] being used to explain a distortion of traditional law [that justifies] assault and rape of women ... These types of [cultural] defenses [set a dangerous precedent], and they denigrate Aboriginal men and Aboriginal culture.

All of the analysts above (LaRocque, Razack, Bolger, and Payne) suggest that race and gender politics are highly visible and most contested in cases of family and sexual violence.

INEQUALITIES OF CRIME, SOCIAL DIVISIONS, AND JUSTICE

Among several puzzles of justice, one that provokes me is whether it is possible to do justice, including alternative forms, in an unequal (and, many would say an unjust) society. There are, in fact, two types of inequality to consider. First, a criminal act itself creates an inequality between an offender and victim. An offender has, in some way, harmed or hurt another, or claimed a position of superiority over another. As Hampton (1998, pp. 38–39) puts it, an offender has said, "I am up here, and you are down there, so I can use you for my purposes." Justice means redressing that inequality and expressing the "victim's equal value" (p. 39). Second, these individual acts called crime take place in, and some would argue are partly caused by, societies marked by inequality and histories of state violence. Can justice truly be achieved in this societal context? Probably not, especially when we appreciate that criminal law and established forms of criminal justice reproduce and amplify social inequalities, not reduce them.

Established (or standard) criminal justice attempts to respond to the first kind of inequality, the one caused by crime itself, although it does so poorly. New justice practices[4] may offer some improvement. They may also be able to relate an individual criminal act to a broader set of community or societal relations. However, we should not expect new justice practices alone to achieve social justice. Striving for this achievement will require other major societal commitments and policies.

Sketched more fully below, an intersectional politics of justice has three parts: it aims to respond to the first kind of inequality by aligning victims' and offenders' interests in ways that are not a zero sum game; it attempts to find common ground between feminist and anti-racist justice claims by identifying the negotiating moves each must make; and it proposes that victims and offenders have positive rights that are not compromised by collectivities.

INDIGENOUS JUSTICE AND RESTORATIVE JUSTICE

Many restorative justice advocates say, wrongly in my view (Daly, 2002, pp. 61–64), that the modern practice of restorative justice *is* an Indigenous justice form. Their claims gloss over the histories and particularities of Indigenous social organization before and after colonial conquest. Moreover, "culture" is wrongly depicted in romantic and static terms, as if it were frozen in time (see also Blagg, 1997; Cunneen, 2003). From the point of view of *process*, there are overlaps between restorative justice and Indigenous justice practices. There are also points of difference, in particular, the role of politics and political aspirations. In the following discussion, I give greater attention to Indigenous justice because few readers are likely to be aware of recent developments, especially by comparison to restorative justice.[5]

Indigenous Justice

As others and I use the term, Indigenous justice refers to modern practices that have emerged in the past 10–20 years in North America and Australia. These practices do not use customary law; rather, with some exceptions, they work within a "white" state's criminal laws and procedures.[6] Indigenous justice refers to a variety of justice practices, normally focused on sentencing, in which Indigenous people have a central role in responding to crime. They include urban sentencing courts, community justice groups' advice to judges in sentencing, Elders' participation in sentencing, and a variety of forms and contexts of sentencing circles. Indigenous justice can be seen as a way to rebuild Indigenous communities and to redress the destruction of Indigenous peoples' culture and social organization brought about by colonialism and state violence (Marchetti & Daly, 2004, 2007).

Indigenous justice practices can be arrayed on a continuum. At one end are practices, such as the Navajo Nation's Peacemaking Division in the United States, which has been developed from within the Navajo Nation, with entry into peacemaking courts by the Navajo police (Coker, 2006). Courts like this are rare: the Navajo Nation has a semi-sovereign relationship with the United States federal government in ways that do not exist for Indigenous peoples in Australia, New Zealand, or Canada. At the other end of the continuum are practices in which Indigenous groups or communities have "input" into sentencing decisions, but these decisions are largely imposed by "white justice." At this extreme of the continuum, the practices may more accurately be termed a form of restorative justice. I agree with Canadian lawyer Jonathan Rudin (2005, p. 99), who says that unless Indigenous people "are given some options and opportunities to develop processes that respond to the needs of that community," the practices should not be termed Indigenous justice. He suggests, for example, that sentencing circles, which are "judge-made and judge-led initiatives," should be termed restorative justice, not Indigenous justice. Rudin is referring to Canadian circle sentencing, which began in the late 1980s and early 1990s, pioneered by judges (especially Judge Barry Stuart) while traveling on circuit to remote areas, although it has since "fall[en] out of favor with the courts" (p. 97) and diminished in use. Although circles may be used less often now in Canada, they were imported, albeit in a highly modified manner into Australia in the late 1990s.

Compared to North America and New Zealand, Australia has the most well developed repertoire of Indigenous justice practices. Although Indigenous participation in sentencing has occurred informally in remote Australian communities for several decades, formalization of these practices began in the late 1990s, both in urban and remote areas. Today, all but one state (Tasmania) has established some type of Indigenous justice practice (see Marchetti & Daly, 2007). To simplify my discussion, I focus on Indigenous sentencing courts, not on all Indigenous justice practices.

To be eligible, an offender must be Indigenous (or in some courts, Indigenous or South Sea Islander) and have entered a guilty plea or have been found guilty. The charge is normally heard in a Magistrates' or Local Court (analogous to a misdemeanor or less serious felony court in the United States); the offence occurred in the geographical area covered by the court; and although there is lay participation, a judicial officer retains the ultimate power in sentencing. During the sentencing process, the judicial officer typically sits at eye-level with the offender, usually at a bar table or in a circle rather than on an elevated bench. Although both a prosecutor and defense attorney are present, their professional role shifts to accommodate a greater degree of interaction between a defendant, his or her supporters, the Elders, other service providers or community members, and a judicial officer. This contrasts with the mainstream court, where the interaction is normally between a judicial officer and an offender's legal representative. Most, but not all Indigenous sentencing courts, do not allow sexual or family violence offences to be heard, among other types of exclusions (see detail in Marchetti & Daly, 2007, pp. 421–422).

A key feature of the courts is the involvement of Elders and the impact they can have on an offender's attitude and behavior. All the courts involve Elders or Respected Persons, but their role and degree of participation varies greatly: it may include advising the judicial officer, talking to and interacting directly with an offender, and taking a support or monitoring role post-sentence. The Elders' participation is one mechanism by which the sentencing process can be made more culturally appropriate. Ideally, a positive impact occurs when an Elder has an existing relationship with an offender and when the offender comes to understand that they have "committed an offence not only against the white law but also against the values of the [Indigenous] community" (Harris, 2004, p. 73). In this way the application of white law is inflected by Indigenous knowledge and cultural respect.

A colleague and I have been researching Australian Indigenous justice practices since 2001. We find that the courts encourage a more open and honest level of communication between the offender and magistrate; place greater reliance on Indigenous knowledge in the sentencing process that includes informal modes of social control both inside and outside the courtroom; and may fashion more appropriate penalties that are better suited to the offender's situation (Marchetti & Daly, 2004). They may have longer-term effects, such as strengthening Indigenous communities by re-establishing the authority of Elders. However, we note that without appropriate services or programs that would benefit an offender in a particular community post-sentence, there is little scope for these courts to impose more effective penalties.

Today, in Australia, there are over 30 sentencing courts operating. In some jurisdictions (Victoria, New South Wales, and more recently, Queensland), the courts receive substantial state funding, largely to pay for an Indigenous staff officer and to support Elders' time and transport. Although Indigenous sentencing courts began in the adult jurisdiction in 1999, youth courts are now being established, and there is interest to extend the idea to more serious offences in the District Court jurisdiction.[7]

Restorative Justice

Restorative justice encompasses diverse practices at different stages of the criminal process, including *diversion* from court prosecution, actions taken *in parallel* with court decisions, and meeting between victims and offenders *at any stage* of the criminal process (e.g., arrest, pre-sentencing, and prison release) (for discussion of problems of definition, see Johnstone, 2003; Johnstone & van Ness, 2007). It can be used by all agencies of criminal justice (police, courts, and corrections). It is also used in non-criminal decision-making contexts such as child protection and school discipline. It is sometimes associated with the resolution of broad political conflict (such as South Africa's Truth and Reconciliation Commission), although transitional justice may be the more appropriate term. Although definitions vary, a popular one, proposed by Tony Marshall (2003, p. 28) is a "process whereby parties with a stake in a specific offence resolve collectively how to deal with the aftermath of the offence and its implications for the future."

The practices associated with restorative justice include conferences, circles, and sentencing circles. (As practiced in Australia, circles are better viewed as a type of Indigenous sentencing court.) The common elements of restorative justice are an informal process; a dialogic encounter among lay (not legal) actors, including offenders, victims, and their supporters; an emphasis on victims describing how the crime has affected them and offenders taking responsibility for their acts; and consensual decision-making in deciding a penalty, which is normally centered on "repairing the harm" caused by the crime.

Comparing Restorative Justice and Indigenous Sentencing Courts

At a general level, there are similarities between restorative justice and Indigenous sentencing courts[8] in that both

- *require an admission* to offending (or in some jurisdictions, an offender choosing "not to deny" an offence);
- *rely on lay actors* (for restorative justice, victims and their supporters, an offender's supporters, and other community members; for Indigenous justice, an offender's supporters, Elders, and other members of the Indigenous community); and
- assume that incarceration is a penalty of last resort.

In addition, both emphasize the need for

- *improved communication* between legal authorities, offenders, victims, and community members, using plain language and reducing some legal formalities;
- *procedural justice*, i.e., treating people with respect, listening to what people have to say, and being fair to everyone; and
- *persuasion and support* to encourage offenders to be law-abiding.

However, there are significant differences in the qualities of "doing justice" and in justice aspirations. For restorative justice, the focus of the interaction and relationship building is between offenders, victims, their supporters, community members, and "the community" (a non-racially specified community),[9] along with professionals such as a police officer and coordinator. For Indigenous sentencing courts, the focus is between offenders, their supporters, Elders, the Indigenous community (including service providers), and "white justice" (typically, embodied in the legal roles of the magistrate, prosecutor, and defense attorney).[10] Doing justice in a restorative process gives attention to victims and to re-building relationships between a victim, an offender, and their community; whereas doing justice in Indigenous sentencing courts gives attention to changing relationships between white justice and Indigenous people, including the offender. Relatively less attention is currently given to addressing the needs of victims in Indigenous sentencing courts, although this may change (Marchetti & Daly, 2007).

For justice aspirations, restorative justice focuses on holding offenders accountable for crime, attempting to repair harms to a victim (or a community), and engaging a process where mutual recognition of both victims and offenders can be facilitated. Its political aspirations are limited to changing justice practices to become more reintegrative and negotiated, to changing individual offenders, and to assisting individual victims. Indigenous sentencing courts have broader and more explicit political aspirations for social change in group relations: to make the court more culturally appropriate (and by implication to break down the whiteness of law and procedure, and to inject it with Indigenous knowledge and values) and to develop greater trust between Indigenous people and dominant white systems of regulation. These elements may, in time, contribute to changing white justice, transforming relations between white justice and Indigenous people, rebuilding Indigenous communities, and ultimately changing the character of race relations (Marchetti & Daly, 2007).

SITES OF CONTESTATION

For several years, I have sought to clarify the different positions that feminist and anti-racist groups have taken toward justice practices (Daly, 2005; Daly & Stubbs, 2006, 2007). Here I consolidate and extend my previous work by identifying three sites of contestation. My examples focus on alternative justice practices at the penalty stage (post-plea) of the criminal process for adults.[11]

Site 1. Inequality Caused by Crime: Victims and Offenders

Addressing the inequality caused by crime is a crucial, if often overlooked, site of contested justice. The points raised in the discussion of Site 1 are relevant to all types of criminal justice processes, i.e., established, restorative, and Indigenous. However, my examples draw from restorative justice, which gives greater attention to victims.

Barbara Hudson (2003) reflects upon whether the multiple objectives of restorative justice can be achieved in one process. She asks, is it "reasonable to expect one process to 'do justice' to both victims and offenders" (p. 177). In doing justice, Hudson has in mind a dual concern with both distributive justice (equity between a victim and offender) and substantive justice (responsiveness to the individual needs of a victim and offender). For distributive justice, she is concerned that restorative justice practices may tip the scales more toward a victim's rights than an offender's: "there is no guarantee that victim interests in adequate reparation can be equitably balanced with offender interests in impositions that do not exceed proportionality to culpability" (p. 188). She suggests further that established criminal justice "admits to the impossibility of this balancing" and attempts to '"do justice' to victims and offenders in separate processes" (p. 188). For Hudson, the heart of the contestation lies in assuming a '"zero sum' approach to victims and offenders, which sees rights for one being at the expense of concern for the other" (p. 178). For substantive justice, Hudson outlines the potential power of restorative justice processes in both the telling of stories and listening to them: "the hearing is at least as important as the saying. The telling of the harm suffered and of the reasons for the offence must make the victim and offender real to each other, if the harm and its causes and circumstances are to be acknowledged as real" (p. 180). Despite this, "there is no guarantee that [an offender and victim] will agree on the version or meaning of events" (p. 184). What is innovative about restorative justice is not that a victim's perspective is presented, but rather that the intention in doing so is "to change the offender's perspective" (p. 184).

Hudson's analysis brings into relief the difficulties of moving beyond a zero sum approach to justice in one process. She is particularly concerned with how offenders may "lose" in restorative practices that do not have a "positive rights" stance for offenders (p. 193).[12] Her views are at odds with those of Annalise Acorn (2004), who is concerned that victims will "lose" in restorative practices. For example, Acorn suggests that restorative justice meetings may give victims an "opportunity ... to vent or blow off steam" toward an offender, but they do not "validate or legitimate the victim's desire to see the perpetrator suffer" (2004, p. 53). Moreover, she believes that offenders are likely to receive more compassion than victims in restorative justice meetings, and that victims themselves may minimize their own need for compassion.

Whereas Hudson is interested in *balancing rights* for offenders and victims, Acorn is interested in "*counterbalancing pain* for the wrongdoer" (p. 47). Whereas Hudson is concerned with introducing safeguards against punishments that may be excessive, Acorn is concerned that punishments may only weakly express a victim's interests to see an offender suffer. Whereas Hudson sees restorative justice as "privileg[ing] the victim's perspective," Acorn believes that victims are not privileged, but used. Their contrasting views reveal an antinomy at the heart of the criminal process: each begins an analysis from the positional interests of an offender or a victim, and it is through the lens of an offender or a victim that the unfolding justice interactions are imagined.

To be fair to Hudson, she does shift positions from the lens of offender to victim and back, and she compares victims and offenders in established justice and restorative justice contexts. In so doing, she offers several ways forward. First, she emphasizes the importance of offenders recognizing "the victim as a real individual .... as real to the offender as those who encourage ... his offending" .(pp. 180–181), alongside a parallel process of the offender being "revealed as a real person to the victim" (p. 181). Second, she believes that by ensuring a balance of rights of offenders and victims, we may move beyond a zero sum game. Third, she considers optimal justice processes in the light of different types of victim–offender relations, those when offences are targeted at a particular victim (e.g., sexual, partner, and family violence; and racial violence) and those that are not specifically targeted. Fourth, she notes the several points of slippage and vagueness by restorative justice proponents, including the meaning of "accepting responsibility," whether more than one meeting is required, and how long "proceedings" would last. Despite procedural safeguards and an emphasis on "undominated speech" in restorative justice meetings, Hudson concludes that there is "no guarantee that a fusion of horizons can be accomplished" (p. 185).

An intersectional politics of justice must fully recognize, not elide or gloss over, the differing positional interests of victims and offenders in the criminal process. These may, may not, or may only be partially "reconciled" in a restorative justice encounter, or many encounters, perhaps running in parallel for victims and offenders. Any such reconciliation must begin with redressing the inequality caused by crime. (This is a key point that Hampton and Acorn raise, but which Hudson does not address.) Such redress may come in many forms, and I shall not consider the debates concerning individualized and just deserts responses (Hudson, 2003, p. 186). Rather, drawing on the arguments of Duff (2003, pp. 48–49), I propose that the inequality caused by crime is redressed, at least ideally, by three types of "suffering" by an offender: remorse, received censure, and making reparation to a victim. Remorse is, in my view, the most important of the three. It is a precious commodity in that it cannot be forced, induced, taken, or imposed; it is the necessary resource that makes it possible to move justice from a zero sum game. When remorse is not forthcoming (or as importantly, is perceived as such), justice is a zero sum game; a victim's anger toward an offender and desire for more suffering increase (Retzinger & Scheff, 1996), along with perhaps excessive demands for punishment. When remorse *is* forthcoming, it is possible to begin to align the interests of victims and offenders.[13]

Site 2. Social Divisions: Race and Gender Politics

The individual inequalities caused by crime take place in a wider political context, in which social divisions, structured by class, race-ethnicity, and gender (among others) form the grounds of contestation. Race and gender politics can be viewed as a group-based overlay on the positional interests of offenders and victims: Indigenous (or racialized minority) groups emphasize offenders' interests; feminist groups, victims' interests. In light of relations of Indigenous (or racialized minority) groups to the state, which are grounded in distrust spawned by a history of white racism, racial prejudice, and discrimination, taking the positional interest of an offender is logical and expected. Likewise, for feminist groups, who awakened consciousness to "the problem that has no name" (sexual and physical abuse by men toward women, particularly in the home), taking the positional interest of a victim is logical and expected. The ways in which these group-based interests relate to restorative justice and Indigenous justice are best revealed by providing examples.

First, drawing from Heather Nancarrow's (2006) research in Australia, we learn why Indigenous and non-Indigenous women have differing views on the potential and pitfalls of restorative justice. In 2000, two Queensland reports – one by the Aboriginal and Torres Strait Islander Women's Taskforce on Violence (2000), and another by the Taskforce on Women and the Criminal Code (2000) – reached different conclusions about the merits of restorative justice for domestic and family violence. The first group, composed entirely of Indigenous women, saw restorative justice as a viable option; and the second, composed almost entirely of non-Indigenous women, did not. Nancarrow's research found that the two groups had different ideas of what restorative justice was and what it could achieve. Whereas the Indigenous women viewed restorative justice as a means of empowering Indigenous people, the non-Indigenous women equated restorative justice with mediation. Nancarrow found that Indigenous women's support for restorative justice stemmed from their distrust of established criminal justice and the harm it currently causes (and has caused in the past), whereas non-Indigenous women had greater trust in the system. Both groups agreed that a combination of restorative justice and established criminal justice was possible; however, the Indigenous women saw restorative justice as the primary response, with established criminal justice as the back-up, whereas the non-Indigenous women saw it just the opposite way.

In addition to showing the reasons for a racialized split in women's views on restorative justice, Nancarrow's research also reveals that when people are talking about restorative justice, they are not talking about the same thing. This is a crucial point, and one of the reasons for the contestation that arises between and among Indigenous and non-Indigenous women on alternative justice forms, more generally. If justice alternatives are viewed by Indigenous groups (including Indigenous women's groups) as activities that operate at some distance from the state or that can be "owned" by Indigenous groups, they are appealing. For non-Indigenous women, by contrast, the task is to enjoin and work with the state to take crime (in particular, violence against women) seriously; not doing so means that such crimes may be re-privatized. Also, and of equal importance, non-Indigenous women may expect that the state can carry through on an agenda of criminalization without causing further harm to them or their families. Indigenous women would be more wary of assuming positive benefits of criminalization.

Second, drawing from research in Australia and Canada on Indigenous justice practices, we see that relatively less attention is given to the role of victims in the sentencing process. The focus instead is on using Indigenous mechanisms of social control and censure to attempt to change offenders, with incarceration understood to be a measure of last resort. How or whether victims are supported, or whether, more generally justice is achieved for victims, is a significant area of contestation between men and women within Indigenous enclaves, which I consider in the discussion of Site 3. Here, we can observe a related problem when judicial officers may attempt to tailor (that is, reduce) penalties to the circumstances of male defendants, especially those who live in remote areas. In Canada, some Indigenous women observe that there appears to be a "discount" when Indigenous men rape or assault Indigenous women (see e.g., LaRocque, 1993, 1997; Nightingale, 1991; Razack, 1994). LaRocque (1997, p. 89) suggests that "in the guise of cultural sensitivity, non-Native judges and lawyers have, as a rule, sympathized with Native rapists and child molesters on cultural grounds ... " Taking a contrary view, Hollow Water (Manitoba) community member Berma Bushie (1997, p. 135) argues that "we don't believe in incarceration, [and] the reason ... is there's no healing in that place ... [and] there's no way that [offenders] can even talk about what they've done."

These examples reveal the complexity of race and gender politics, and in particular, the shifting and differing positions taken by Indigenous women on established and alternative practices. On the one hand, Indigenous women may, more than non-Indigenous women, see the value of alternative justice practices, especially when these can translate into more meaningful ways of addressing crime and community disorder. At the same time, these alternatives may appear to protect "their" men from deserved penalties or from removal from the community. Their men (especially the more powerful leaders), in turn, may form alliances with non-Indigenous judicial officers and lawyers, who align themselves with the positional interests of offenders, although this is couched in terms of community interests and culture.

Site 3. Individual Rights and Collectivities

Examples from Canada and Australia reveal the gender politics that arise in Indigenous women's relationship to "community." Site 3 is related to Site 2 in that racialized women's justice claims are often pulled more toward offenders than victims because offenders come to represent the "collectivity" of racialized group interests. It is important to recognize, however, that individual rights claims may be marshaled differently, depending on the context. One context is women's rights to bring forward experiences of violence within racialized groups or collectivities (victims' rights). A second is an offender's rights when confronting a collectivity such as the state or a community.

Gender Politics and Victims' Rights
In Australia and Canada, feminist claims for justice have been equated with women's individual rights; and anti-racist claims, with collective interests or rights of Indigenous people. What this translates to, concretely, is whether to prioritize offenders (in the interests of collective social harmony) or victims (in the interests of women's rights to safety). Paraphrasing Emma LaRocque (1997, p. 87), Indigenous women are put in "an untenable position of having to choose between gender and culture."

As documented by Marchetti (2008) for Australia, during the investigations and research that was part of the Royal Commission into Aboriginal Deaths into Custody (1991), Indigenous women put community interests ahead of "women's issues." As a consequence, their experiences and concerns with family violence were not brought forward; rather they raised "concerns such as racism in the police force, housing, employment, education, and substance abuse" (Marchetti, 2008, p. 12). They did not wish to "encourage any line of inquiry that would reflect poorly on their communities, and in particular, their Indigenous men" (p. 14).

In Canada, the debates over collective and individual rights have been sparked by the use of several Indigenous justice practices for cases of violence against women and children (Cameron, 2006). In communities in and around Hollow Water, Manitoba, a community-wide process was established in the late 1980s to address widespread problems of sexual abuse within and across families and generations. Called Community Holistic Circle Healing, it uses a "decolonization therapy" that emphasizes "cultural values" in the "healing journeys" of victims and offenders (Lajeunesse, 1996, pp. 18, 59). The process requires that an offender admit to offending and commit to a period of intensive counseling; parallel process are also set in motion to support victims. Although the Hollow Water Circle Healing process has received praise from restorative justice and Indigenous justice advocates, some Indigenous women say that community interests are given precedence over women's rights. For circle sentencing, Rashmi Goel (2000, p. 320) says that the "sentencing circle represents a significant step in the ability of Aboriginal communities to regain control over dispute resolution and justice matters. ... Success in the circle means success for the individual offender, and another step forward in recognizing Aboriginal self-government." However, this puts great pressure on Indigenous communities to "make the sentencing circle work," and in particular, to show its effects in reducing recidivism. One consequence, Goel says, is that victims' interests are silenced, especially victims of family and sexual violence: "the victim is obscured by a central focus on *the offender as a victim* of colonial society" (p. 324, emphasis added). The "circle encourages the Aboriginal woman to place her community interests ahead of her own" (p. 317) (see also Crnkovich & Addario, 2000; Stewart, Huntley, & Blaney, 2001).

Despite these problems, Goel considers the positive value of circles. They can be a forum to raise community awareness about family violence, provide community-based services, and offer women some means of redress. However, Goel believes that circles will only become meaningful and effective when women enter the circle as equals. The same point was made some time ago in the *Report of the Aboriginal Justice Inquiry of Manitoba* (1991), where as Razack (1994, p. 913) suggests, Indigenous women's "responses speak of healing and community but also speak of safety of women and of equality; they are different in a significant way from the forgiving approach [advanced by advocates of circles] because they attempt to come to terms with women's realities at the intersection of racism and sexism."

Compared to Canada, relatively less criticism has been raised by Australian Indigenous women on the ways in which male community leaders may use Indigenous sentencing practices to their advantage. Circles and other Indigenous sentencing practices are more recent in Australia than Canada; as a consequence, less is known about them and the ways in which cases are handled. Having observed recent developments, I would say that Australian Indigenous initiatives have been created with a greater degree of participation by women, and with more explicit attention to women's interests (see also Blagg, 2002). At the same time, like Indigenous Canadian women, Australian Indigenous women are in structurally ambivalent relationship to their communities and their men when responding to sexual and family violence.[14] For example, Melissa Lucashenko (1997, pp. 155–156) says that "Black women have been torn between the self-evident oppression they share with Indigenous men – oppression that fits uneasily ... into the frameworks of White feminism – and the unacceptability of those men's violent, sexist behaviors toward their families." The experience of racial oppression is shared with men; community or culture can be a refuge from racism and a source of strength in challenging a dominant white society. At the same time, because some men may hurt and harm women and children, community is not a refuge or a safe place.

A key element in understanding the complexities of race and gender politics is to observe the way in which the terms "victim" and "offender" are discursively reconfigured and mobilized. I have said that the general stance of Indigenous (or racialized minority) groups is to emphasize offenders' interests in the criminal process. At the same time, in individual cases, Indigenous defendants may deflect or minimize culpability by constituting themselves as victims of white colonization (Goel, 2000). Describing the impacts of colonization or continued forms of neo-colonial relations is not the problem. The problem instead is that when an offender makes a discursive shift from offender to victim, the actual victim is obscured. The zero sum game is played out with an offender taking the place of both offender and victim, with the actual victim having been removed (discursively) from the game.

Offenders' Rights

A second context of rights claims is when an offender faces the collectivity of the state (as victim). This is the context that Hudson (2003) has in mind in calling attention to the need to balance offender's and victim's rights in alternative justice practices. She suggests that although established criminal justice "does not necessarily afford the actual victim a hearing, it assumes the perspective of the victim" (p. 184). Further, she argues that established criminal justice "prioritizes the victim perspective in the sense that it makes the penalty relate to the harm done to victims, allowing for offender interests by the contrivance of a standard victim" (p. 186). Although restorative justice may individualize cases better than established justice, both solve "the problem of equilibrium ... by coming down clearly on one side – that of the victim" (*ibid.*).[15] Taking the positional interests of an offender, Hudson is concerned that unless offenders have "positive rights," a zero sum game will be played out, with the rights of the collective (the state or community) eclipsing those of an offender.

INTERSECTIONAL POLITICS OF JUSTICE

To address conflicts and competing interests that emerge in the sites of contestation, an intersectional politics of justice requires *resources* (offender remorse; knowledge and capacities of victims, offenders, community people; and state supports); *movement* of group-based interests to other positional interests; and *positive rights* for victims and offenders that are not compromised by collectivities. My framework is schematic, provisional, and unadorned: an intersectional politics of justice could easily become larger, more complex and sophisticated, and informed by a variety of social and political theories.

For redressing *the inequality caused by crime*, a required element that may begin to align the interests of an offender and victim is an offender's remorse. One of three types of offender "suffering" identified by Duff, remorse is the resource that shifts justice away from a zero sum game. I agree with Acorn and Duff that redressing the inequality caused by crime is achieved by a "sign" from the offender that s/he has harmed another person: it is a sign of recognition to the victim as a "real person" (as Hudson proposes) and a sign of suffering (even if this is only symbolic, as in a sincere apology). Without "real" offender remorse, neither distributive nor substantive justice can be achieved. I agree with Hudson (2003) that positive rights for victims and offenders are required, but within an intersectional justice framework, these are exercised and used as resources in Site 3.

For *social divisions*, including feminist and anti-racist social movement politics, there are numerous relationships to consider, but I shall focus on the two examples discussed above. Differences in group-based claims of Indigenous and non-Indigenous women can move toward common ground once non-Indigenous women began to recognize and take the positionality of Indigenous women.[16] What this means concretely is that non-Indigenous women need to see the state as not only invested with male interests, but also with class interests, white interests, and whiteness. It also means that non-Indigenous women appreciate the limits of criminalization and formal legality: in particular, this means that "getting tough" on offenders may translate into further harm to socially disadvantaged women. There are other related consequences of this shift in perspective as it affects service provision for victims. Finally, non-Indigenous women need to see the limits of an analysis of male violence against women that focuses solely on partner violence, not the broader set of relations and harms that are part of family violence (Kelly, 2002). Indigenous women will also need to move by becoming familiar with and strategic about the uses of formality legality. This is particularly relevant in establishing women's rights in a collectivity. Each group needs to recognize the other as having important resources (knowledge and capacity) to achieve a shared objective of a safer and more secure society for women and children.

The common ground of male interests in justifying violence against women (i.e., those of the judiciary and community leaders), which may cross boundaries of class and race, must change. Men must recognize and take the positionality of women. This is not as difficult as it seems. For some time, men have taken the positional interests of women, although in highly restricted ways by protecting or defending the honor of "their women" and children. Men need to shift from the positionality of *their* women and children, to that of all women and children.[17] At a Family Violence Forum,[18] Indigenous leader Mike Dodson made comments that showed intersectional thinking and ways forward. He said that family violence "is not just a black boy problem. White fellas are struggling, and we can learn from each other."

For *individual and collective interests*, an intersectional politics of justice assumes that victims and offenders have positive rights, which are not compromised by collectivities. This is easier said than accomplished. Gender relations, and in particular, women's subordinate position in white or racialized collectivities, is a seemingly natural condition. Invoking women's individual rights is often viewed in negative terms: as elitist (white, middle class, feminist) and as anti-male, anti-family, and anti-community. Few women would wish to identify with this string of negatives.

At the Family Violence Forum, Indigenous leader Jackie Huggins said "we are not going anywhere without our men in dealing with family violence." To "stand with our men" does not mean to be subsumed within or engulfed by a collectivity. It is an image that reflects intersectional thinking: a both/and status of standing side by side with men, i.e., as a woman and a member of a collectivity. Intersectional thinking is also apparent in Razack's (1994, p. 913) characterization of Canadian Indigenous women's interests in both "healing and community" *and* "safety of women and equality" in addressing crime and violence.

While the above examples are about the relationship of individuals as crime victims to collectivities, intersectional thinking is also required for offenders in their relationship to collectivities. Drawing from Hudson (2003), positive rights can be a resource for offenders to avoid a zero sum game between victims and offenders.

With an intersectional framework, we can see the ways in which restorative and Indigenous justice improve upon established criminal justice, and where further improvements can be made. The quality of remorse is evoked, at least ideally, when an offender and victim are "real" to each other (restorative justice) or when an offender confronts an Elder (Indigenous justice). The emphasis placed on honest communication and dialogue gives the justice process immense discursive power, which is lacking in established criminal justice (Hudson, 2003).

Indigenous justice practices are not only discursive, but they may challenge and attempt to change a white legal perspective. Blagg (2005, p. 3) terms this "constructive hybridization," and it refers to the ways in which "Aboriginal values and principles can be incorporated into the non-Aboriginal justice system." Constructive hybridization reveals intersectional thinking. However, it must include Indigenous women's interests and avoid inappropriate uses of cultural arguments. Restorative justice practices typically work within a dominant white perspective, but they could benefit by using constructive hybridization.

Indigenous justice practices can be improved by bringing the voice or perspective of the victim into the process. This is especially important so that an offender does not take up the position of offender and a victim of colonial society, which has the effect of obscuring the victim. It may also serve to break the common ground of male interests (i.e., those comprising white justice and black community leaders).

Both Indigenous and restorative justice rely on the capacities and actions of victims, offenders, and communities in responding more appropriately and meaningfully to crime. However, Hudson (2003, p. 190) calls attention to the danger of "putting too much responsibility onto victims and offenders and their 'communities of care' for crime reduction," which absolves the state of its responsibilities and obligations. In particular, the state must provide adequate resources for effective rehabilitation of offenders and for services and support for victims. This obligation stems, in part, from the state's "complicity in racist and sexist cultures" and its role in deepening "socio-economic inequities" (p. 191). The state too must begin to engage in intersectional thinking.

NOTES

1. This chapter expands upon previous work (Daly, 2005; Daly & Stubbs, 2006; Marchetti & Daly, 2007). My thanks to Brigitte Bouhours, Elena Marchetti, Heather Nancarrow, and Gitana Proietti-Scifoni for their comments on an earlier draft.
2. There are many complexities in the victim–offender relationship which I gloss over in this chapter. In actual cases, victims and offenders often depart from idealized conceptions and assumptions (see Christie, 1986; Green, 2007; Daly, 2008).
3. In her more recent work, Razack (2007) extends her discussion of women, gender, culture, and the state to debates among and between feminist, Muslim, and immigrant groups, in which contestation arises over the meanings and trade-offs of "refuge" for women in secular states and religious communities.
4. Throughout this essay, I use new, alternative, or innovative justice practices to refer to restorative justice, Indigenous justice, and other related forms.
5. Indigenous is capitalized except when it is not capitalized by others in quoted material. Community participation can be from an Elder or a Respected Person, but for simplicity, I refer to Elders. This portion of the chapter draws on material in Daly (2002), Daly, Hayes, and Marchetti (2006), and Marchetti and Daly (2007).
6. For analyses of customary law and modern forms of Indigenous justice, see Law Reform Commission of Western Australia (2006a, 2006b) and Northern Territory Law Reform Committee (2003).
7. Inevitably, when Indigenous courts are discussed in Australia, someone will ask why there are no courts for other racialized minority groups. Chris Vass, who worked with an Indigenous community in South Australia to launch the first Indigenous sentencing court in 1999, said to me, "I don't see anything wrong with the courts recognizing people from different cultures and dealing with that specific person in a slightly different way. All courts should adopt a slightly different approach so *that* person and *that* culture feel that that they're being listened to rather than coming into an alien environment" (Daly interview with C. Vass, September 28, 2001, emphasis added).
8. This section draws from Marchetti and Daly (2007), where comparisons are drawn among restorative justice, Indigenous justice, and therapeutic jurisprudence.

9. There are significant debates in the restorative justice literature over the meaning of community, which I shall not address here (see Walgrave, 2002).

10. Terms such as doing justice, white justice, whiteness, white system, white state, community, and the community are put in quotation marks when they first appear; after that, I use quotation marks for these works sparingly.

11. Among the contexts and areas I do not include are youth diversionary conferences, proposed restorative justice guilty pleas (Combs, 2007), bail procedures, and a variety of prison or pre-release meetings.

12. Hudson (2003, p. 193) defines a "positive rights agenda" as seeing "all humans has having rights which do not have to be earned, cannot be forfeited, and must be respected."

13. Following Hudson's (2003, pp. 179, 182–184) point that we must distinguish between different types of victim–offender relations in depicting optimal justice responses, and in particular, between on-going intimate violence and "one-off" incidents, my remarks have in mind the latter types of victim–offender relations. As others have emphasized (e.g., Acorn, 2004, p. 74; Stubbs, 2007), remorse and apology are part of a cycle of violence in partner abuse.

14. Of course, all racialized women in dominant white societies are likely to be in this structurally ambivalent relationship, but my analysis focuses on Indigenous women. In dominant white societies, the meaning of community for white women differs in that refuge may be sought in a variety of non-racialized communities.

15. In a structural sense, Hudson is right that the state assumes the perspective of the victim; but in practice, whether for established or restorative justice, the experience of victims is rarely of justice coming down on their side.

16. This discussion could be extended to different racial–ethnic contexts and specificities for dominant and minority groups, but I focus on Indigenous and non-Indigenous women as exemplars.

17. This needs to be done in ways that do not reinscribe the superiority of white western men, who aim to "protect" women and children from black, non-western, or Other men (see Razack, 2007).

18. The Forum was convened by the Queensland Centre for Domestic and Family Violence Research, Central Queensland University, Mackay, May 2004.

REFERENCES

Abel, R. (Ed.) (1982). *The politics of informal justice* (Vols 1 and 2). New York: Academic Press.

Aboriginal and Torres Strait Islander Women's Taskforce on Violence. (2000). *Aboriginal and Torres Strait Islander women's taskforce on violence report (Boni Robertson, Chair)*. Brisbane: Department of Aboriginal and Torres Strait Islander Policy and Development.

Acorn, A. (2004). *Compulsory compassion: A critique of restorative justice*. Vancouver: UBC Press.

Bell, V., & Campbell, K. (Eds). (2004). Out of conflict: Peace, transition and justice. *Special Issue of Social & Legal Studies, 13*(3).

Blagg, H. (1997). A just measure of shame? Aboriginal youth and conferencing in Australia. *British Journal of Criminology, 37*(4), 481–501.

Blagg, H. (2002). Restorative justice and Aboriginal family violence: Opening a space for healing. In: H. Strang & J. Braithwaite (Eds), *Restorative justice and family violence* (pp. 191–205). Cambridge: Cambridge University Press.

Blagg, H. (2005). *A new way of doing justice business? Community justice mechanisms and sustainable governance in Western Australia.* Background Paper No. 8. Perth: Law Reform Commission of Western Australia.

Bolger, A. (1991). *Aboriginal women and violence.* Darwin: Australian National University, North Australian Research Unit.

Braithwaite, J., & Daly, K. (1994). Masculinities, violence and communitarian control. In: T. Newburn & E. A. Stanko (Eds), *Just boys doing business? Men, masculinities and crime* (pp. 189–213). New York: Routledge.

Bushie, B. (1997). A personal journey and CHCH reflections: Berma Bushie. In Ministry of the Solicitor General of Canada. *The four circles of Hollow Water* (pp. 129–156). Ottawa: Public Works and Government Services.

Cameron, A. (2006). Stopping the violence: Canadian feminist debates on restorative justice and intimate violence. *Theoretical Criminology, 10*(1), 49–66.

Charlesworth, H., & Chinkin, C. (2000). *The boundaries of international law: A feminist analysis.* Manchester: Manchester University Press.

Chinkin, C., & Charlesworth, H. (2006). Building women into peace: The international legal framework. *Third World Quarterly, 27*, 937–957.

Christie, N. (1986). The ideal victim. In: E. A. Fattah (Ed.), *From crime policy to victim policy: Reorienting the justice system* (pp. 17–30). Basingstoke: MacMillan.

Coker, D. (2006). Restorative justice, Indigenous justice, and other "alternative" interventions in domestic violence cases. *Theoretical Criminology, 10*(1), 67–85.

Combs, N. (2007). *Guilty pleas in international criminal law.* Stanford: Stanford University Press.

Crenshaw, K. (1989). Demarginalizing the intersection of race and sex: A black feminist critique of antidiscrimination doctrine, feminist theory, and antiracist politics. *University of Chicago Legal Forum, 129*, 139–167.

Crenshaw, K. (1991). Mapping the margins: Intersectionality, identity politics, and violence against women of color. *Stanford Law Review, 43*, 1241–1299.

Crnkovich, M., & Addario, L. with Archibald, L. (2000). *Inuit women and the Nunavut justice system.* Ottawa: Research and Statistics Division, Department of Justice.

Cunneen, C. (2003). Thinking critically about restorative justice. In: E. McLaughlin, R. Fergusson, G. Hughes & L. Westmarland (Eds), *Restorative justice: Critical issues* (pp. 182–194). London: Sage Publications.

Daly, K. (1989). Criminal justice ideologies and practices in different voices: Some feminist questions about justice. *International Journal of the Sociology of Law, 17*, 1–18.

Daly, K. (1992). What would have been justice? Remarks prepared for the Plenary on Sexual Harassment in the Thomas hearings. *Law & Society Annual Meeting*, Philadelphia, May. Available at www.griffith.edu.au/professional-page/professor-kathleen-daly/publications (under other papers).

Daly, K. (2002). Restorative justice: The real story. *Punishment & Society, 4*(1), 55–79.

Daly, K. (2005). A tale of two studies: Restorative justice from a victim's perspective. In: E. Elliott & R. Gordon (Eds), *Restorative justice: Emerging issues in practice and evaluation* (pp. 153–174). Cullompton: Willan Publishing.

Daly, K. (2008). Girls, peer violence, and restorative justice. *Australian & New Zealand Journal of Criminology, 41*(1), in press.

Daly, K., Hayes, H., & Marchetti, E. (2006). New visions of justice. In: A. Goldsmith, M. Israel & K. Daly (Eds), *Crime & justice: A guide to criminology* (3rd ed, pp. 439–464). Sydney: Law Book Company.

Daly, K., & Immarigeon, R. (1998). The past, present, and future of restorative justice: Some critical reflections. *The Contemporary Justice Review, 1*(1), 21–45.

Daly, K., & Stubbs, J. (2006). Feminist engagement with restorative justice. *Theoretical Criminology, 10*(1), 9–28.

Daly, K., & Stubbs, J. (2007). Feminist theory, feminist and anti-racist politics, and restorative justice. In: G. Johnstone & D. Van Ness (Eds), *Handbook of restorative justice* (pp. 149–170). Cullompton: Willan.

Duff, R. A. (2003). Restoration and retribution. In: A. von Hirsch, J. Roberts, A. Bottoms, K. Roach & M. Schiff (Eds), *Restorative justice and criminal justice: Competing or reconcilable paradigms?* (pp. 43–59). Oxford: Hart Publishing.

Freiberg, A. (2001). Problem-oriented courts: Innovative solutions to intractable problems? *Journal of Judicial Administration, 11*, 8–27.

Freiberg, A. (2005). Problem-oriented courts: An update. *Journal of Judicial Administration, 14*, 196–219.

Garland. (1996). The limits of the sovereign state. *British Journal of Criminology, 36*(4), 445–471.

Garland. (2001). *The culture of control: Crime and social order in contemporary society*. Chicago: University of Chicago Press.

Goel, R. (2000). No women in the center: The use of Canadian sentencing circle in domestic violence cases. *Wisconsin Women's Law Journal, 15*, 293–334.

Green, R. G. (1998). *Justice in Aboriginal communities*. Saskatoon: Purich Publishing.

Green, S. (2007). The victim's movement and restorative justice. In: G. Johnstone & D. van Ness (Eds), *Handbook of restorative justice* (pp. 171–191). Cullompton: Willan.

Hampton, D. (1998). Punishment, feminism, and political identity: A case study in the expressive meaning of the law. *Canadian Journal of Law and Jurisprudence, 11*(1), 23–45.

Harrington, C. (1985). *Shadow justice: The ideology and institutionalization of alternatives to the court*. Westport: Greenwood.

Harris, M. (2004). From Australian courts to Aboriginal courts in Australia – Bridging the gap? *Current Issues in Criminal Justice, 16*(1), 26–41.

Hesse, C., & Post, R. (Eds). (1999). *Human rights in political transition: Gettysburg to Bosnia*. New York: Zone.

Hudson, B. (2003). *Justice in the risk society*. London: Sage Publications.

Huggins, J. (1994). A contemporary view of Aboriginal women's relationship to the white women's movement. In: N. Grieve & A. Burns (Eds), *Australian women: Contemporary feminist thought* (pp. 70–79). Melbourne: Oxford University Press.

Johnstone, G. (Ed.) (2003). *A restorative justice reader: Texts, sources, context*. Cullompton: Willan.

Johnstone, G., & van Ness, D. (Eds). (2007). *Handbook of restorative justice*. Cullompton: Willan.

Kelly, L. (2002). Using restorative justice in Aboriginal communities. In: H. Strang & J. Braithwaite (Eds), *Restorative justice and family violence* (pp. 206–222). Cambridge: Cambridge University Press.

Lajeunesse, T. (1996). *Community holistic circle healing, in Hollow Water, Manitoba: An evaluation*. Ottawa: Solicitor General of Canada.

LaRocque, E. (1993). Violence in Aboriginal communities. *In the National Round Table on Aboriginal Health and Social Issues, The path to healing* (pp. 72–89). Ottawa: Canada Communication Group.

LaRocque, E. (1997). Re-examining culturally appropriate models in criminal justice applications. In: M. Asch (Ed.), *Aboriginal and treaty rights in Canada: Essays on law, equity, and respect for difference* (pp. 75–96). Vancouver: UBC Press.

Law Reform Commission of Western Australia. (2006a). *Aboriginal customary laws: Discussion paper overview*. Perth: Law Reform Commission of Western Australia.

Law Reform Commission of Western Australia. (2006b). *Aboriginal customary laws: The interaction of Western Australian law with Aboriginal law and culture: Final report*. Perth: Law Reform Commission of Western Australia.

Lucashenko (1997). Violence against Indigenous women: Public and private dimensions. In: S. Cook & J. Bessant (Eds), *Women's encounters with violence: Australian experiences* (pp. 147–158). London: Sage.

Maher, L. (1997). *Sexed work: Gender, race and resistance in a Brooklyn drug market*. Oxford: Clarendon Press.

Marchetti, E. (2008). International race and gender analyses: Why legal processes just don't get it. *Social & Legal Studies, 17*(2), in press.

Marchetti, E., & Daly, K. (2004). Indigenous courts and justice practices in Australia. *Trends and Issues in Crime and Criminal Justice No. 277*. Canberra: Australian Institute of Criminology.

Marchetti, E., & Daly, K. (2007). Indigenous sentencing courts: Toward a theoretical and jurisprudential model. *Sydney Law Review, 29*(3), 415–443.

Marshall, T. (2003). Restorative justice: An overview. In: G. Johnstone (Ed.), *A restorative justice reader: Text, sources, context* (pp. 28–45). Cullompton: Willan.

McCall, L. (2005). The complexity of intersectionality. *Signs: Journal of Women in Culture and Society, 30*(3), 1771–1800.

Moreton-Robinson, A. (2000). *Talkin' up to the white woman: Aboriginal women and feminism*. St. Lucia: University of Queensland Press.

Morrison, T. (Ed.) (1992). *Race-ing justice, en-gendering power*. New York: Pantheon Books.

Nancarrow, H. (2006). In search of justice for domestic and family violence: Indigenous and non-indigenous women's perspectives in Australia. *Theoretical Criminology, 10*(1), 87–106.

Nightingale, M. (1991). Judicial attitudes and differential treatment: Native women in sexual assault cases. *Ottawa Law Review, 23*, 71–98.

Northern Territory Law Reform Committee. (2003). *Report of the committee of inquiry into Aboriginal customary law*. Darwin: Northern Territory Law Reform Committee.

O'Malley, P. (1999). Volatile and contradictory punishment. *Theoretical Criminology, 3*(2), 175–196.

Payne, S. (1992). Aboriginal women and the law. In: C. Cunneen (Ed.), *Aboriginal perspectives on criminal justice* (pp. 31–40). Sydney: Institute of Criminology.

Razack, S. (1994). What is to be gained by looking white people in the eye? Culture, race, and gender in cases of sexual violence. *Signs, 19*(4), 894–923.

Razack, S. (1998). *Looking white people in the eye: Gender, race, and culture in courtrooms and classrooms*. Toronto: University of Toronto Press.

Razack, S. (2007). The 'Sharia law debate' in Ontario: The modernity/premodernity distinction in legal efforts to protect women from culture. *Feminist Legal Studies, 15*, 3–32.

Report of the Aboriginal Justice Inquiry of Manitoba. (1991). *Report of the Aboriginal Justice Inquiry of Manitoba.* Winnipeg: Public Inquiry into the Administration of Justice and Aboriginal People.

Retzinger, S. M., & Scheff, T. (1996). Strategy for community conferences: Emotions and social bonds. In: B. Galaway & J. Hudson (Eds), *Restorative justice: International perspectives* (pp. 315–336). Monsey: Criminal Justice Press.

Roberts, P. (2003). Restoration and retribution in international criminal justice: An exploratory analysis. In: A. von Hirsch, J. Roberts, A. E. Bottoms, K. Roach & M. Schiff (Eds), *Restorative justice and criminal justice: Competing or reconcilable paradigms?* (pp. 115–134). Oxford: Hart Publishing.

Royal Commission into Aboriginal Deaths in Custody. (1991). *Royal Commission into Aboriginal deaths in custody: National report(* (Vols 1–5). Canberra, ACT: Australian Government Publishing Service.

Rubio-Marin, R. (Ed.) (2006). *What happened to the women? Gender and reparations for human rights violations.* New York: Social Science Research Council.

Rudin, J. (2005). Aboriginal justice and restorative justice. In: E. Elliott & R. M. Gordon (Eds), *New directions in restorative justice: Issues, practice, evaluation* (pp. 89–114). Cullompton: Willan Publishing.

Stewart, W., Huntley, A., & Blaney, F. (2001). *The implications of restorative justice for Aboriginal women and children survivors of violence: A comparative overview of five communities in British Columbia.* Ottawa: Law Commission of Canada.

Stubbs, J. (2007). Beyond apology? Domestic violence and critical questions for restorative justice. *Criminology and Criminal Justice, 7*(2), 169–187.

Sullivan, D., & Tifft, L. (Eds). (2006). *Handbook of restorative justice: A global perspective.* New York: Routledge.

Taskforce on Women and the Criminal Code. (2000). *Report of the taskforce on women and the criminal code.* Brisbane: Office of Women's Policy, Queensland Government.

Walgrave, L. (2002). From community to dominion: In search of social values for restorative justice. In: E. G. M. Weitekamp & H.-J. Kerner (Eds), *Restorative justice: Theoretical foundations* (pp. 71–89). Cullompton: Willan.

Wexler, D. (1990). *Therapeutic jurisprudence: The law as a therapeutic agent.* Durham: Carolina University Press.

Winnick, B. J., & Wexler, D. (Eds). (2003). *Judging in a therapeutic key: Therapeutic jurisprudence and the courts.* Durham: Carolina Academic Press.

Yazzie, R., & Zion, J. (1996). Navajo restorative justice: The law of equality and justice. In: B. Galaway & J. Hudson (Eds), *Restorative justice: International perspectives* (pp. 157–173). Monsey: Criminal Justice Press.

FROM WAR TO PEACE: INFORMALISM, RESTORATIVE JUSTICE AND CONFLICT TRANSFORMATION IN NORTHERN IRELAND

Graham Ellison and Peter Shirlow

ABSTRACT

In the discussion that follows we provide an overview of the operation of informal justice and 'punishment violence' in Northern Ireland which has been a deep-seated a semi-permanent aspect of the violent political conflict and which has persisted well into the transition to peace. Eschewing a mono-causal framework we argue that 'punishment violence' can only be explained and hence understood in terms of the organizational dynamics of the various armed groupings; the economic and social deprivation caused by Northern Ireland's declining economic base and the economic costs of the conflict and finally by the deficiencies in the provision and nature of public policing. We then turn our attention to restorative justice as a panacea to the problem of 'punishment violence' and examine the effectiveness of a number of schemes and initiatives that currently operate in Northern Ireland. Finally, we suggest that the capacity of armed groups to demobilize and demilitarize and embrace

Restorative Justice: From Theory to Practice
Sociology of Crime, Law and Deviance, Volume 11, 31–57
Copyright © 2008 by Emerald Group Publishing Limited
All rights of reproduction in any form reserved
ISSN: 1521-6136/doi:10.1016/S1521-6136(08)00402-8

*non-violent means of dealing with conflict depends to a significant extent
on the leadership skills of ex-combatants themselves.*

INTRODUCTION

On 28th July 2005, the Irish Republican Army (IRA) released a statement
announcing a formal end to its 30-year military campaign.[1] During the
course of the conflict in Northern Ireland, upwards of 3,000 people were
killed and many thousands more injured and an untold number left
psychologically scarred (Smyth & Fay, 2000). While the overall number of
fatalities does not compare with other ethnic conflicts (Bosnia and Rwanda,
for instance) for such a small jurisdiction with a population of 1.6 million
people, the human and economic costs of violence on everyday life have
been incalculable. The conflict knew no geographic boundaries with one
paramilitary organization (the IRA) operating well beyond the confines of
Northern Ireland to launch attacks on targets in Britain and continental
Europe, with the 1993 bombing of London's financial centre causing an
estimated £1 billion worth of damage.[2] However, at last Northern Ireland
is emerging from the shadows. Levels of economic investment are high,
unemployment is at its lowest level for decades and Belfast has been
transformed from a ringed fortress into a lively and modern cultural city.
Of course, the IRA's statement needs to be seen in context. Recent election
results have witnessed Sinn Féin (the IRA's political wing) become the
largest Nationalist party in Northern Ireland. Buoyed by such electoral
successes and concerned about the implications (both domestically and
internationally) of continuing its military campaign in the face of international terrorism – particularly the Al Qaeda attacks on New York,
Madrid and London – the IRA statement was an inevitable, if strategic,
adjustment to the *realpolitik* of a changing global security environment.
Certainly, compared to what went before, the past decade has seen a
demonstrable decline in violence in Northern Ireland. Deploying Johan
Galtung's (1976) typology of a 'positive' and 'negative' peace it might be
more accurate to speak of an absence of 'war' rather than the attainment of
a normatively constructed 'peace' but it is fair to say that on a day-to-day
level, violence in Northern Ireland has greatly reduced in scale and intensity
compared to the years prior to 1996.

Nevertheless while the overall situation in Northern Ireland has stabilized
to a significant degree, there have been a number of issues that have slowed

the overall pace of political transformation. Policing and police reform in particular, has continued to be a protracted and divisive issue, with Sinn Féin only agreeing to lend its support to the Police Service of Northern Ireland (PSNI) and participate in the governance and accountability structures in January 2007 – some eight years after the proposals of the Independent Commission on Policing (ICP) were published (Ellison, 2007). Similarly, a number of unresolved legacy issues continue to dominate debates around policing as with the nefarious links between elements within RUC/PSNI Special Branch – the unit of the police devoted to counter-terrorism and loyalist paramilitary organizations. In fact, this issue was the subject of a damning report by the Police Ombudsman in early 2007 (Office of the Police Ombudsman for Northern Ireland, 2007).

Likewise, while paramilitary organizations may have ceased their 'military' activities, in recent years reservations have been expressed about the involvement and participation of paramilitary organizations and ex-combatants in various forms of organized criminal activity.[3] However, this is something of a grey area in research terms and whatever information we do have comes exclusively from official police sources who may have their own particular agendas to pursue. What is not in doubt is that a huge illicit market operates in Northern Ireland made all easier by a shared (and unguarded) border with the Irish Republic. The situation is thus conducive to smuggling, racketeering and other forms of organized crime. This has been compounded by a spate of high-profile bank heists (in one of the largest in European history the perpetrators £26.5 million from the Northern Bank in Belfast) which has seen Northern Ireland dubbed 'Sicily without Sunshine' in the local media and generated public anger and political disquiet. Whether these activities represent a form of Mertonian rational adaptation, with paramilitary organizations progressing instrumentally from 'political' to organized crime, or the result of ex-combatants acting without the sanction of their organization, or a combination of both, it remains difficult to say (particularly, in the absence of verifiable, independently researched evidence).

Similarly, in what forms the main thrust of this chapter, the participation of paramilitary organizations in punishment violence: the dispensation of extra-legal 'justice' and 'punishment' through shootings and beatings has continued to provide a cause for concern. In many ways the operation of informal justice and the punishment attacks that followed it have been a defining feature of the conflict over the course of the past 30 years. Such punishment attacks have been enacted by members of armed organizations – very often with the tacit support of the community – against individuals who were believed to have been involved in criminality or anti-social activity *within* the community. As such, they are qualitatively distinct from the broader patterns of inter-communal violence, attacks on members of the security forces and indeed disciplinary attacks on members of paramilitary organizations that were a mainstay of the conflict. As avowedly brutal as such attacks were they rarely resulted in death, although in many cases individuals were left permanently disfigured, while the specialist orthopaedic unit at Belfast's Royal Victoria Hospital was to gain considerable experience in treating such injuries over the years.

In what might at first seem a rather anomalous occurrence, after a dip in the immediate aftermath of the first paramilitary ceasefires (post-1994) the number of punishment attacks, including shootings and beatings, rose to levels that surpassed those during the earlier phase of conflict (Figs. 2 and 3). In addition, there appeared to be something of a descent into vigilantism with the IRA widely acknowledged – though not definitively proved – to have been behind an organization that went by the moniker of Direct Action Against Drugs and which was believed to have been responsible for the murders of 11 suspected drug dealers between 1995 and 1999 (Hollywood, 1997). While the situation in relation to informal justice and 'punishment' attacks has improved dramatically in recent years, it is nevertheless the case that in a period of political transition a declaration of intent to 'end' a military campaign by the various actors involved does not necessarily translate into a cessation of all activities by armed groups. In this respect the discussion that follows interrogates the often brutal dynamics of informal justice in Northern Ireland and considers how these have been steered towards mechanisms of non-violent dispute resolution through the adoption of restorative justice techniques and principles (see also McEvoy & Mika, 2002; McEvoy & Eriksson, 2008). The chapter is divided into two sections. In Section 1 we provide some background and context for those readers perhaps unfamiliar with the nuances of the Northern Ireland situation by outlining how and why a system of informal justice emerged during the phase of the political conflict. Avoiding a mono-causal explanation we argue that any satisfactory explanation needs to be located within the context of three interlocking dynamics: intra-organizational imperatives of the armed groups; broader economic and social structural factors and problems with the nature and character of state policing. We then consider the backcloth to a number of restorative justice initiatives that attempted to steer armed groups on a course of non-violent dispute resolution within their respective communities. In Section 2 we provide some quantitative data on the numbers of punishment attacks that have taken place in Northern Ireland.

We suggest that these have tended to follow the contours of the political process and that at some level the move to embrace restorative justice initiatives can be seen as the strategic result of a cost-benefit calculation by the various actors involved. Later in Section 2 we consider the positive leadership role that ex-combatants can themselves play in steering armed groups away from violence during a period of political transition. In the conclusion we suggest that Northern Ireland provides useful international lessons in non-violent dispute resolution and the adoption of restorative justice strategies within marginalized and disadvantaged communities.

1. INFORMAL JUSTICE IN NORTHERN IRELAND: BACKGROUND AND CONTEXT

There is now a broad literature and general acknowledgement that the existence of non-state ordering mechanisms and structures is a common feature in those societies undergoing political schism or where the legitimacy of the state and its agencies is contested (e.g. de Sousa Santos, 1982). In this sense the situation in Northern Ireland has been little different from many other transitional societies given the levels of socio-political conflict experienced there from the late 1960s to the signing of the negotiated constitutional settlement (The Belfast Agreement) of 1998 and the associated reforms in relation to policing and criminal justice (ICP, Criminal Justice Review). It is within the context of the maintenance of a 'contested order' (Weitzer, 1987) that informal justice and ordering, the associated 'punishment beatings' and attacks and the particular problems in relation to state policing need to be located. However, for the sake of brevity, both the emergence and operation of a system of informal justice in Northern Ireland can be outlined by three interlocking dynamics: the internal organizational dynamics of the respective paramilitary groupings; the impact of crime and anti-social activity on urban working-class communities and particular problems associated with the form and nature of state policing.

    In the first place, it should be noted at the outset that the underlying rationales for the development of informal justice within republican and loyalist communities and enacted by their respective paramilitary organizations, cannot really be homogenized and to a significant extent depend on the ideological position of the organization in question and its position vis-à-vis the state. Organizational cohesiveness and legitimacy was constructed and manufactured through the structures and symbolic manifestations of informal justice. Thus, the operation of informal justice is intimately tied up with a movement's sense of 'self' and the complex dynamics of power and legitimacy that are at play in the construction of its identity and self-validation. Expressed simply, the development and practice of informal justice for republicans was tied up with the broader struggle against what was perceived as British 'occupation'. It is difficult to see in any logical sense, how republicans could have allowed the formal justice agencies – in particular the RUC – to operate unhindered in their respective communities, given the place that such agencies occupied in traditional republican discourse and that the representatives of those self-same agencies were considered legitimate targets for attack. In other words, by denying the formal structures a place, the republican movement and in particular the IRA, could claim its place as 'legitimate' defenders and protectors of the community and define a particular territory as outside the purvey or beyond the reach of the formal state apparatus. By contrast, pro-state, loyalist paramilitary organizations occupied a much more ambiguous position in relation to the state and formal criminal justice agencies (Bruce, 1992). By and large, loyalists were reasonably happy with the 'idea' of the RUC – the belief that the force represented in symbolic and ideational terms the continuation of the link with Britain – and as such it was able to police relatively unhindered within working-class loyalist communities. For loyalists then, the immediate justification for informal justice was not about defining a territory as 'no-go' for the state, but rather the imprimatur was *more* about the internal 'policing' of their members. That said, there is some parallel with republican armed groups here insofar as loyalists too became concerned with the impact of crime, and in particular, the rise of a hard-drugs problem and criminality within their areas. For working-class loyalists while the RUC may have been regarded as a legitimate police force, it was nevertheless seen as one that was disconnected, and in many respects disinterested, in the problems of crime that afflicted working-class loyalist areas. Indeed, the RUC from the mid-1970s had undergone something of an *embourgeoisement* with many officers earning higher salaries than doctors (and often twice or thrice that of academics!) and living far removed from the communities they were policing in gated towns reminiscent of James Mangold's *Cop Land.*

Second, Belfast from the 1970s suffered like many comparable UK cities from post-industrial blight, urban deprivation and long-term structural unemployment brought about by the decline of the traditional manufacturing sector as a consequence of broader sectoral changes in the global economy. Between 1971 and 1984 over 74,000 manufacturing jobs were lost in Northern Ireland (Canning, Moore, & Rhodes, 1987).

In purely subjective terms these changes impacted *more* upon working-class loyalists given that this group had historically represented something of a labour aristocracy and enjoyed virtually exclusive rights to employment in the traditional manufacturing sector (e.g. ship-building and engineering). But the cumulative effect cut across the community divide and levels of structural long-term male unemployment in Northern Ireland was in excess of 20% by the late 1970s and early 1980s (Northern Ireland Statistics and Research Agency, 1988). In Belfast the situation was even worse with 'much of inner and West Belfast [an] industrial wasteland' (O'Dowd, 1980, p. 58) with adult male unemployment in some Catholic electoral wards of the city running in excess of 50%. For Protestant males, unemployment rates in the city, while lower than for their Catholic counterparts were nevertheless higher than the Northern Ireland average, at between 17.4% and 30% (O'Dowd, 1980, p. 58). Criminologists have not been strangers to the impact of sectoral changes in the economy on crime (e.g. see Young, 1999). Beatrix Campbell in her excellent *Goliath* paints a very human picture of the ways in which decimation of traditional working-class employment in the coal and steel industries in the North of England has affected traditional communities (Campbell, 1993). One key impact of this structural dislocation – particularly among young males – was to engender feelings of alienation, marginalization, exclusion and disaffection and the consequent participation in various forms of criminality and anti-social behaviour.

Of course, we cannot discount the economic costs of the conflict which merely added to and exacerbated an already precarious economic situation. The relentless bombing campaign pursued by the IRA and the specific singling out of economic targets meant that business confidence was low and levels of inward investment into Northern Ireland, virtually nil. Employment where it existed, was heavily dependant upon state subsidies and certainly while the conflict persisted there was little prospect of urban regeneration or any long-term solution to Northern Ireland's economic malaise. Again, the point that we wish to emphasize here is that Northern Ireland's already dire economic situation was made worse by the decades of socio-political conflict that impacted even more directly upon those who were already marginalized and excluded. For some young people, their futures bleak and prospects limited, reacted as many young people do in similar situations and turned to youth offending and anti-social activity. Others, engaged in expressions of misplaced bravado and embarked on such activities simply as a way of challenging the authority of paramilitary organizations (i.e. the IRA or UVF) since they were seen as 'authority figures' and which meant that they were often singled out for particular attention (Monaghan, 2002). More seriously, the phenomenon referred to as 'joy' – or perhaps more accurately 'death' driving – in republican areas was a considerable cause for concern. Not only because it involved the risk of death and injury to innocent motorists and pedestrians, but because the young people involved were also at risk of being shot by members of the security forces, as happened in a number of cases.

The third aspect that needs to be considered relates both to the provision of public policing in urban working-class areas and also the style and form that such policing was to take. Again this particular issue, or at least one manifestation of it, is not peculiar or isolated to the Northern Irish case. As policing scholars have acknowledged for decades, the relationship between the police and the urban poor has long been problematic, a situation that is often exacerbated when issues of race and ethnicity are factored in (Brogden, 1982; Skolnick & Fyfe, 1993; McLaughlin, 2007). Considered historically, however, policing on the island of Ireland has long been contested and overlaid with particularly political and symbolic overtones (e.g. see Palmer, 1988). Indeed, as one of us has argued elsewhere (Ellison & Martin, 2000) issues around justice, and in particular policing, arose from being peripheral to central concerns of the Northern Ireland campaign for civil rights in the late 1960s and arguably for many nationalists and republicans have remained central to a resolution of the conflict ever since. Quite simply, the RUC saw its mandate or core-practice as 'defeating terrorism' over the prevention and detection of ordinary crime, with much serious crime being ignored or tolerated by units within the organization for wider instrumental purposes (Ellison & Smyth, 2000; McGarry & O'Leary, 1999).[4] In organizational and resource terms the thrust of the organization was geared much more to the former, with considerably less emphasis on the latter (e.g. the widespread adoption of routine policing activities such as issuing tickets to speeding motorists are a comparatively recent phenomenon in Northern Ireland). Even allowing for the fact that it was notoriously difficult for the RUC to patrol republican areas of Belfast (and could only do so with support from the British Army) high crime rates, youth offending and anti-social activity in republican areas was viewed by many in the RUC as a collective community punishment; the price of not lending support to the force. Furthermore, even ordinary crime could have its uses with young males who were suspected of dealing drugs, or engaging in other criminal activities, having these overlooked by the RUC so long as they were willing to provide information on the activities of paramilitary organizations. This practice became known colloquially as the recruitment of '£10 touts'.[5]

We have suggested thus far that explanations of the phenomenon of informal justice in Northern Ireland need to consider three interlocking dynamics: (1) The internal organizational exigencies of paramilitary groupings and the need to maintain a semblance of control and legitimacy within their respective communities. (2) Conditions of economic marginalization, youth alienation and unemployment as a consequence of economic downturn and which were exacerbated by the proliferation of the conflict itself. (3) A security vacuum in policing and community safety terms that reflected the traditional difficulties of policing urban working-class environments, but which were complicated by the RUC's organizational imperative to 'defeat terrorism' and whose activities brought it into conflict with many in the nationalist community in particular.

1.1. Informal Justice in Practice: Responding to Anti-Social Behaviour and Crime

It was noted earlier that informal justice operated according to different sets of rationales according to broader exigencies of the paramilitary organization in question. Similarly, the ways in which informal justice has been organized and structured has tended to vary between the various paramilitary factions also, being somewhat more administrative and procedural in the case of republican paramilitary organizations, particularly the IRA (Munck, 1984; McEvoy & Mika, 2002). Indeed, as far as the IRA was concerned it would be a mistake to regard the operation of informal justice and punishment attacks as entirely undisciplined and spasmodic. Some effort at adhering to a rudimentary process was attempted and from the earliest days of the conflict the IRA operated what was called 'the civil administration' unit which '…was established to hear complaints of criminality or anti-social activity from the local community, conduct investigations and carry out the designated punishment' (McEvoy & Mika, 2002, p. 536). Aping in some ways aspects of the formal justice system (i.e. around notions of proportionality, investigation, evidence gathering), the 'civil administration' unit operated a tariff system with warnings issued to those individuals deemed to have been involved in criminal or other anti-social activity, or who engaged in some other transgression. Non-compliance with the warning could have dire and often brutal consequences. The 'punishments' ranged from banishment from the community with the individual concerned often having to seek sanctuary in England or Scotland, to beatings with iron bars, baseball bats or hurling sticks or having concrete blocks dropped on them. In other cases individuals were shot in the thighs, kneecaps, elbows or ankles with low-velocity handguns (see McEvoy & Mika, 2002, pp. 535–536).

It is somewhat difficult to quantify the total number of banishments and 'punishment' attacks (i.e. shootings and beatings) that have taken place over the years given the difficulties in compiling accurate statistics. However, according to official data there were 3,090 recorded 'punishment' shootings between 1973 and 2005 and 2,328 'punishment' beatings between 1983 (when records began) and 2005. Needless, to say the brutal nature of such 'punishments' brought paramilitary organizations in for sustained criticism from official agencies, local politicians and human and civil rights organizations such as Amnesty International and Human Rights Watch. As the peace process unfolded from the first paramilitary ceasefires in 1994 it was made abundantly clear to the political representatives of the IRA and the UVF that such attacks would have to cease if they were to stand any realistic chance of being included in the political negotiations. Indeed, the US Senator George Mitchell, who chaired the preliminary round of talks leading to the Belfast Agreement, was to urge the political representatives of the various paramilitary factions '... that "punishment" killings and beatings stop and to take effective steps to prevent such actions' (cited in McEvoy & Mika, 2002, p. 537).

1.2. From 'Punishment' Attacks to Restorative Justice

The period from the mid-1990s onwards marks something of a sea change in attitude by representatives of the various paramilitary organizations in Northern Ireland towards punishment violence. This, however, as we have already noted, was heavily influenced by political exigencies in the context of the unfolding peace process. In 1996 a group, comprising an academic from Queen's University, Belfast and representatives from the Northern Ireland Association for the Care and Resettlement of Offenders (NIACRO) embarked on a training programme with republican activists – and with the apparent sanction of the IRA – in order to consider how anti-social and criminal activities could be dealt with through non-violent means. The training programme included a consideration of crime prevention, restorative justice, human rights, humanitarian law, mediation and non-violent dispute resolution (McEvoy & Mika, 2002) and a number of proposals were subsequently published as 'The Blue Book' and circulated widely amongst republican activists and the Irish and British Governments. 'The Blue Book' was endorsed by the Sinn Féin leadership and four pilot projects were established in republican areas under the rubric of Community Restorative Justice Ireland (CRJI), which employed restorative justice and community mediation techniques practices to deal with anti-social and criminal behaviour to avoid the often violent response that would have hitherto have been the case. Community members who had been victimized or who had some other grievance were encouraged to report in the first instance to CRJI rather than the IRA, who would then engage in a process of mediation between the perpetrators/s and the offended parties in order to seek a non-violent resolution to the problem. The relative success of the pilot projects resulted in the programme being expanded to other republican areas. The situation with restorative justice and non-violent dispute resolution has arguably been much less coherent on the loyalist paramilitary side and the schemes and initiatives that have been rolled out, have been of a smaller-scale and involving only one of the loyalist paramilitary organizations (the UVF) with the Ulster Defence Association (UDA) refusing to participate. Nevertheless, from 1996 a pilot project involving restorative justice and non-violent dispute resolution was established in the staunchly loyalist Shankill area of Belfast under the Greater Shankill Alternatives Programme. Again, the pilot scheme appeared to have some initial success in drastically reducing the number of 'punishment' attacks and it was later extended to a number of loyalist areas under the aegis of Northern Ireland Alternatives (NIA).

The operation of restorative justice initiatives by CRJI and NIA has recently been subject to a full-scale independent evaluation (see Mika, 2006). The evaluation provides a useful corrective to those critics who are sceptical about the potential of restorative justice in a post-conflict situation and who suggest it has an altogether more maleficent dimension insofar as it provides a conduit for paramilitary organizations to take control over local communities (Kennedy, 1994). However, what we find is that the projects themselves operate with a high level of support from within the local community – particularly in those areas where the PSNI are still viewed problematically – and perhaps more importantly their operation is far removed from the shambolic and often amateurish representations that can be found in some of the literature (for a useful deconstruction of the various critiques that have been applied to restorative justice in Northern Ireland, see McEvoy & Mika, 2002). As we can see from the chart in Fig. 1 restorative justice initiatives that operate in Northern Ireland are highly

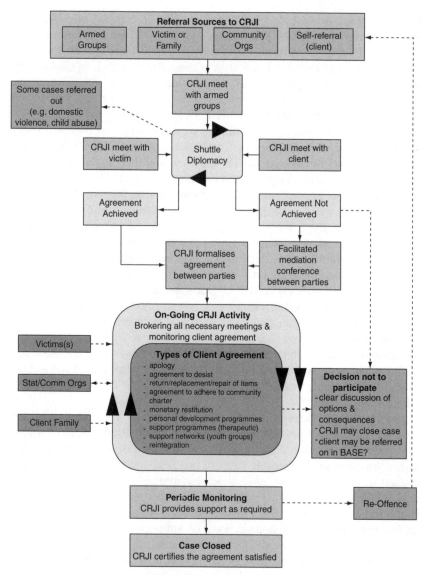

Fig. 1. The Restorative Justice Process in Northern Ireland. *Source:* Mika (2006).
Reproduced with the kind permission of the Institute of Criminology and Criminal
Justice, School of Law, Queen's University, Belfast.

organized and operate according to a definite process and fixed policies and procedures.

Each organization involved in the provision of restorative justice has a clear code of practice, and as well as taking due cognizance of human rights considerations, both the rights of the offender (client) and the victim are prioritized at all stages in the process. Fig. 1 provides some idea of the various stages involved in the restorative justice process. In general, CRJI meets with the various parties involved to the dispute – including the representatives of armed groups – and depending on the willingness of the victim and client to participate, there are a number of possible interventions such as a facilitated mediation conference; recommendations that the client undergoes a personal development programme or therapeutic support programmes, in the case of drug and alcohol abuse, for example. CRJI and NIA are self-limiting in the 'types' of interventions they participate in and do not become directly involved in cases involving domestic violence, serious sexual assault or child abuse. Instead these are referred directly or indirectly to the appropriate statutory agencies. Nevertheless for the humdrum of routine ordering, associated crime problems and anti-social behaviour, these restorative initiatives offer a potentially more inclusive dynamic, rooted firmly in local experience and lived reality. They also have the capacity, if brutalizing and corrupting tendencies can be countered and guarded against (which we would argue has been the case in Northern Ireland) to adopt much more grounded rehabilitative and restorative approaches than those of state writ large, and to 'envision new ways of policing rooted in unrestricted human rights, ethnic tolerance, and citizen service [with these imperatives going beyond the immediate concerns of peacemaking as traditionally understood]' (Call & Stanley, 2001, p. 152). Certainly, the level of support provided by these restorative justice initiatives provides victims with a sense of empowerment in the sense that they feel they are being listened to, and offers offenders (clients) the opportunity to make amends in ways that encourage them to reflect on their wrongdoing and in doing so may offer a diversion from future offending. In many fundamental respects both victims and offenders have become passive participants in the formal criminal justice process which leaves the former feeling angry and resentful, while doing little to steer the latter away from more concentrated offending patterns. Of course, whether these projects could enjoy the same level of success if they were rolled out on a larger scale is an open question. But certainly, in the specific context of Northern Ireland with a bitter legacy of paramilitary violence and inter-communal strife, they have provided a useful antidote to the deficiencies of the formal criminal justice and legal process.

Perhaps more importantly in the context of this chapter, the restorative justice projects appear to have been broadly successful in their key aim to substantially reduce the number of 'punishment' attacks that have taken place and to wean armed organizations away from violent interventions as part of a broader conflict resolution process. For instance, of the 199 formal case interventions reported to CRJI between 2003 and 2005 'punishment' attacks were prevented in 82% of cases. For NIA out of a total of 127 cases the comparable figure is 71% (Mika, 2006, pp. i–ii). As Mika acknowledges, 'NIA and CRJI have caused a noticeable drop in the number of beatings and shootings compared to what was happening in the neighbourhoods outside of their service catchments' (Mika, 2006, p. ii).

2. THE POLITICAL DYNAMICS OF PUNISHMENT ATTACKS IN NORTHERN IRELAND

Since the start of the peace process in Northern Ireland the IRA has effectively held together a broadly consistent republican position and for the most part avoided factional splits. Even on the issue of republican acceptance of the PSNI – the most emotive issue of recent years, and one of the most powerful gestures of the entire process – republican discipline and control has been maintained. This political leadership has translated to community level, ensuring that the IRA has been able to deliver on their ceasefire promises and ensure the cessation of republican political violence across Northern Ireland.

By contrast, loyalism, always a more fragmented bloc (Bruce, 1992; Hall, 2006) became even more diffuse in the post-ceasefire period, with feuds and factional splits occurring at a number of critical moments and resulting in the emergence of a large regressive/criminal element. Discontented forces within loyalism, such as the Loyalist Volunteer Force (LVF), have openly tried to undermine transformative loyalism through championing a discourse that depicts peaceful transition as duplicitous (Gallaher & Shirlow, 2006). However, reactionary loyalist discourse has typically been disorganized and incoherent and has failed to mobilize a full-scale return to violence. Such violence as has occurred has typically been directed inwards, in internal loyalist feuding and power-grabs, rather than towards the republican or Catholic population.

An important factor in the transformation of armed groups and promotion of non-violence is the extent to which the military leadership is considered credible by the rank-and-file. Such credibility has been essential to dissuading a return to large-scale violence as it provides direction to armed actors to pursue non-violent activities, as well as legitimizing anti-violence discourse on a national scale. Evidently, both the UVF and IRA have significantly reduced and even removed the capacity of their organizations to undertake organized armed action. In the explicit transition from 'armed struggle' to 'unarmed struggle', these groups have opened the door for the continued interpretation of identity through a variety of social, cultural and political approaches. To measure the peace process only in terms of political agreements and milestones ignores the day-to-day, incremental, essential work of community activists in preventing violence on the ground.

Data relating to punishment shootings was compiled since 1973 by the RUC and more recently by the PSNI (Figs. 2 and 3). This data has certain problems both in terms of recording (poor RUC record keeping in early 1970s and pre-computerization), under-reporting due to fear of reprisal and also acceptance of the punishment received. As was noted earlier, there were 3,090 recorded punishment shootings between 1973 and 2005. There was a

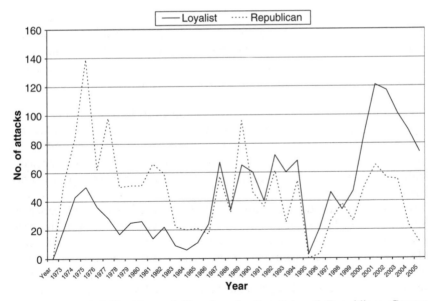

Fig. 2. Recorded 'Punishment' Shootings by Loyalist and Republican Groups 1973–2005. *Source:* Police Service of Northern Ireland.

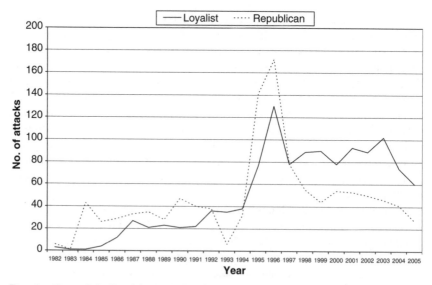

Fig. 3. Recorded 'Punishment' Beatings by Loyalist and Republican Groups
1982–2005. *Source:* Police Service of Northern Ireland.

dramatic fall in such shootings after the ceasefires of 1994 but a significant
peak by 2002, thereafter which they began to decline and fewer than 5 such
incidents have been recorded after 2005 (Fig. 2). The recording of
punishment beatings began in 1983, and between then and 2005, there
were 2,328 recorded incidents (Fig. 3). What is evident from the data in
Fig. 3 is that there was a sharp dip in the number of beatings committed by
republicans prior to the first IRA ceasefire in 1994. However, post-1994, for
both republicans and loyalists such attacks increased dramatically and
reached unprecedented levels between 1996 and 1997. They eventually
stabilized between 1997 and 2005, albeit at higher levels than at any other
stage in the conflict.

    The peak in punishment beatings in 1996/1997 correlated directly with a
virtual disappearance in shootings in that year. Evidently, the infancy of the
peace process had led to an initial disengagement away from armed assault.
However, one of the reasons why punishment attacks across the board were
able to continue at relatively high levels was that for strategic political
reasons successive Northern Ireland Secretaries of State failed to rule that
such attacks constituted a breach of the ceasefires with no significant or
meaningful sanction against those organizations persisting with them.

The more rigorous scrutiny and condemnation of such violence during attempts to restore devolution was directly linked to the reduction in republican punishment-based violence. What this might lead us to conclude, albeit tentatively, is that punishment attacks have been used in a rational-strategic fashion by protagonists to the conflict both to win political concessions and to withhold them in the case of the state.

The significant increase in punishment shootings after 1996 can be understood and explained by any number of factors but in particular, by the sense of *anomie* experienced by some ex-combatants in the aftermath of the peace process and the perceived loss of their role and status; the rise in anti-social behaviour following demilitarization; the influx of a drug culture that had been relatively underdeveloped during the conflict due to high levels of police and army surveillance and the loosing of the bonds of social control during the transition to 'peace' that had been central to community solidarity during the conflict.[6] In some cases it was understood among former combatants that anti-social elements took the opportunity to engage in unacceptable behaviour given the impression in the mid-1990s that the paramilitaries had been neutered. It should also be acknowledged that some of this violence may have been engaged in as a final 'push' to remove criminal elements and deter others form activities such as drug dealing, while in other cases it can be related to internecine feuding between rival organizations. For example, feuding between the rival loyalist paramilitary groups accounts for a number of shootings and beatings observed between 2000 and 2004. This related to a vicious drugs and turf war between the UDA/UFF and the UVF initially in the loyalist Shankill area of Belfast but which soon spread to other areas of Northern Ireland including Ballymena, Carrickfergus and Coleraine and resulted in at least seven deaths.

One of the issues raised by the phenomenon of informal justice and punishment attacks in Northern Ireland is that the ability to reduce such violence is feasible and doable, but this can only be achieved after a series of internal debates about the consequences of such violence and its long-term implications. Undoubtedly, the cessation of the military campaigns by both the IRA and the UVF resulted in a dramatic reduction in the numbers of deaths. After 1994 these declined by 90% for republicans and 84% for loyalists (Shirlow & McEvoy, 2008). This reduction can best be understood as the product of wider engagement via political negotiation and compromise. Paradoxically, however, the decline in the number of deaths due to the political situation was mirrored by an increase in the number of 'punishment' beatings and attacks within republican and loyalist communities. The demilitarization of communities, the subsequent growth in drug usage and the removal of high levels of surveillance led to an expansion in anti-social behaviour and criminality. Moreover, a reactionary element within both paramilitary factions opposed the peace process and persisted with punishment violence in a desire to locate and maintain status. However, the leadership and direction of a number of senior ex-combatants meant that the restorative justice approach eventually took hold within main armed groups and eventually the use of punishment violence was reduced significantly. This would suggest that the application and pursuit of restorative justice can be uneven but it does succeed when it is linked to wider political shifts and in the case of Northern Ireland a holistic model of conflict transformation.

3. RESTORATIVE JUSTICE AS CONFLICT TRANSFORMATION

There is an endurable link between the evolution and sustainability of restorative justice projects and programmes and paramilitary organizations such as the IRA and UVF. This involvement in and development of such approaches to anti-social behaviour is tied to wider processes of transition that are committed to peace building and political settlement. In Northern Ireland, it is important to note that many former combatants have dedicated time, support and enthusiasm along a broad front that stretches across a range of issues linked to securing the rights and entitlements of their respective communities. In developing social justice campaigns and programmes former combatants have provided examples and models of leadership that aim to prevent the resumption of punishment attacks and whilst doing so provide alternative non-violent approaches.

The removal of such violence was driven by moral issues but it is also evident that internal and external political pressure and sanctions against the political representatives of these movements had a significant impact. In particular the Democratic Unionist Party's (DUP) refusal to let Sinn Féin join the executive of the Northern Ireland Assembly until IRA activity ceased, incentivized the removal of punishment violence and it is not surprising that such violence has virtually disappeared since the restoration of the Northern Ireland Assembly in May 2007. Moreover, there were internal struggles within these organizations regarding the acceptance and/ or rejection of the efficacy or punishment violence. Those who effectively led their organizations away from violence engaged in a definable leadership role framed by collaborative thinking, symbolic intent, internal debate and the re-framing of organizational roles and functions. Evidently the leaders of these organizations had to bring with them a membership whose attitudes to ending violence was uneven, ambivalent and potentially divisive. Therefore, the leadership of such groups encouraged the airing of views, pinpointed various reactions to those views and ensured that those who were opposed to such views were increasingly identified as a minority.

There are several key points regarding the evolution of restorative justice approaches and wider peace building strategies. First, as argued by Shirlow and McEvoy (2008) there was a need to locate former prisoners and combatants in new roles in order to stabilize a nascent transitional peace processes. Obviously finding roles to play within civic society, such as restorative justice, provided a sense of purpose for those who had been involved in a protracted and complex conflict. The failure of such roles and positions to materialize may have provided space for wreckers to destroy group loyalty and thus the capacity to positively shape wider transformations. Indeed the Secretary-General of the United Nations, Kofi Annan, argued in 2004 during a speech in Northern Ireland that a sustainable peace could not be delivered without 'providing the fighters with an alternative, peaceful means of earning their living (cited in Shirlow & McEvoy, 2008, p. 164).

Secondly, the policing vacuum remained despite the reforms of the ICP and peace building strategies and restorative justice programmes filled such a void. This vacuum related at one level to a more general hostility to the police; a belief that they did not wish to deliver an effective service in particular working-class communities and the legacy of conflict which saw the developmental trajectory of public policing itself steered primarily towards a counter-insurgency role with little emphasis on crime prevention and community safety (Mulcahy, 2006). Thirdly, former combatants had, especially within republican areas, a status and level of respect that provided the standing required to provide the leadership needed to sustain and maintain restorative justice projects. Fourthly, these former combatants were prepared to take risks in sustaining such projects especially within the loyalist community were threats against restorative justice activists from criminal gangs were forthcoming. In exploring the shift away from punishment violence we contend that the evolution and development of restorative justice schemes cannot be detached from issues that stretch beyond anti-social behaviour.

The role of former combatants in restorative justice programmes is important given that society in Northern Ireland, due to ethno-sectarian disputation, is inherently territorial. Identities and attitudes to issues such as policing remain constructed around territoriality and social class. Such territoriality replicates the ongoing significance of place to social networks and mental and emotional bindings within communities. There is no doubting that the use of 'punishment' violence was not solely a reaction to a policing vacuum but also of a desire to control space given that territorial control was a crucial element in identity, power and politics within Northern Ireland. In effect punishment violence was 'a symbol of political domination and political practice' (Shirlow, 2001, p. 69), which was most acutely experienced at in areas within which republican and loyalist identities were strongly defined and symbolically embedded. Punishment violence was for some within such organizations a physical and symbolic recognition of their political legitimacy. The decision to remove such violence and promote non-violent approaches produced concerns among those who were suspicious of the wider peace process and related policing reforms and who interpreted the shift into non-violent approaches as a loss of status and authority.

The leadership driven and accepted re-direction of paramilitary activity away from violence undermined the use of punishment attacks but was not in itself not simply directed via a hierarchical structure but through agreed grass-roots activism. As such, former combatants undertaking roles such as community workers, interface workers or youth leaders were tied into a wider rights-based approach that also included those involved in community-based restorative justice programmes. Each of these approaches were guided by the desire and concern to reduce multifarious forms of violent conflict. In some instances those who opposed such positive shifts and/or who encouraged the maintenance of armed struggle were at times dealt with via violence or the threat of it and exclusion. The IRA shooting and harassment of dissident republicans and the more obvious loyalist feuds between those supportive of peace and those who wished to maintain conflict illustrated the ironic use of violence to end violence. Such ruthlessness indicated the significant departure away from previous armed campaigns and the intent to de-stabilize those intent upon undermining wider conflict transformation strategies.

For the political representatives of the IRA (Sinn Féin) and the UVF (Progressive Unionist Party, PUP) the desire to end punishment attacks was part of an ongoing process related to policing reforms and the outplaying of the wider peace process. In 1999 Sinn Féin, for example, stated that:

> Sinn Féin has total and absolute commitment to pursue our objectives by exclusively peaceful and democratic means in accordance with the Good Friday Agreement.

> For this reason, we are totally opposed to any use of force or threat of force by others for any political purpose. We are totally opposed to punishment attacks.[7]

A senior member of Sinn Féin, Martin McGuiness, had made a public denunciation of punishment attacks as early as 1985.[8] David Ervine a former leader of the PUP described punishment attacks as 'immoral and reprehensible'. However, the local media constantly played upon these condemnations as hollow utterances. Such negative commentary disguised much of the hidden and internal work that political leaders in each of these movements undertook. Indeed according to one prominent former republican combatant the condemnation of republicans and loyalists produced

> A result contrary to what our critics wanted. The elements that demanded the exclusion of Sinn Féin due to IRA violence actually never wanted that violence to go away. Their criticism of republicans actually helped undermine those who were not as progressive as others within the movement. You see, the political leadership could say 'look we are being excluded by unionists because of IRA violence so we are letting them dictate our future. So if we stop the punishment stuff we can get power and representation and undermine them. (Interview with the authors, August 2006)

There is no doubting that respective political leaders prepared, cajoled and sometimes even bullied sections of their respective constituencies to stop punishment violence. The leadership drive to remove violence was met with some hostility between those who saw wider political engagement as a betrayal of key principles. Moreover, many activists who lived within areas with high rates of anti-social behaviour remained concerned that the cessation of punishment violence who lead to the exacerbation of such behaviour. Furthermore, there were those who understood the process of demilitarization as undermining their status and standing within communities in which they lived. Dealing with such persons was achieved through internal discipline and even exclusion. However, an important impact was the nature of wider political shifts and the intersection between '... agency and structure, the ways in which individual actors transform themselves from armed actors to negotiators, often as a result of changed political circumstances' (Shirlow & McEvoy, 2008, p. 21).

The role that former combatants have played within the evolution of restorative justice has been obvious (McEvoy & Eriksson, 2008). Many of the loyalist and republican negotiators of the Belfast Agreement were former prisoners/combatants. Most of these individuals have openly stated that such negotiation skills were learned and honed in their dealings with the prison authorities when imprisoned (Sinnerton, 2002). It is also clear that leaderships within each movement has 'stretched' their base through the employment of extensive dexterity in overcoming hostile attitudes to restorative justice. This involvement in community life is crucial to understanding the role such former combatants have undertaken. As one former republican prisoner commented:

> Locally ex-prisoners are involved in every aspect of their communities. Community restorative justice is an example where ex-prisoners are involved – trying to provide an alternative form of response to anti-social behaviour. Housing committees, community groups. I mean they are activists. They went to jail for activism – a different type of activism but they are passionate about righting wrong, about bringing about change for people in these areas. And that type of culture is there still, despite people being released. They are giving leadership to people in their areas and they are leading by example, they are getting involved. (cited in Shirlow & McEvoy, 2008, p. 111)

The community-based restorative justice programmes in republican and loyalist areas are a useful illustration of the kind of leadership under discussion. Since their inception, the presence of former prisoners in these programmes has been a defining feature (McEvoy & Mika, 2002). The quality of their work has increasingly garnered recognition, even from the most critical of sources:

> we have received evidence which we find convincing that community restorative justice can under the right conditions help offer alternatives to paramilitary violence and intimidation. To the extent that it can do this, can operate accountably and to acceptable standards, fully respect human rights, and can demonstrate to people that they need not look to paramilitaries to deliver reasonable behaviour within their communities, we believe that it can have a valuable part to play. (Independent Monitoring Commission (IMC), 2004, p. 36)

The notion of credibility is central to this behavioural response rather than an instrumental approach to military leadership. Put simply, unless those who bring the peacemaking message have credibility amongst current paramilitary activists and can frame it appropriately within the organization's way of thinking, the message will not be heeded. As one former loyalist prisoner commented:

> I think the analysis we give to the UVF has been good. It has been instrumental in a lot of interface issues and in that some responses have been measured. Since the ceasefires you can see the effect of good leadership. Other than interface stuff the organisations have been very disciplined. That has involved former prisoner analysis. If it wasn't for the rednecks things would be a lot better. (cited in Shirlow & McEvoy, 2008, p. 201)

Again the work of former prisoners and former combatants in the community-based restorative justice programmes is instructive. As well as working and volunteering in these programmes, former prisoners have been central to efforts at persuading paramilitary organizations to desist from punishment violence, to refer 'complainants' from the community to the programmes and to consider their own internal organizational attitudes towards violence. Such a process of persuasion or leadership in trying to move paramilitary organizations onwards is neither smooth nor easy. Nor is involvement in peace-making work without its personal risks, particularly for former loyalist prisoners. As one argued:

> You could be shot dead – it's as simple as that! If you criticise about drug houses or individuals involved in drugs then those type of people want to do you as much damage as possible – they have the most to lose from the political and peace processes. It applies across the board. It terms of military leadership for example, if you try to clamp down on these people, the ones who are making a living from drugs or whatever, then you are making enemies. The biggest risk is going too far ahead of your constituency. (cited in Shirlow & McEvoy, 2008, p. 121)

Despite these difficulties, it is through the leadership and persuasion efforts of former prisoners involved in initiatives such as restorative justice that we have seen significant reductions in punishment violence in the areas where the projects are operational, as well as changes (for the better) in the ways in which local paramilitary organizations conduct their 'policing' activities such as referring cases to one of the schemes rather than punishing alleged anti-social offenders (McEvoy & Mika, 2002). As Burns (1978) has argued, '… transforming leadership ultimately becomes moral in that it raises the level of human conduct and ethical aspirations of both leader and led, and thus has a transforming effect on both' (p. 20).

Evidently the idea of 'moral leadership' being provided by former combatants may appear as counter-intuitive. However, such a viewpoint is ultimately a normative one as opposed to one based around the *realpolitik* of a situation that warrants a more rational understanding of political violence and the complexity of moral impetus and community reading. Furthermore, it is precisely because of their experience of a violent past that many former combatants are ideally placed to provide leadership around such issues given that their desire to undermine the use of violence cannot be denoted as cowardice. Accordingly, their rejection of the efficacy of violence as a strategy is itself a powerful exercise in both moral leadership and community capacity building.

4. CONCLUSIONS

The earlier discussion has considered the phenomenon of informal justice and punishment attacks that were a feature of the conflict in Northern Ireland. We have suggested that the existence and persistence of such attacks needs to be located within the dynamics of conflict, and do not sit easily with simplistic or mono-causal explanations. In particular we have argued that the internal organizational imperatives of the various armed groups and the need to exercise control within their respective communities; urban deprivation and economic malaise caused by Northern Ireland's position in the global economy and the economic effects of the conflict itself, together with major and fundamental problems with the nature, character and provision of public policing provision all contributed to a situation whereby punishment attacks could occur with impunity. We have also suggested that the peaks and troughs of punishment attacks needs to be set in the broader context of transition and political change and can be seen as both a response to political developments and a catalyst for them. The relative success of the transition process in Northern Ireland has attracted considerable international interest, both in terms of police reform (Ellison, 2007) but also restorative justice (McEvoy & Mika, 2002; McEvoy & Eriksson, 2008) and holds out a number of 'best-practice' lessons that can with some tweaking, be emulated internationally. However, the development of restorative justice initiatives and projects within Northern Ireland has met with considerable opposition (see McEvoy & Eriksson, 2008) and in some respects it has been an uphill struggle. The state has proved reticent about ceding too much authority to local communities, a point that can also be seen in the context of police reform; while a number of local political parties have suggested that such initiatives are merely a back-door route for paramilitary organizations to exercise control within their respective communities. Such a view, however, is to miss the point on a number of levels. The reality of the conflict and the transition to peace is that ex-combatants needed to become engaged with paths out of violence, and as we have suggested many were to play an extremely important and influential leadership role in this respect. Furthermore, in many fundamental respects the operation of restorative justice projects contains all the best-practice lessons of community-partnerships and local crime reduction initiatives that have become the hallmark of New Labour's crime and justice policy. The fact that many initiatives – particularly in republican areas – do not necessarily engage fulsomely with the police makes them no less worthy and in many cases such schemes demonstrate the level of partnership between local communities and the statutory/non-statutory agencies that the formal criminal justice sector can only dream of. It has taken time, but the experience from Northern Ireland demonstrates that restorative justice initiatives can make a real difference to levels of crime and anti-social activity. However, perhaps more fundamentally they have contributed to a reduction in the brutal and often barbaric forms of informal justice and punishment violence. In this sense they should be lauded.

NOTES

1. See BBC News, http://news.bbc.co.uk/1/hi/northern_ireland/4724599.stm (accessed 6th April 2006).
2. BBC News, 'IRA bomb devastates City of London' 24th April 1993. http://news.bbc.co.uk/onthisday/hi/dates/stories/april/24/newsid_2523000/2523345.stm (accessed 6th April 2006).
3. See for instance, the Report of the all party House of Commons Northern Ireland Affairs Committee, *The Financing of Terrorism in Northern Ireland* (Northern Ireland Affairs Committee, 2002, Fourth Report, House of Commons, HC 978-I, Session 2001-02). The Northern Ireland Policing Board, has noted in its most recent policing plan that organized crime is one of the biggest challenges facing the PSNI (see Northern Ireland Policing Board, *Policing Plan 2006-2008*, Belfast). To deal with the scale of the problem the government has recently established an Assets Recovery Agency in Northern Ireland and an Organized Crime Task Force.
4. This was a main criticism in the recent Ombudsman's investigation which suggested that a number of officers in the RUC's special branch colluded with members of loyalist paramilitary organizations in the murder of Catholic civilians.
5. In Northern Ireland the term 'tout' is used pejoratively for an informer. There have been documented cases of RUC officers offering bribes or inducements to young people in order to obtain information on the activities of individuals suspected of involvement in paramilitary activity.
6. This latter aspect is a documented feature of many post conflict and transitional societies. For comparative evidence from South Africa see Shaw (2000).
7. http://news.bbc.co.uk/1/hi/northern_ireland/522791.stm
8. http://www.abc.net.au/lateline/content/2005/s1326151.htm

REFERENCES

Brogden, M. (1982). *The police: Autonomy and consent*. London: Academic Press.
Bruce, S. (1992). *The Red Hand: Loyalist paramilitaries in Northern Ireland*. Oxford: Oxford University Press.

Burns, J. (1978). *Leadership*. New York: Harper & Row.

Call, C. T., & Stanley, W. (2001). Protecting the people: Public security choices *after civil wars*. Available at http://www.watsoninstitute.org/pub/CallGlobalGovArticle.pdf

Campbell, B. (1993). *Goliath: Britain's dangerous places*. London: Methuen.

Canning, D., Moore, B., & Rhodes, J. (1987). Economic growth in Northern Ireland: Problems and prospects. In: P. Teague (Ed.), *Beyond the rhetoric: Politics, the economy and social policy in Northern Ireland*. London: Lawrence & Wishart.

de Sousa Santos, B. (1982). Law and revolution in Portugal: The experiences of popular justice after 25th April 1974. In: R. Abel (Ed.), *The politics of informal justice* (Vol. 2). New York: Academic Press.

Ellison, G. (2007). A blueprint for democratic policing anywhere in the world?: Police reform, political transition and conflict resolution in Northern Ireland. *Police Quarterly, 10*, 243–269.

Ellison, G., & Martin, G. (2000). Policing, collective action and social movement theory: The case of the Northern Ireland civil rights campaign. *The British Journal of Sociology, 51*(4), 681–699.

Ellison, G., & Smyth, J. (2000). *The crowned harp: Policing Northern Ireland*. Pluto: London.

Gallaher, C., & Shirlow, P. (2006). The geography of loyalist paramilitary feuding in Belfast. *Space and Polity, 10*(2), 149–169.

Galtung, J. (1976). *Peace, war, and defence. Essays in peace research* (Vol. 2). Copenhagen: Christian Ejlers.

Hall, M. (Ed.) (2006). *Loyalism in transition: A new reality?* Island Pamphlets No.79. Newtownabbey: Island Publications.

Hollywood, B. (1997). Dancing in the dark: Ecstasy, the dance culture, and moral panic in post ceasefire Northern Ireland. *Critical Criminology, 8*(1), 62–77.

Independent Monitoring Commission (IMC). (2004). Third Report, House of Commons, HCC 1218, November, London: HMSO.

Kennedy, L. (1994). Nightmare within nightmare: Paramilitary repression within the working-class communities. In: L. Kennedy (Ed.), *Crime and punishment in West Belfast*. Belfast: The West Belfast Summer School.

McEvoy, K., & Eriksson, A. (2008). Who owns justice?: Community, state and the northern Ireland transition. In: J. Shapland (Ed.), *Justice, community and civil society: A contested terrain*. Cullompten: Willan.

McEvoy, K., & Mika, H. (2002). Restorative justice and the critique of informalism in Northern Ireland. *British Journal of Criminology, 42*(3), 534–562.

McGarry, J., & O'Leary, B. (1999). *Policing Northern Ireland: Proposals for a new start*. Belfast: Blackstaff Press.

McLaughlin, E. (2007). *The new policing*. Sage: London.

Mika, H. (2006). *Community based restorative justice in Northern Ireland: An evaluation, institute of criminology and criminal justice*. Belfast: The Queen's University.

Monaghan, R. (2002). The return of "Captain Moonlight"-informal justice in Northern Ireland. *Studies in Conflict and Terrorism, 25*(1), 41–56.

Mulcahy, A. (2006). *Policing Northern Ireland: Conflict, legitimacy and reform*. London: Willan Publishing.

Munck, R. (1984). The lads and the hoods: Alternative justice in an Irish context. In: M. Tomlinson, T. Varley & C. McCullagh (Eds), *Whose law and order? Aspects of crime control in Irish society*. Belfast: Sociological Association of Ireland.

Northern Ireland Statistics and Research Agency. (1988). *Northern Ireland annual abstract of statistics.* Belfast: NISRA.

O'Dowd, L. (1980). Shaping and reshaping the orange state: An introductory analysis. In: L. O'Dowd, B. Rolston & M. Tomlinson (Eds), *Northern Ireland: Between civil rights and civil war.* London: CSE Books.

OPONI. (2007). *Statement by the police ombudsman for Northern Ireland on her investigation into the circumstances surrounding the death of Raymond McCord Junior and related matters.* Belfast: OPONI.

Palmer, S. H. (1988). *Police and protest in England and Ireland, 1780–1850.* Cambridge: Cambridge University Press.

Shaw, M. (2000). *Crime, and policing in post-apartheid South Africa: Transforming under fire.* London: Hurst.

Shirlow, P. (2001). Fear and ethnic division. *Peace Review, 13*(8), 67–74.

Shirlow, P., & McEvoy, K. (2008). *Beyond the wire. Former prisoners and conflict transformation in Northern Ireland.* London: Pluto.

Sinnerton, H. (2002). *David Ervine: Unchartered waters.* Belfast: Brandon Books.

Skolnick, J. H., & Fyfe, J. J. (1993). *Above the law: Police and the excessive use of force.* New York: Free Press.

Smyth, M., & Fay, M. T. (2000). *Personal accounts from Northern Ireland's troubles: Public conflict, private loss.* London: Pluto Press.

Weitzer, R. (1987). Contested order: The struggle over British security policy in Northern Ireland. *Comparative Politics* (April), 281–298.

Young, J. (1999). *The exclusive society: Social exclusion, crime and difference in Late Modernity.* London: Sage.

THE AGENDAS OF THE RESTORATIVE JUSTICE MOVEMENT

Gerry Johnstone

ABSTRACT

This chapter examines how the aspirations of the restorative justice movement are broader than tends to be acknowledged in debates about the virtues and vices of restorative justice. It suggests that, along with trying to change the social response to crime, the movement is concerned to bring about transformations in the way conflict is handled in a range of institutions, in approaches to political reconciliation, in social organisation and in our understanding of the self. Also, along with introducing new procedures for handling social problems, the movement is concerned to bring about profound changes in the way problems are construed.

INTRODUCTION

This chapter is about restorative justice as a social movement, i.e. as a collective enterprise that is seeking to transform various aspects of contemporary society (Johnstone & Van Ness, 2007, p. 5).[1] My concern is to describe, in very broad terms, the sorts of transformations the restorative

Restorative Justice: From Theory to Practice
Sociology of Crime, Law and Deviance, Volume 11, 59–79
Copyright © 2008 by Emerald Group Publishing Limited
All rights of reproduction in any form reserved
ISSN: 1521-6136/doi:10.1016/S1521-6136(08)00403-X

justice movement (hereinafter, the RJM) is attempting to bring about. In particular, I am concerned to elucidate the *scope* and *nature* of these transformations. I will show that the ambitions of the RJM include, but also extend well beyond, changing the way contemporary societies deal with criminal behaviour. It is also concerned to change the way we deal with wrongdoing, deviant behaviour, conflict and unsatisfactory performance in a variety of institutional settings. With regard to the nature of the changes sought in these spheres, I show that the RJM is concerned, not only to change our procedures for dealing with crime and other social problems, but also to bring about fundamental changes in the way we construe these problems and in our conceptions of what constitutes a good solution. The RJM also seeks to transform the way post-conflict societies approach the task of political reconciliation. Moreover, the movement is seeking to bring about a set of far-reaching changes in ourselves and in existing social relations.

In this chapter, I purposely restrict myself to *describing* various transformations that the RJM seeks to bring about and eschew discussion of the feasibility and desirability of these changes (cf. Johnstone, 2002). There is a reason for this. In recent years there has been a surge of literature debating the virtues and vices of restorative justice. Although important and interesting, this debate is marred, in my view, in that it tends to revolve around a very narrow idea of what the RJM is trying to achieve. Often, the focus of debate is as narrow as the use of restorative processes (or sometimes only one of these processes) as dispositional processes within the criminal justice system. Even when the focus of debate is broader, it is still often widened only enough to encompass phenomena such as reparative sanctions in criminal justice and the use of restorative processes in other institutional settings such as schools. This chapter seeks to demonstrate the poverty of such a restricted focus by providing a fuller (but still by no means comprehensive) descriptive account of the agendas of the RJM than that which tends to be relied upon in debates about the merits and shortcomings of restorative justice.[2]

But while restricting myself to description, I do not confine myself to 'thin description' of the agendas of the RJM – description which simply outlines the 'surface' of the transformations which the RJM promotes. Rather, I am interested in a thicker description: one which encompasses the ideas underlying proposals for change, including ideas about what those changes will achieve. Indeed, in many places I seek to *explain* the agendas of the RJM in terms that I think are more coherent and comprehensible than the way these agendas are typically explained by members of the RJM.

What I want to avoid doing, in this chapter, is making any judgement of the value of the proposed transformations or about which, if any, of these transformations the RJM should pursue.

I will suggest that the RJM is pursuing at least five distinct agendas. They are distinct, however, for analytical purposes only; in reality, these agendas interweave and overlap. Also, each agenda is internally complex and could be broken down further. Nevertheless, I will suggest that these agendas are sufficiently distinct – and internally sufficiently coherent – to serve as a basis for fruitful discussion.[3] They are:

1. To promote the use of restorative processes within the social response to crime.
2. To encourage a new way of construing crime and related problems and new conceptions of what constitutes a good solution to such problems.
3. To promote the use of restorative processes and principles in a variety of institutional settings as a way of handling deviant behaviour, conflict and 'under-performance'.
4. To promote restorative justice as part of the solution to the problem of achieving political reconciliation in the aftermath of mass violence and oppression.
5. To create a just society, defined as a society in which all human needs are met, and – as an aspect of this – to transform the way people understand their selves and their relation to the world around them.

AGENDA 1: RESTORATIVE PROCESSES AND THE SOCIAL RESPONSE TO CRIME

The most familiar agenda of the RJM is to transform the social response to crime by promoting the use of processes such as victim–offender mediation (VOM), conferencing and circle sentencing. At the heart of these processes is the idea that offenders and their victims have a meeting facilitated by a trained mediator or facilitator.[4] In VOM, the mediator assists the victim and offender to resolve the conflict between them and to decide together what the offender should do to help repair the harm they have caused. As part of this process, victims and offenders are helped to express their feelings about what happened and to present their perception of events.

Conferencing is similar to VOM in that offenders take part in a facilitated meeting, usually and ideally with their victims also involved although sometimes with a surrogate victim. However, conferencing differs from VOM in significant ways. In particular, others are invited to take part in the meeting. The list can include family members of both offender and victim, members of community support groups, police officers and other justice officials, welfare workers and so on. Also, an explicit objective of conferencing is to improve the attitudes and behaviour of the offender. Conferencing, it is claimed, helps achieve this goal by making offenders more conscious of the harm and suffering their behaviour has caused to others whilst at the same time making them aware that many people care about them and are willing to support them in efforts to repair the harm they have done and improve their future behaviour. As with VOM, conferencing is also conceived as a forum in which people affected by crime can express their feelings.

In circle sentencing, a judge invites members of the community in which a crime has occurred to come into court and, sitting in a circle and taking turns to speak, express what they feel about the crime and the offender and indicate what they think can and should be done about the matter. The judge then takes the community's views into account when deciding upon a sentence. Circle sentencing shares some of the goals and ideas of VOM and conferencing. Another fairly explicit aspiration of circle processes is to strengthen communities that have been damaged by crime and other social problems.

Broader Aspects of This Agenda

By promoting the use of such processes as a key part of the social response to crime the RJM is seeking to instigate some more general changes in the nature of that response. First, it is seeking to turn back the tide of professionalisation of crime control and criminal justice that has advanced relentlessly for centuries. One of the key ideas underlying these processes is that the people affected fairly directly by criminal behaviour, and in some versions members of the wider community, should be directly involved in tasks such as holding offenders to account and deciding what should be done about an incident of criminal behaviour. Concomitantly, professionals and state officials should become less directly involved in the handling of criminal cases. Their role should switch to one of facilitating restorative dialogue between offenders, their victims and members of the community. This agenda, then, is rooted in a broader critique of professionalisation of responsibility for dealing with social problems (and related phenomena such as rationalisation and bureaucratisation) and in an associated revival of interest in lay participation in policy (Richardson, 1983).

The second more general change the RJM is after is a reversal of the tendency to keep offenders and their victims as separate as possible in the process for dealing with the offence. Restorative processes contrast significantly with many criminal justice processes in that they bring victims and offenders together, in a safe environment, to talk to each other. At least part of the wider goal here is to 'humanise' people – who are in conflict – to each other: to enable each to recognise the humanity of the other and to break through the stereotypes, fears and misunderstandings that frustrate efforts to bring peace where there is conflict. Here, the agenda of the RJM is rooted in a broader set of ideas about mediation (Bush & Folger, 1994) and peacemaking (Govier, 2006).

A third more general change being sought through the promotion of restorative processes is less obvious. One of the broader goals is to provide certain communities with a way of handling offences which is more appropriate to their culture (Consedine, 2000). Proponents of restorative justice frequently suggest that talking things out in a family and community circle is a traditional way of handling problems of troublesome behaviour amongst the New Zealand Maori, First Nation people in North America, and other indigenous peoples. Restorative processes enable the reactivation of these traditional methods. Here, the agenda of the RJM links up with broader agendas to do with revitalisation of the traditional customs of colonised peoples (Zion, 1998; cf. Cunneen, 2007).

Why Restorative Processes?

According to their advocates, restorative processes are extraordinarily powerful. It is claimed that, provided they are used in appropriate cases and skilfully conducted, they can have a profound transformative effect on the perspective of those who take part in them. Offenders who enter the process not only lacking remorse but wholly indifferent to the harm they have done often emerge feeling deep regret for their behaviour, committed to repairing the harm they have done and determined to refrain from further criminal conduct. Victims who enter the process deeply traumatised emerge feeling that they are on the path to recovery. Those who enter the process with vengeful feelings tend to emerge with a more charitable attitude towards the offender and many indeed are keen to help the offender in their efforts improve their conduct and lifestyle. Members of the community tend to emerge much more confident of their capacity to handle difficult social problems. Observers, even those who are initially quite sceptical, tend to be deeply moved by what they see and often join the RJM.[5]

More generally, restorative processes are claimed to be more effective than 'traditional' criminal justice processes in achieving many of the objectives of the criminal justice system.[6] They are better at preventing reoffending, holding offenders accountable, and assuring victims and members of the public that something meaningful has been done in response to the crime (Braithwaite, 2003a). In addition, it is suggested, these processes achieve further valuable goals that the criminal justice system does not even attempt to achieve. For instance, they provide opportunities for people to express and have validated their feelings about what happened, thereby helping people deal with the emotional consequences of being involved (as victim, offender or bystander) in a criminal incident.

AGENDA 2: A NEW CONCEPTION OF CRIME AND JUSTICE

The second agenda is again focused on transforming the social response to criminal behaviour. However, it seeks an even more profound change in the nature of that response than is sought in agenda 1. What is sought is a change in the way the problem of crime is construed and a concomitant change in our conception of what constitutes a good solution. To describe this agenda we need first to describe what it is that the RJM seeks to replace: the traditional way of construing the problem of crime and traditional notions of what constitutes a good solution.

The Traditional Model of Crime and Justice

If we were to ask 'what is wrong with committing crime?', and look to the discourse and practices of traditional criminal justice for an answer, we might arrive at something like the following.[7] Within society, there is a set of rules called the criminal law. These are issued by the state and prohibit people from doing certain things on the ground that these things are injurious to other members of society, i.e. to their life, wellbeing, liberty or possessions. Crime is a voluntary infraction of these rules. It is therefore an injurious act. But, it is much more than that; it is an act of conscious disobedience of the state's authority. Crime is an act of defiance; in committing a crime, a person does something which they have been expressly forbidden to do by the state.

What, then, constitutes a good solution to the problem of criminal behaviour? In the traditional model, what one is seeking from a solution are a number of things. Above all, the authority which has been defied must be reasserted – the state must do something to display its entitlement to prohibit certain forms of behaviour within its jurisdiction and to have those prohibitions obeyed. In addition, something should be done to discourage or prevent the person who has broken the law – and perhaps others with similar motives and opportunities – from further breaches. Also, the offender must be deprived of any benefit or pleasure they obtained from committing the crime.

In contemporary societies, the preferred method of achieving these goals is state punishment of the offender. Such punishment consists of the deliberate imposition of some painful sanction (such as imprisonment or a monetary fine) upon the lawbreaker. Through punishment, the state re-asserts its authority. Punishment also has the capacity to discourage crime, by deterring the offender and others from future criminal acts. Some forms of punishment can also prevent crimes in other ways, e.g. by incapacitating those who have shown a propensity to break the law. Also, punishment offsets any benefit or pleasure which the offender may have derived from his or her act of lawbreaking.

An untrammelled power to punish lawbreakers would, however, give the state the capacity to dominate its citizens in a way that is inconsistent with notions of individual rights and liberties that emerged in Europe from the sixteenth century and were subsequently further developed, articulated and theorised. Hence, at least in liberal-democratic societies, it tends to be insisted that the state's power to punish be restricted and regulated. Various 'principles of justice' have been developed to govern the power to punish. These include: people can only be punished for a breach of a published criminal law; they must be proclaimed guilty in a public court, having had the opportunity for a fair and impartial trial; the severity of punishment must be proportionate to the seriousness of the crime or based on what is necessary for deterrence; and the severity of punishment cannot be modified to take account of factors that are deemed, by principle, to be irrelevant (such as purely personal characteristics of the offender or the victim's attitude – be it one of forgiveness or vengeance).

In sum, then, a good solution to the problem is crime is a solution which achieves the goals of criminal justice, such as reassertion of authority that has been defied, though punishment of the offender in accordance with the widely acknowledged principles of justice.

The RJM's Proposed Alternative Model

For the RJM, the core problem with this model is that it fails to capture what it is that makes crime wrong. Crime is certainly a violation of the state's authority – but this is not what makes it *so* wrong. Rather, what mainly makes crime wrong is that it is a violation of another *person*. As Howard Zehr puts it, in effort to describe the 'private' dimensions of crime (dimensions which for him are its essence and which are not properly highlighted in the traditional model): 'crime is in essence a violation: a violation of the self, a desecration of who we are, of what we believe, of our private space' (Zehr, 1990, p. 24).

We need to be clear about what Zehr (along with others in the RJM) is arguing here. The point is not simply that crime injures other people; that much is clearly recognised by the traditional model and to state it would hardly be saying anything interesting. Rather, his point is that the traditional model pays far too little attention to this fact, that it tends to focus much more on the fact that crime is an offence against an impersonal entity such as the state, and that when remedies are being devised they are remedies for the injury done to the state – not remedies for the injury done to the individual victim. What Zehr is suggesting, then, is that we should construe crime as *primarily* an act whereby one person violates another person, and only secondarily as an offence against the state. Building upon this point, Zehr and others in the RJM have sought to highlight and describe the nature and consequences of such violation. Crime, they argue, is deeply traumatic. This is not only because of the material injury it causes (the property that has been stolen or damaged, the body that has been wounded, etc.) but because of the psychological and emotional harm it causes to its victims (see also Strang, 2002) and perhaps also because of what it says about the offender's attitude towards the victim.[8]

The RJM, then, encourages us to construe crime in a different way – a way which focuses attention on the 'private' dimensions of crime: the damage and trauma its causes to its direct victims and those closely connected to them. If we adopt this way of construing crime, it follows that we need a new conception of what the solution to the problem of crime is. A solution designed to reassert the authority of the state is not obviously going to be a solution to the problem of the violation of another person. For the RJM, a good solution to the problem of crime is, in fact, one which repairs the harm done by crime. In other words, a good solution is one which repairs not only the material harm done by crime, but also the psychological, emotional and symbolic harm inflicted on the victim. A good solution is one that promotes healing of the trauma caused to victims by criminal violations. This, I think, is one reason why members of the RJM frequently talk about 'healing justice' as an alternative to punitive justice (Van Ness & Strong, 2006, pp. 3–4).

The problem with the punishment of offenders, then, is not simply – and not even mainly – that in practice it frequently fails to achieve some objectives of traditional criminal justice (e.g. it often fails to deter). Rather, the key problem is that (according to the RJM) it is not aimed at redressing the most significant wrong of crime: the traumatic violation of another person. We need a new solution to the problem of crime, one that is designed to repair the harm crime causes to other people.

For the RJM, the best solutions are in fact those organised around the processes described in agenda 1. These processes, provided they are used consciously as part of a wider project of reparation, are particularly suited to repairing the harm and healing the trauma caused by crime. However, within the terms of agenda 2, these processes are not ends in themselves, but rather means (and probably the best means currently available) of achieving the goals of reparation and healing. They are valuable only to the extent that they do in fact achieve such goals. And, within the terms of agenda 2, it is feasible that other processes could be promoted if they too are demonstrated to be effective in repairing the harm of crime (Johnstone & Van Ness, 2007, pp. 12–15).

AGENDA 3: PROMOTING RESTORATIVE JUSTICE PROCESSES AND PRINCIPLES IN A VARIETY OF SETTINGS

The third agenda looked at here is similar to the first, in that its concern is to promote the use of restorative processes. However, in this agenda the aim is to promote these processes, not only within the social response to crime, but in a much wider range of settings including schools, the workplace and elsewhere in the community where conflict may arise.[9] For example, there is a large movement to develop the use of restorative processes in schools for handling problems such as bullying and truancy (Morrison, 2007), in prisons for dealing with 'internal' problems such as breaches of prison rules (Johnstone, 2007), as a way of handling complaints by the public against the police as well as breaches of discipline by police officers (Pollard, undated), and for the handling of grievances in the workplace.[10]

A feature of this agendas is that, whilst the initial focus has been on problems analogous to criminal behaviour (e.g. bullying and breaches of prison rules), there are usually attempts to extend the use of restorative processes to the handling of problems which are not in any obvious sense problems of deviant conduct. One example of this is from the use of restorative processes in the workplace. The organisation 'Restorative Solutions',[11] promotes restorative justice as an alternative or complement to existing conflict management strategies as a way of handling grievances in the workplace. Some of these grievances clearly have their source in deviant conduct such as employee misconduct, workplace bullying and sexual harassment. However, some of the 'grievances' arise from rather different types of problem: problems such as absenteeism, aggressive management and 'performance issues'. Although this seems a small step, it is in fact highly significant. It envisages the use of restorative processes, not simply as a tool which can be used to deal more effectively with behaviour that clearly infringes certain rules or norms, but as a tool that can be used to manage people more effectively in order to achieve the positive goals of an organisation.

A further aspect of this agenda is the tendency to move from promoting the use of restorative processes to handle specific problems when they arise (as an alternative to standard disciplinary processes, complaints handling procedures, strategies of conflict management, etc.) to trying to reform entire organisations in line with restorative principles. Examples of this are whole-school approaches to restorative justice (Hopkins, 2004; Morrison, 2007, p. 329) and restorative prison projects (Edgar & Newell, 2006; Johnstone, 2007; Van Ness, 2007). Here, the aim becomes to transform entire organisation or institutions – many of them which operate on hierarchical, regimental lines – in line with restorative principles.

It is interesting to compare this third agenda with agenda 1 in terms of its ambitiousness. Looked at in one way, this seems like a less ambitious agenda. Significant transformation in the way we handle crime is difficult to achieve. The sort of transformation sought by the RJM is especially difficult to achieve in contemporary societies because it involves a more constructive approach to offenders at a time when there is a political consensus about the need to be tough with those who break the law. In this context, it is tempting to see the move to develop restorative processes in other contexts as an attempt to salvage the RJM by focusing its efforts on settings where there might be less resistance to experimentation with restorative processes.

Looked at in another way, this might be seen as a more ambitious agenda than agenda 1. If we ignore petty misdemeanours and regulatory offences, crime – for all the concern about it – is still a pretty exceptional event. A change in the way we handle crime, whilst it may have profound long-term effects, is not likely to affect many people *directly* in the short term. So, whatever political opposition it might meet with, the attempt to develop restorative processes in the context of crime is not likely to meet with intense resistance at the level of implementation, other than from some professionals.[12] However, the promotion of restorative processes in schools, workplaces, etc., has direct implications for a great number of people. Poor performance, aggressive management, etc., are phenomena that very many of us are affected by (either as aggressive managers/poor performers and/or as those affected by aggressive management and poor performance of others). This third agenda, then, will require selling the idea of restorative justice to a much wider range of people.

AGENDA 4: RESTORATIVE JUSTICE AND POLITICAL RECONCILIATION

There are signs of the RJM becoming increasingly interested in the potential contribution of restorative justice to projects of political reconciliation. The problem of political reconciliation arises in societies which have been torn apart by mass violence and gross violations of human rights. Rwanda, the countries that were formerly part of Yugoslavia, South Africa and Northern Ireland are typical examples (Minow, 1998; Govier, 2006). However, it also arises in less obvious settings, such as in the context of racial alienation in the USA which is profoundly affected by the legacy of slavery (Brooks, 2004). Trudy Govier provides a useful, succinct statement of the problem:

> [P]eople living in the same society need to cooperate; to cooperate, they need to trust; and in the aftermath of violence and oppression, that is difficult. To say that people alienated by wrongdoing are in no position to trust and cooperate is an understatement. Efforts towards reconciliation can be understood as attempts to end alienation and resentment and build relationships characterised by some degree of trust. (Govier, 2006, p. 7)

Within this field, there are profound debates about such core issues as what the goal of reconciliation is (what sort of reconciliation is it appropriate to strive for?) and how best to achieve it. One of the central problems is to find a way of dealing with past wrongdoing which provides victims (including family and community members of direct victims) with some feeling that justice has been done, but at the same time does not create fresh obstacles to reconciliation.

In the aftermath of mass violence and gross violations of human rights, when some order has been restored, victims of wrongdoing tend to demand 'justice'. What they usually have in mind is the criminal trial and punishment of perpetrators of wrongdoing according to their just deserts (Minow, 1998). As we shall see, meeting these demands, even where it is feasible to do so, is often deemed undesirable because it creates an obstacle to political reconciliation. Hence, there is a strong temptation to urge victims of wrongdoing simply to forget about the past or grant perpetrators of past wrongdoing an unconditional amnesty. Moreover, some victims at least are so wearied and traumatised by what has happened that they are tempted to accept these solutions, for the sake of future peace.

Many, however, consider such approaches as morally objectionable – victims are denied their right to justice. Some argue further that such approaches can in fact be an obstacle to enduring political reconciliation. The victims of wrongdoing tend to be so embittered by the failure of those in charge to grant them justice that they refuse to cooperate with or trust others in society. Even where they go along with such approaches in the short term, there is always the danger that in the longer term old resentments will re-surface and result in fresh spates of violence.

The problem is that meeting victims' demands for justice is often not feasible, and even if feasible can itself create new obstacles to political reconciliation. In the aftermath of mass violence, bringing a significant proportion of perpetrators to 'justice' is often simply not possible. While it may be possible to bring a small handful of perpetrators to 'justice', where the proportion is a very small one the process smacks of selective punishment, which is itself inconsistent with broader notions of justice (Minow, 1998). A further problem is that many perpetrators of wrongdoing may themselves also be victims of wrongdoing. Indeed, this is highly likely in a society in which two or more groups have engaged in campaigns of violence against the others over a period of time.

Even in situations where it might be possible to bring a significant proportion of perpetrators of wrongdoing to justice, there may be strong arguments for not doing so. In particular, it may be necessary to forgo 'justice' if any degree of political reconciliation is going to be achieved. For instance, one group which is party to a violent conflict might agree to cease using violence, and start cooperating with others, only on the condition that its members are exempt from 'justice' for wrongs committed as part of a conflict. Even if they do not make such demands, the process of bringing to trial and punishing perpetrators of wrongdoing is likely to be a divisive one that imperils the goal of political reconciliation. Another problem is that the group which is to be subjected to justice may control vital resources – or be the only group which has certain essential knowledge and skills – which the society may require to rebuild itself. A decision to punish them may result in society losing those resources and skills.

In search of solutions to this dilemma, many in the field of political reconciliation have turned to restorative justice as an alternative to criminal trials and punishment. One of the key attractions of restorative justice is that it may have the potential to satisfy victims' demands for justice without alienation or destroying perpetrators of wrongdoing. What is understood by restorative justice, in this context, is an approach to justice that, first, calls upon perpetrators to acknowledge the wrongness of what they have done and then to make serious efforts at symbolic reparation. Reparation involves apologising for doing wrong and demonstrating the sincerity of that apology by doing things such as paying monetary reparation, doing other positive things for victims and victimised groups, and even undergoing something burdensome. Restorative justice is accomplished, however, only when those who acknowledge and make serious efforts to repair the harm they have done are reintegrated (or integrated for the first time) into society – or at least when there has been some gesture of reacceptance.

The appeal of restorative justice to those concerned with political reconciliation is, however, due to much more than the fact that it is potentially a less divisive way of achieving justice. The fit between restorative justice and reconciliation is much tighter than this. In the early experiments with restorative justice in the 1970s, reconciliation between victims and offenders was a central goal. Indeed, the early experiments were called 'victim/offender reconciliation projects' (VORPS) (Peachey, 2003). Advocates of restorative justice continue to tell stories about victims of crime – sometimes quite atrocious crimes – not only becoming less hostile towards the perpetrators of these crimes, as a result of restorative justice, but becoming friends with them.[13] Many members of the RJM do have a much more cautious attitude towards the goal of reconciliation. Van Ness and Strong (2006, p. 72) for instance, suggest that the more appropriate and realistic goal for restorative justice should be to get victims and offenders to respect each other, see each other as persons and identify with the experiences of the other. However, this still represents a move in the direction of reconciliation (away from hostility) and is presented as a benefit that often comes from restorative justice, even if promoting reconciliation is not pursued as a central goal.

Activists and theorists interested in reconciliation and sustainable peace who have turned to the concept of restorative justice as a fruitful framework for thinking through these issues are not necessarily members of the RJM.

Many, for instance, might regard restorative justice as only one strategy among many for achieving their goals, and may be quite wary about placing too much faith in it. Also, those pursuing political reconciliation who have shown an interest in restorative justice tend to have little interest in, or awareness of, the development of restorative justice in more 'domestic' contexts. However, their interest in restorative justice creates an opportunity for the RJM to extend restorative processes, principles and ideas into a new terrain.

Within the RJM, there has been increasing interest in recent years in developing restorative justice in this direction.[14] The strength of this tendency should not be overestimated. Issues of political reconciliation still barely feature in major international conferences of the RJM. And, the areas focused upon so far have been fairly obvious one: societies torn apart by recent violent conflict. For instance, the RJM has been extremely slow to recognise issues such as the debate about reparation for slavery as issues in which it should be taking the lead. However, this is an emergent agenda of the RJM and one which may develop rapidly.

AGENDA 5: TRANSFORMING OUR SOCIETIES AND EVERYDAY LIVES

The fifth agenda, like the third, envisages an expansion of the mission of restorative justice: an application of restorative justice principles beyond the sphere of crime, deviance and social control. However, it envisages a broader and deeper transformation than that of agenda 3. Whereas agenda 3 promotes the use of restorative processes in a variety of institutional settings – settings where deviance, conflict and under-performance have to be dealt with – agenda 5 seeks the application of restorative justice to questions of social organisation and personal lifestyle. Moreover, it seeks a profound transformation in these spheres. Here, I will attempt to provide a very brief indication of the sorts of changes that are envisaged.

According to advocates of this agenda, the goal of the RJM should be, not simply to design and promote interventions that are more effective in restoring justice in the aftermath of crime, but to create a more just society. As John Braithwaite has put it:

> [R]estorative justice is not simply a way of reforming the criminal justice system, it is a way of transforming the entire legal system, our family lives, our conduct in the workplace, our practice of politics. Its vision is of a holistic change in the way we do justice in the world. (Braithwaite, 2003b, p. 1)

The argument of those who urge the RJM to pursue this agenda is that the more conventional restorative justice project (e.g. agendas 1 and 2) is too limited and conservative. Restorative justice seeks to repair the harm created and revealed by unjust acts. However, it is argued, it focuses attention upon a very limited range of unjust acts – those that are officially classified as criminal, while ignoring much behaviour that is not classified as criminal but is equally unjust and causes great harm.[15] In fact, according to some advocates, countless harmful acts occur everyday as part of normal social interaction in a society which is *structurally violent* (Sullivan & Tifft, 2001; Gil, 2006).

However, the problem is not simply that the RJM will fail to provide redress for victims of such harm if it confines its goals to reforming the social response to (officially designated) criminal behaviour. In addition, it will actually help legitimate structural violence. This is because – at least for some advocates of this fifth agenda – behaviour that is officially classified as crime is itself ultimately caused by structural violence.[16] David Gil (2006) claims that crime should be understood as 'counter-violence': a reaction to social-structural violence that interferes with the fulfilment of human needs (p. 505). However, rather than this counter-violence being directed at those responsible for social-structural violence (who are, in any event, difficult to identify) it tends to be (mis)directed at others who are perhaps also victims of social-structural violence. Criminal justice is then depicted by Gil as 'repressive social-structural violence in response to counter-violence, aimed at controlling punishing and "correcting" perpetrators of counter-violence and deterring further counter-violence' (*ibid.*). If this is the case, what the RJM is doing, when it pursues agendas 1 and 2, is seeking to improve and humanise 'repressive social-structural violence'. This very focus deflects attention from and helps to legitimate the initial social-structural violence which sets off the chain: social-structural violence → counter-violence → repressive social-structural violence in response to counter-violence (cf. Pavlich, 2005).

What the RJM needs to do, then, if it is to act consistently with its ideas and objectives, is ensure that its efforts to do justice in the aftermath of crime are accompanied by, or perhaps even subordinated to, efforts to tackle social-structural violence, i.e. it should seek to transform structurally violent, unjust societies. As some advocates of this agenda put it, restorative justice needs to become transformative justice (Sullivan & Tifft, 2006b).

What does this involve? The goal for Gil, and for others such as Sullivan and Tifft (2001) who share his view of the proper agenda of restorative justice – is to transform our social arrangements so that the needs of all people in the world (their biological-material needs, social-psychological needs, productive-creative needs, security needs, self-actualisation needs and spiritual needs) are fulfilled. Gil suggests that this goal could be achieved through a worldwide redistribution of the world's resources and burdens:

> The institutional requirements of global justice could be met by sharing the aggregate of the resources, knowledge, work, and goods and services of the global community in ways conducive to meeting everyone's needs, and realizing everyone's innate capacities. People everywhere would thus have equal social, economic, and political rights, responsibilities, opportunities, and constraints, and no one would be dominated and exploited by others. (Gil, 2006, p. 503)

What are the obstacles to this? According to Sullivan and Tifft (2001), the fundamental obstacle is an ideological one. We are accustomed to thinking about justice in a different way. Our relationships and daily lives are organised around rights-based and deserts-based notions of justice. We believe that people in possession of certain resources have a right to those resources, so that to transfer them to others without their consent is to violate their rights which is morally objectionable. In addition, people tend to subscribe to deserts-based notions of justice, according to which 'it is believed that a person should receive benefits, privileges and burdens and have access to resources on the basis of merit or desert, according to the efforts he or she has put forth' (*ibid.*, p. 99). Sullivan and Tifft argue that such notions of justice are flawed and should be replaced by a needs-based conception of justice, of the sort described by Gil.

But, even amongst those who find this way of thinking attractive, there is a tendency to assume that achieving complete justice (as defined in the needs-based conception) is either impossible or would require violent revolution. One objection is that there are simply not enough resources in the world to meet the needs of all. Accordingly, we have to find some other principle for distributing scarce resources, perhaps involving some complex mixture of needs-based, desert-based and rights-based approaches.[17] A related objection is that, given human nature, people will lack the motivation to develop and produce resources if these resources are allocated purely according to need, with no consideration of merit. On this view, a desert-based distribution is a matter of social prudence, even if it does result in some people not having even their basic needs met.

A further objection is that any attempt to redistribute resources according to a needs-based conception of justice would be violently resisted by the privileged: those who benefit from our existing 'oppressive processes and relations'. Hence, social justice, as defined in the needs-based conception, could only be achieved through the use of violence and coercion. Some, of course, are perfectly happy to endorse such violence in the pursuit of justice. But this creates problems for members of the RJM, because it conflicts with another central principle of restorative justice: that goals should be pursued in a non-coercive, non-violent and peaceful way. To endorse violence in the pursuit of justice would be to take one outside of the RJM.

Gil's response to such objections is to challenge the assumption that global resources are necessarily limited. One effect of meeting the needs of all, he suggests, would be to increase the capacity of people to create resources which can be used to meet the needs of all:

> Contrary to intuitive assumptions and fears, redistribution of resources, knowledge, work, and goods and services in accordance with principles of global justice need not cause major declines in the quality of life of privileged people and nations. Global wealth is not a fixed, zero-sum quantity and quality but is enhanced quantitatively and qualitatively as the productive potential of underdeveloped people and countries is liberated. Redistribution would have to be implemented gradually, thoughtfully, and non-coercively, as more and more people come to discover that social justice would serve their inherent needs and real interests and would, therefore, enrich everyone. (Gil, 2006, p. 503)

Sullivan and Tifft (2001) are well aware, however, that this sort of transformation requires a profound change, not only in our political outlook, but in our perception of ourselves (ch. 8). The argument here is a complex one, but the following passage might convey something of its essence:

> Because restorative justice requires that the unique needs of each person be taken into account and met, those who seek to create restorative relationships must begin with social arrangements that are structurally inclusive ...
>
> But adopting such a perspective does not come without significant effort, without a radical reframing or our views of self and the other, that is, of our political economy of relationship. Anyone who seeks to adopt a restorative, needs-based perspective on justice must first confront the self that hierarchically ranks the worth of some over that of others and treats the categories created by such rankings as a fact of human nature ...
>
> If we wish to create a just community in which restorative justice is a cornerstone, we must make a commitment to not reforming but dissolving the self. (Sullivan & Tifft, 2001, pp. 163–165)

Rupert Ross (1996) – although coming at this issue for a very different direction – would no doubt concur. In his exploration of aboriginal conceptions of justice, he suggest that we (people in contemporary western societies) have great difficulty in comprehending, let alone practicing, the sort of 'healing' or peacemaker' justice that he encountered in his exploration of the vision of justice adhered to by various aboriginal peoples. This is because the vision is grounded in a fundamentally different way of understanding ourselves and our place in the world.[18] According to Ross, the very structure of our language – with its preponderance of judgmental nouns and adjectives – is an obstacle to our grasping properly the teachings of aboriginal peoples, whose language is characterised by a dearth of such nouns and adjectives (*ibid.*, pp. 101ff.). Ross provides a multitude of other examples of how our entire way of seeing and representing the world, which is difficult for us to escape, conditions us to think of justice in a certain way, which is antithetical to the healing–peacemaker justice of aboriginal peoples, within which adopting a needs-based conception of social justice would seem more natural.

The implication of Sullivan and Tifft's and Ross's work is that, creating a society in which the requirements of restorative justice (as they are understood by Gil and Sullivan and Tifft) are met, requires a profound political, cultural and psychological transformation – and that the different aspects of this transformation must go hand-in-hand.

CONCLUSION

My main aim has been a simple one: to show that the RJM has multiple agendas and that these differ significantly, in terms of their focus, scope and depth. Nevertheless, these agendas are linked in that they emanate from the same social movement. There are certain core ideas which tie them together.

I also want to suggest that those who debate the virtues and vices of restorative justice need to be aware of the full range of transformations which the RJM seeks to bring about. This is not, of course, to suggest that those interested in particular agendas – such as the agenda to introduce restorative processes in the workplace to resolve issues of workplace conflict or the agenda to employ restorative approaches to justice as part of the solution to problems of political reconciliation in the aftermath of genocide and mass violence – need to discuss or evaluate the entire programme of the RJM. But they should be aware that in discussing a particular agenda, they are not discussing restorative justice per se, but only one dimension of it.

This chapter is also intended to provide some of the groundwork for a sociological study of the social movement for restorative justice. The emergence, rapid growth and rising social prominence of the RJM is an extraordinary phenomenon. A study of its composition, goals, ideology, etc., will probably tell us much about the changing nature of the societies in which the RJM has gained a foothold. A starting point for such a study must be an adequate account of what it is that the RJM seeks to achieve.

NOTES

1. For the definition of social movements, see Crossley (2002, ch. 1).
2. In this chapter, I have opted for the modern usage of 'agenda' as singular, with 'agendas' as the plural.
3. I do not intend to imply that any of the agendas I describe has been fully worked out. Within each, there are many areas where the agenda is vague or where, internally, there is lack of agreement on the precise nature of the transformation sought.
4. These processes are described in many places in the literature of the RJM. For useful introductory descriptions see McCold (2006), Newburn (2007, pp. 752–758), Van Ness and Strong (2006, ch. 4) and Zehr (2002, ch. 3).
5. Robinson (2003, pp. 375–377) provides a useful summary of the 'virtues of restorative processes'.
6. The RJM – and those who comment on it – often describes established ways of thinking about and practicing criminal justice as the 'traditional' model of criminal justice. Although this term is ambiguous (since it could also refer to pre-modern criminal justice, towards which the RJM has a very different attitude) I will use it in the remainder of this chapter without scare quotes.
7. On the following, see Johnstone and Ward (2008).
8. Bennett (2007) provides a very useful expansion and rectification of the theory of the damage done by crime present in the work of Zehr. Whilst clearly sympathetic to the RJM, Bennett draws upon the work of more traditional 'retributivist' philosophers of punishment such as Peter Strawson, Jeffrie Murphy and Jean Hampton.
9. See the objectives of the restorative justice consortium in a document available at www.restorativejustice.org.uk/ – accessed 31 October 2007.
10. http://www.restorativesolutions.us/organizations.html – accessed 31 October 2007.
11. This organisation has 'pioneered restorative justice in government, schools, community organizations, faith communities and within individuals'.
12. This professional resistance is, of course, a huge potential obstacle.
13. See Daly (2003) on stories told about restorative justice.
14. See, for instance, Llewellyn (2007), McEvoy and Newburn (2003) and Sullivan and Tifft (2006a, section V).
15. The argument here has significant overlaps with that of critical criminologists such as Hillyard and Tombs (2004) who maintain that the official category of crime includes many acts which cause relatively little harm, and excludes many acts which cause serious harm to people.
16. Others such as John Braithwaite, whilst they seem highly sympathetic towards this fifth agenda, would not (I guess) fully subscribe to this explanation of conventional criminal behaviour.

17. Within such an approach, there would still be space for a radical redistribution of resources.
18. Sawatsky (2008) is a fascinating study of notions and practices of healing justice.

REFERENCES

Bennett, C. (2007). Satisfying the needs and interests of victims. In: G. Johnstone & D. Van Ness (Eds), *Handbook of restorative justice* (pp. 247–264). Cullompton, Devon: Willan Publishing.
Braithwaite, J. (2003a). Restorative justice and a better future. In: G. Johnstone (Ed.), *A restorative justice reader* (pp. 83–97). Cullompton, Devon: Willan Publishing.
Braithwaite, J. (2003b). Principles of restorative justice. In: A. von Hirsch, J. Roberts, A. Bottoms, K. Roach & M. Schiff (Eds), *Restorative justice and criminal justice: Competing or reconcilable paradigms* (pp. 1–20). Oxford: Hart Publishing.
Brooks, R. (2004). *Atonement and forgiveness: A new model for black reparations*. Berkeley, CA: University of California Press.
Bush, R., & Folger, J. (1994). *The promise of mediation: Responding to conflict through empowerment and recognition*. San Francisco: Jossey-Bass Publishers.
Consedine, J. (2000). Restorative justice: An interview with Jim Consedine. *America, 182*(6), 7–12.
Crossley, N. (2002). *Making sense of social movements*. Buckingham: Open University Press.
Cunneen, C. (2007). Reviving restorative justice traditions? In: G. Johnstone & D. Van Ness (Eds), *Handbook of restorative justice* (pp. 113–131). Cullompton, Devon: Willan Publishing.
Daly, K. (2003). Restorative justice: The real story. In: G. Johnstone (Ed.), *A restorative justice reader* (pp. 363–381). Cullompton, Devon: Willan Publishing.
Edgar, K., & Newell, T. (2006). *Restorative justice in prisons*. Winchester: Waterside Press.
Gil, D. (2006). Toward a 'radical' paradigm of restorative justice. In: D. Sullivan & L. Tifft (Eds), *Handbook of restorative justice: A global perspective* (pp. 499–511). London: Routledge.
Govier, T. (2006). *Taking wrongs seriously: Acknowledgement, reconciliation, and the politics of sustainable peace*. Amherst, NY: Humanity Books.
Hillyard, P., & Tombs, S. (2004). Beyond criminology? In: P. Hillyard, C. Pantazis, S. Tombs & D. Gordon (Eds), *Beyond criminology: Taking harm seriously* (pp. 7–22). London: Pluto Press.
Hopkins, B. (2004). *Just schools: A whole school approach to restorative justice*. London: Jessica Kingsley.
Johnstone, G. (2002). *Restorative justice: Ideas, values, debates*. Cullompton, Devon: Willan Publishing.
Johnstone, G. (2007). Restorative justice and the practice of imprisonment. *Prison Service Journal* (November), 173.
Johnstone, G., & Van Ness, D. (2007). The meaning of restorative justice. In: G. Johnstone & D. Van Ness (Eds), *Handbook of restorative justice* (pp. 5–23). Cullompton, Devon: Willan Publishing.
Johnstone, G., & Ward, T. (2008). *Law and crime*. London: Sage (forthcoming).

Llewellyn, J. (2007). Truth commissions and restorative justice. In: G. Johnstone & D. Van Ness (Eds), *Handbook of restorative justice* (pp. 351–371). Cullompton, Devon: Willan Publishing.

McCold. (2006). The recent history of restorative justice: Mediation, circles and conferencing. In: D. Sullivan & L. Tifft (Eds), *Handbook of restorative justice: A global perspective* (pp. 23–51). London: Routledge.

McEvoy, K., & Newburn, T. (Eds). (2003). *Criminology, conflict resolution and restorative justice*. London: Palgrave.

Minow, M. (1998). *Between vengeance and forgiveness: Facing history after genocide and mass violence*. Boston, MA: Beacon Press.

Morrison, B. (2007). Schools and restorative justice. In: G. Johnstone & D. Van Ness (Eds), *Handbook of restorative justice* (pp. 325–350). Cullompton, Devon: Willan Publishing.

Newburn, T. (2007). *Criminology*. Cullompton, Devon: Willan Publishing.

Pavlich, G. (2005). *Governing paradoxes of restorative justice*. London: Glasshouse Press.

Peachey, D. (2003). The Kitchener experiment. In: G. Johnstone (Ed.), *A restorative justice reader* (pp. 178–196). Cullompton, Devon: Willan Publishing.

Pollard, C. (n.d.). *Restorative justice and police complaints*. Available at www.iirp.org/library/t2000/t2000_cpollard.html. Accessed on 5 November 2007.

Richardson, A. (1983). *Participation*. London: Routledge.

Robinson, P. (2003). The virtues of restorative processes, the vices of "restorative justice". *Utah Law Review, 1*, 375–388.

Ross, R. (1996). *Returning to the teachings: Exploring aboriginal justice*. Toronto: Penguin.

Sawatsky, J. (2008). *The ethic of traditional communities and the spirit of healing justice*. Ph.D. thesis, Unpublished. University of Hull, UK.

Strang, H. (2002). *Repair or revenge: Victims and restorative justice*. Oxford: Oxford University Press.

Sullivan, D., & Tifft, L. (2001). *Restorative justice: Healing the foundations of our everyday lives*. Monsey, NY: Willow Tree Press.

Sullivan, D., & Tift, L. (Eds). (2006a). *Handbook of restorative justice: A global perspective*. London and New York: Routledge.

Sullivan, D., & Tift, L. (2006b). Transformative justice and structural change. In: D. Sullivan & L. Tift (Eds), *Handbook of restorative justice: A global perspective* (pp. 495–497). London and New York: Routledge.

Van Ness, D. (2007). Prisons and restorative justice. In: G. Johnstone & D. Van Ness (Eds), *Handbook of restorative justice* (pp. 312–324). Cullompton, Devon: Willan Publishing.

Van Ness, D., & Strong, K. (2006). *Restoring justice* (3rd ed.). Cincinnati, OH: Anderson.

Zehr, H. (1990). *Changing lenses: A new focus for crime and justice*. Scottdale, PA: Herald Press.

Zehr, H. (2002). *The little book of restorative justice*. Intercourse, PA: Good Books.

Zion, J. (1998). The use of custom and legal tradition in the modern justice setting. *Contemporary Justice Review, 1*(1), 133–148.

CROSSING CULTURAL BOUNDARIES: IMPLEMENTING RESTORATIVE JUSTICE IN INTERNATIONAL AND INDIGENOUS CONTEXTS

Gabrielle Maxwell

ABSTRACT

It was nearly twenty years ago that Howard Zehr (1990) wrote the first book about Restorative Justice (Changing Lenses), John Braithwaite (1989) wrote about "Crime, Shame and Reintegration" and New Zealand introduced the family group conference – a restorative process for resolving matters when children and young people became involved in offending.[1] These events marked the transition from a theoretical debate about alternatives to Western models of criminal justice to the recognition of a new theory, a new set of values and a new practical alternative to the Western-style court system. Since then, theory has evolved and many other jurisdictions have experimented with various processes for delivering restorative justice (Johnstone & Van Ness, 2007). Perhaps the most common form, especially for young people has been the use of the restorative conference in youth justice. From its beginnings in New Zealand, it has spread to Australia, Brazil, Canada, England, Ireland,

Restorative Justice: From Theory to Practice
Sociology of Crime, Law and Deviance, Volume 11, 81–95
Copyright © 2008 by Emerald Group Publishing Limited
All rights of reproduction in any form reserved
ISSN: 1521-6136/doi:10.1016/S1521-6136(08)00404-1

Macao, Norway, Scotland, Sweden, Singapore, South Africa, Tonga, Thailand and the United States of America. Many different forms of restorative family conferencing for young people who have offended have emerged in these different states, provinces and countries for many different types of offences and for people from many different cultures. In this chapter, I want to briefly review what has been learnt about the transferability of the process. In particular, what are the questions that have been largely resolved and what issues still remain unresolved? And what are the key conditions which must be met for the process to work in different jurisdictions and among different peoples and what aspects of the process tend to vary to reflect the diversity of cultures and customs within and between peoples in various areas?

RESOLVED QUESTIONS

Will Families and Extended Families Participate?

Those working in the welfare and criminal justice systems have often queried whether families will attend and participate. Those professionals providing traditional helping options often struggle in their attempts to reach out to families who have been dissatisfied by their own past contacts with the justice system and who have also become disillusioned as a result of their experience with governmental "helping" services. These are often people who have themselves fallen foul of the law, been interviewed or suspected of child neglect, and have been or had children or relatives removed from their own families in the past. They are suspicious and distrustful of any contacts with police, courts and welfare. A second and related concern of professionals is that these families are themselves dysfunctional and unlikely to make any constructive contribution to a decision-making process.

In practice, these fears have proved unfounded. A repeated finding is that family group conferences are able to bring together a number of people who have an interest in resolving a crisis which is real and immediate for them, involves those for whom they care and enables them to participate in taking and implementing decisions (Hudson, Morris, Maxwell, & Galaway, 1996). This confirms the theory behind restorative justice practice which suggests that if people are actively enabled to resolve issues themselves as opposed to being the recipient of state decisions, then there is a real preparedness to be part of the process, not just in terms of attending but in terms of meaningful involvement.

Will Offenders and Victims Be Able to Be Effectively Involved?

In the traditional justice system, neither offenders nor victims are effective participants in the process of discussing what has happened or in making decisions about the future. Most studies that have asked such questions report that the language of the court is incomprehensible; the process mystifying and active involvement is minimal or non-existent. For the offender, involvement is usually confined to an agreement to the plea entered by a lawyer and, for victims; it is, at best, limited to the edited police account of the impact the offence has had on them. There is an enormous contrast here with what happens at family group conferences. Provided victims are encouraged and enabled to attend, they do so and they participate actively in the process. Our research (Maxwell, Robertson, Kingi, Morris, & Cunningham, 2004) showed that 87% of the victims who attended said that they agreed with the decision.

Being present at restorative meetings offers victims further potential benefits: some of their emotional needs may be met; for example, they may be provided with the opportunity for some healing, for some understanding of what happened and why, and for some closure. Our 2004 data shows that 81% felt better as a result of participating in the process. The following quotes some of the reasons why victims felt they benefited:[2]

To know what is happening is to be involved.

The conference managed to clear the air for us and let us talk about things.

It is a positive way to sort feelings through.

I got the ill feelings out of my system.

The offender is made to face the victim rather than a faceless judge.

I felt better after seeing them. I wasn't scared any more – I didn't fear them.

It was satisfying to see the offender sorry.

It would work well if it was my son. I'd want every opportunity to put him back on the right track.

There are, however, a number of situations in which victims are likely to feel worse: when they do not feel that the offender is truly sorry, when their concerns have not been adequately listened to, when people are not interested in or sympathetic to them, or when they do not have sufficient support. Most of these concerns reflect poor practice by those responsible for managing the process. Successful restorative justice processes put victims at the heart of what happens.

Offenders also find benefits in attending conferences, although some express the view that it would have been easier to simply go to the court and receive a penalty rather than face their victim. The process is certainly not an easy one for the offender but it is one that can be transformative; as one observer comments:

> I have observed offenders clearly distressed – some in tears – when confronted with the consequences of the offending, I have observed offenders show all the external signs of deep embarrassment when the victims spoke of what the offence meant for them in the presence of the offender's family or "community of interest" and I have observed offenders sit at the feet of victims to ask for their forgiveness.

Despite feeling nervous about the conference and often finding it a difficult process to cope with, afterwards offenders also report real benefits for them from the process. Our 2004 data shows that 94% of young people reported that people were there who cared about them and supported them, 93% that they understood what was decided; 74% reported that they were treated fairly; 77% felt they were able to make up for what they had done and 77% felt that they were given another chance:[3]

> It was quite open and quite good … you get to talk openly.

> It seemed pretty fair with people sitting around talking about things.

> I didn't want to see the victims but it did have an impact, especially seeing [the elderly victim].

> It was really good. I got to see the victim. I could apologize.

> The family group conference allowed me to get out of a bad place to a safe place.

> The conference helped a lot. Afterwards I just got stuck into life and got closer to my family.

Power and Control

Some commentators have expressed a concern that a forum which can be controlled by family members will perpetuate patterns of power and control that have sustained a dynamic that led to offending and perpetuated patterns of social inequity which disadvantage women, children and the weak. On the contrary, Pennell and Burford (1996) report that family members in their conferences were able to move from shame:

> for failing to protect and nurture, for having committed violence, for suffering victimization, or for witnessing violation. Mothers and wives, in particular, held themselves and were held as culpable for not creating a family setting of caring and safety. The structure of the conferences made it possible not only to confront individual shame but also for other members of the family group to accept some of the responsibility ... This context generated a sense of shame across the extended family for not having acted in the past to safeguard its relatives ... With such links across the family group affirmed, the participants could reach out to each other [to encourage] growth for change.

Certainly our experience from attending many family group conferences is that women and children are far more likely to participate than in conventional courtroom settings. Indeed it is the women who often dominate the family discussions and are seen as the central figure in the family group because of their role in nurturing and caring for the family. This is in contrast to the courtroom where, if any family member speaks, it is more likely to be the man when he is present.

With respect to children, we saw more of a problem. The patterns of the past together with the shame for offending often meant that, without real encouragement, the young person did not speak on his own behalf or did so minimally. There are indeed problems of the transfer of patterns of social inequality into the family group conference setting. On the other hand, the voices of women, children, victims and culture are often heard more clearly in family group conferences than in alternative types of situations intended to resolve conflict.

Other Unfounded Fears

In all jurisdictions, criticisms are raised about the potential dangers of using family group conferences in the youth justice system. Recurring themes raised are about whether or not agreements will be honoured and tasks completed or that victims will demand savage penalties with the result that there will be increase in re-offending because the deterrent effect of harsh penalties for subsequent offences will be lost. However, in all the jurisdictions that have experimented with or adopted conferencing and reported on outcomes, these fears have proved to be unfounded. Rather, results indicate that when the process is restorative, agreements are honoured and tasks completed, then re-offending is actually less probable. Nor do the victims usually demand harsh penalties – on the contrary, as indicated above, they often show amazing forgiveness and generosity.

ISSUES TO BE RESOLVED

How Should the Conference Process Be Managed?

Two core values of restorative justice have particularly important implications for how the process is managed. These are the respect for all peoples which imply and emphasis on cultural relevance and an acceptance of cultural difference, and the participation of all those affected by the events: the victims, offenders and others in the community or close to the central figures. The involvement of men, women and even children who are not professional participants in the justice system and who may have very different cultural expectations requires a flexible and adaptable process that is contrary to conventional notions of justice. More recently Tonga has adopted a Youth Justice Diversion process incorporating restorative principles. Preliminary findings suggest that this has been welcomed by all parties (Maxwell, 2007).

Giving control to participants over the decision making also requires flexibility about outcomes. Traditionally, fixed and rigid rules have been justified on the grounds that they ensure fairness in the process and solutions that are equitable and proportional to the offence for all offenders. However, what is fair and equitable can also be judged through the eyes of those most affected by the offending: the victims and offenders themselves. I would suggest, that if restorative solutions are to be seen as fair by the central participants, they will inevitably be diverse and, consequently, potentially lacking in equity and proportionality if judged by objective yardsticks. How to arrive at specific solutions for specific circumstances is a question discussed further in the following sections.

ACCOMMODATING CULTURAL DIFFERENCES

Family group conference processes can be adapted to different indigenous and minority cultural practices more readily than the formal processes of the court. But to do so successfully is not necessarily simple and has not always been effectively implemented because of different power structures, perceptions, values and practices reflected within Western and indigenous systems. In Australia, various jurisdictions report variable success in developing a process that is comfortable for the many different Aboriginal clients in traditional communities because of the remoteness of the communities, the different meaning given to appointment arrangements and the alienation of the people from white justice. For instance, Wundersitz in 1995 commented that in the urban communities of South Australia, the family group conferences were little different for Aboriginals and white Australians despite their very different life styles and concerns.

In New Zealand there has been criticism that family group conferences have not been managed in ways that conform with traditional practice of Maori or those from other cultural backgrounds. It has been suggested that the high proportion of Maori staff managing the process and the inclusion of Maori greetings and blessing is little more than tokenism and that can rarely be described as a truly Maori process. This is despite the undisputed origins of many aspects of the conference process in traditional Maori procedures (Consedine, 1995). On the other hand, on occasion, the management of the conference process is sometimes passed over to a Maori social service group and, in Auckland, the Samoan community have developed a version of a family group conference based on the ifoga (indigenous restorative process) for members of their community (Consedine, 1995).

It is ironic that the format of family group conferences in Manitoba that, perhaps, most faithfully replicated indigenous cultural practice of the Ojibwa had a very low rate of acceptance by the courts for their recommendations (Longclaws, Galaway, & Barkwell, 1996). On the other hand, in smaller communities of Alaska and Northern Canada, Peace Circles have been adapted as a restorative process by members of the judiciary (Stuart, 1996; Lilles, 2001).

In the Pacific (Maxwell & Hayes, 2006; Dinnen, 2003), many of the various Melanesian and Polynesian cultures report the widespread use of extended family and village processes of meeting to resolve disputes and heal conflict. These systems are used, not only for the infringements of custom by individuals or small groups that could be seen as crime, but also for the resolution of all types of dispute between families, clans, villages and tribes, including disputes that have the potential to lead to civil conflict. The variety of forms is large but, in general, the processes either directly bring together the families involved or are managed through the local tribal structure.

For instance in Samoa, the village fono (council of matai who are the head of families) determines both laws and responses to breaches: justice can be summary and harsh or it can involve a peace-making process, for example ifoga. Ifoga involves offenders and their family coming with gifts and kneeling before the home of the family that has been wronged until such time as they are taken into the home. Then negotiations proceed until a settlement is reached and the restoration of peace is signified by a feast involving all parties. In Melanesia, the authority structures are very different but throughout the Pacific Islands of both Polynesia and Melanesia, traditional systems share common elements of enabling peace and reconciliation to be arrived at through a process involving apologies and compensation.

On the other hand, a conference on restorative justice in Vanuatu in 2000 (Dinnen, 2003) did not favour a simple return to past practices that had often been oppressive and discriminatory rather than respectful and empowering. But nor did the participants favour a continued reliance on Western processes that were seen as lacking legitimacy and unable to respond in ways that respected customary values and practices. Rather, they favoured a creative integration of the best of both. New systems that involved communities and were built around restorative values were seen as a way of overcoming the problems created by the weaknesses of both indigenous and Western models in the societies of today.

The examples considered here indicate that restorative practices are frequently a part of the experience of most indigenous and tribal societies. Practices vary but core values and ingredients of participation, repair and reintegration are to be found in traditional processes almost everywhere. Aspects of these practices can often find a place in the modern justice systems of the world if restorative values and key ingredients open up participatory alternatives to courtrooms. However, doing so is not necessary easy.

In countries where the indigenous peoples and other ethnic minorities are not the dominant group (for instance, New Zealand and Australia) their experience has been that more time and resources are required if family group conferences are to be held using traditional protocols and in traditional time frames. These requirements are not readily accepted by managers responsible for funding. There is also the matter of the cultural appropriateness of the relatively scarce services which are available. However, in countries where indigenous practices are still operative, these traditional forms are not always restorative, they do not necessarily mesh with current definitions of offending, comply with demands for equity across all peoples or take into account the inevitable shift in values in all societies that has been a consequence of globalization.

Thus blending indigenous and modern restorative practices is not simple; inevitably systems belong to those with whom the locus of power resides. Some redistribution of both resources and power is required for cultural difference to be validated and for equitable systems to be developed. These issues are part of wider debate about sovereignty and self-determination for indigenous peoples within the Western world and about the recognition of the cultural legitimacy of the values and practices of minority groups in the larger society. But they are also about adapting the practices of the past to a consideration of the human rights we see as universal in today's societies.

THE LOCATION OF FAMILY GROUP CONFERENCE MANAGEMENT

One issue that remains unresolved is where best to locate the management of family group conferences. Various options are: in a government department of welfare, with the police, with courts or in an independent public sector organisation or managed through referrals to non-governmental organisations or community groups. All these options have been seen as having disadvantages. Welfare departments are often seen as controlling people's lives and removing children from their families. The police, similarly, are often perceived as agents of state control. Courts are too often seen as coercive and punitive. Independent organisations may have difficulty in encouraging and developing the trust of the state gatekeepers who control referrals, especially when the conferencing process lacks a legislative base. Commentators from various jurisdictions all have reservations about their current management processes.

In New Zealand, family group conferences are managed through Child, Youth and Family Services (CYF). This branch of government is responsible for all welfare, adoption and youth justice services and the oversight of operations, record keeping and management of community funding. In the area of youth justice they receive referrals for family group conferences from police and courts, are responsible for arranging the conferences, arranging social services, liaising with other justice and community organisations involved with young people who offend or are seen as at risk of offending, and managing community and residential care.

They employ teams of youth justice coordinators and youth justice social workers throughout New Zealand.

However, because of their other role, and particularly because of their general responsibility for children and young people in need of care and protection, there has often been competition for resources, especially over a period where CYF had limited funding while notifications of children in need of care and protection increased markedly. I would suggest that there are always likely to be risks if youth justice activities are not in an independent organisation with dedicated funding and for this reason have favoured proposals to create an independent public sector organisation to manage youth justice as is the case in New South Wales, Australia and Northern Ireland to take two examples. I believe autonomy can give an independent profile and authority to youth justice and ensure that other duties do not impact on the delivery of youth justice services.

STATUTORY AUTHORITY

In some jurisdictions, there are provisions for police or prosecutorial discretion in referring cases to court or taking alternative actions (for instance issuing a warning, giving a more formal caution, arranging a diversion or making a referral for a programme). Where there are some such provisions or accepted arrangements, it is possible to informally make arrangements for pre-sentence restorative meetings. In several jurisdictions, trials of restorative justice options have been arranged in this way. There are also jurisdictions where judicial discretion over court hearings has allowed for restorative meetings in communities to be part of the process (for instance in the Circle sentencing courts of North America). European jurisdictions have been more limited by the restrictions inherent in their legal systems but some have nevertheless, found options under the law for including restorative justice referrals.

Ultimately, however, most jurisdictions that have adopted restorative practices have made legislative changes. The New Zealand system that requires youth justice family group conferences for all serious matters in the youth justice system is perhaps the example that, more than any other, mainstreams the restorative process (although more recently Northern Ireland has adopted legislation that largely follows the New Zealand model, http://www.youthjusticeagencyni.gov.uk/youth_justice_system/). Other jurisdictions, for example most of the Australian jurisdictions, allow for referrals of limited types of cases and these are not always the more serious matters that often have been found to benefit more from a resolution of matters through a conference (Hayes, 2007).

One of the concerns frequently expressed in jurisdictions where there is no process for mandatory referral of a defined class of offenders to family group conferences is that referrals may occur haphazardly and arbitrarily. In South Australia, for instance, there appears to have been selective referral of less serious cases and numbers vary over time (Wundersitz & Hetzel, 1996). Similar concerns have been expressed about the provisions for the use of referral orders for restorative processes in the United Kingdom (Dignan, 2004) and for family group conferences under provisions for alternative actions in Canada (Bala, 2004). Pilot projects in South Africa report variable referrals of cases and variable responses of the courts to recommendations of the cases that were conferenced.

There seems little doubt that New Zealand is in a strong position in having:

• A legislative requirement that all cases that appear before the court will be referred in addition to other repeat and/or moderately serious matters.
• Providing for direct referral of less serious matters to a family group conference.
• A requirement that, in sentencing, the court shall have regard to any decision, plan or recommendation made or formulated by the family group conference (in practice, the court does not normally depart from agreed and recommended family group conference plans and decisions without a substantive legal reason).
• An explicit statement of restorative values and principles that affect all aspects of the youth justice system; including police and youth court actions.

BEST PRACTICE ISSUES

A number of best practice issues are emerging from the experience of the system in New Zealand and these are generally endorsed by those working in other jurisdictions. These include the need for:

• A clear understanding by all those professionals involved in the conference of the values and philosophy of the youth justice system.
• Quality preparation for the family group conference which includes meetings with victims, offenders and family members, the gathering of all

necessary and relevant information and the consideration of alternative
options for outcomes.
- Procedures that are respectful of all who are involved.
- Ensuring that arrangements are made for monitoring the outcomes of
family group conferences.
- A clear understanding by all the professionals involved in their respective
roles in the process and the development for each professional group of
best practice guidelines.
- Training, both entry and refresher, to develop and maintain best practice
and reinforce the underlying values that reinforce the restorative potential
of the process.
- The development of a strong team approach among all the professionals
that have a role in youth justice; both at local and national level.

TO WHAT EXTENT SHOULD COMMUNITIES BE INVOLVED?

An essential element of a restorative system is the participation of those who
have been affected by the crime. The question then arises as to who these
people should be. Clearly the victim and the offender are two important
parties. So too are those who play an important role in the day-to-day life of
the offender and supporters chosen by the victim.

However, there has been considerable debate about the breadth of the net.
Many of the historical and indigenous models have involved the whole
community. This still seems appropriate in small communities and has the
real strength that all those whom the offender meets on a daily basis are a
party to the process. In this way, the force of social pressures and
expectations can become part of the process of change.

However, who are the community in larger social groups? Should those
processes involving community panels and community representatives be
regarded as appropriate ways of delivering restorative justice? Or,
alternatively, are such processes prone to being co-opted to the same values
that underpin the present criminal justice system – or even, worse, could
they become kangaroo courts or examples of vigilantism?

Because of the potential dangers in involving those not connected to the
parties, we have favoured a focus on communities of interest. The important
concept is that of connectedness – it is those who are connected to the
offender and the victim who needs to be involved in the restorative process if

it is to find solutions that truly make amends and achieve the reintegration of offenders and victims the social group.

WHAT ABOUT RE-OFFENDING?

Another way in which it is easy to discount new processes is to choose re-offending as the main yardstick by which to judge them. There are a number of problems with this approach. I will comment on two major ones.

First is that the restorative process is only one of many factors in an offenders life – bad friends, traumatic life events and the failure to succeed are just some of the subsequent life events that can lead someone to re-offend. In the longer term, current life events are likely to outweigh something that occurred in the past.

The second mistake is to assume that just because a restorative process has been used, there should be less re-offending. Evidence from a six-year follow up of participants (Maxwell & Morris, 1999) suggests that the probability of re-offending can be affected by family group conferences, but this is only so when the victim is present, the offender is remorseful and the family group conference leaves a mark on the memory of the young person. In other words, the use of a potentially restorative process will not always be successful in changing hearts and minds.

CONCLUSION

The results of experiments in a variety of jurisdictions demonstrate that the family group conference (or some form of it) can be successfully implemented in a variety of different countries, by a number of different cultural groups and using an array of different processes. A restorative option which was created in New Zealand and was importantly influenced by New Zealand Maori has found a place in cultures and societies which are very different. In part, this may be because it evokes a past when the clan, the tribe, the village or the community gathered to resolve among themselves the wrongs that could otherwise threaten their cohesion. It is a process that belongs to a time when the alternative to finding a restorative process was to face dissolution as a group that could effectively protect its own members from external threats. Echoes of the same system are to be found in the Polynesian cultures throughout the Pacific, among the aboriginal communities of South Australia, the Inuit of Northern Canada, the Ojibwa of central Canada, the indigenous peoples of North America, the Bantu peoples of South Africa and the Bedouin tribes of the Middle East (Johnstone & Van Ness, 2007). How is this so? A major factor is that restorative justice is about an underlying set of values that are markedly different from those implicit in the traditional system: values that emphasise not only taking responsibility and repairing harm but also treating people with respect, and working toward reconciliation and healing. Another key ingredient is the emphasis on the participation of all those affected by the offending and the expectation that they will, together, arrive at a consensus about issues of repair and restoration. A third important element is the flexibility and variety of the restorative process itself: it does not need to be constrained within a universal format but can be allowed to adapt to the customs of the people who are participating in it.

Adopting a restorative approach make demands on legal systems and conventional views of justice which are unusual. It requires flexibility in the way in which matters are resolved. It moves away from traditional outcomes, such as punishment and deterrence, from restorative processes is unrealistic. And it demands an emphasis on the good of the wider society as opposed to a narrow emphasis on issues that directly affect the victim and the offender.

NOTES

1. Family group conferences are also used in the child welfare system when options are being considered for children thought to be in need of care or protection.
2. These quotes come from both our 1993 (Maxwell & Morris, 1993) and our 2004 (Maxwell et al., 2004) research.
3. Of course not all felt positive and the research identified many conferences where matters were not well handled and outcomes were not positive. It also identifies the key practice features that can enable better outcomes.

REFERENCES

Bala, N. (2004). Dealing with child and adolescent offenders outside of youth court: The Canadian experience. In: T. W. Lo, D. Wong & G. Maxwell (Eds), *Alternatives to prosecution*. Singapore: Marshall Cavendish Academic.

Consedine, J. (1995). *Restorative justice: Healing the effects of crime*. Christchurch, NZ: Ploughshare Publications.

Dignan, J. (2004). Alternatives to the prosecution of unruly children and young persons: The position in England and Wales. In: T. W. Lo, D. Wong & G. Maxwell (Eds), *Alternatives to prosecution*. Singapore: Marshall Cavendish Academic.

Dinnen, S. (2003). *A kind of mending: Restorative justice in the Pacific Islands*. Sydney: Pandanus Books.

Hayes, H. (2007). Reoffending and restorative justice. In: G. Johnstone & D. Van Ness (Eds), *Handbook of restorative justice* (Chapter 22). Cullhompton, Devon: Willan Publishing.

Hudson, J., Morris, A., Maxwell, G., & Galaway, B. (Eds). (1996). *Family group conferences: Perspectives on policy and practice*. Annandale, NSW: The Federation Press.

Johnstone, G., & Van Ness, D. (Eds). (2007). *Handbook of restorative justice*. Cullompton, Devon: Willan Publishing.

Lilles, H. (2001). Circle sentencing: Part of the restorative justice continuum. In: A. Morris & G. Maxwell (Eds), *Restorative justice for juveniles: Conferencing, mediation and circles*. Oxford: Hart Publishing.

Longclaws, L., Galaway, B., & Barkwell, L. (1996). Piloting family group conferences for young Aboriginal offenders in Winnipeg, Canada. In: J. Hudson, A. Morris, G. Maxwell & B. Galaway (Eds), *Family group conferences: Perspectives on policy and practice*. Annandale, NSW: The Federation Press.

Maxwell, G. (2007). Tonga project – responses to youth offending. An interim report to the Ministry of Justice and Crown Law in Tonga. Available on www.ips.ac.nz

Maxwell, G., & Hayes, H. (2006). Restorative justice developments on the Pacific region: A comprehensive survey. *Contemporary Justice Review, 9*(2), 127–154.

Maxwell, G., & Morris, A. (1993). *Families, victims and culture: Youth justice in New Zealand*. Wellington: Social Policy Agency and Institute of Criminology.

Maxwell, G. M., & Morris, A. (1999). *Understanding re-offending*. Wellington: Institute of Criminology, Victoria University of Wellington.

Maxwell, G. M., Robertson, J., Kingi, V., Morris, A., & Cunningham, C. (2004). *Achieving effective outcomes in youth justice*. Final report to the Ministry of Social Development. Wellington: Ministry of Social Development.

Pennell, J., & Burford, G. (1996). Attending to context: Family group decision making in Canada. In: J. Hudson, A. Morris, G. Maxwell & B. Galaway (Eds), *Family group conferences: Perspectives on policy and practice* (Chapter 10). Annandale, NSW: The Federation Press.

Stuart, B. (1996). Circle sentencing in Canada: A partnership of the community and the criminal justice system. *International Journal of Comparative and Applied Criminal Justice, 20*, 291ff.

Wundersitz, J., & Hetzel, S. (1996). Family conferencing for young offenders: The South Australian experience. In: J. Hudson, A. Morris, G. Maxwell & B. Galaway (Eds), *Family group conferences: Perspectives on policy and practice* (Chapter 7). Annandale, NSW: The Federation Press.

PART II:
EVALUATING RESTORATIVE PROGRAMMING

EVALUATION OF A RESTORATIVE MILIEU: RESTORATIVE PRACTICES IN CONTEXT

Paul McCold

ABSTRACT

CSF Buxmont Academy operates eight school/day treatment programs that use restorative practices, which includes a culture in which restorative characterizes staff interaction with students, and staff-to-staff and student-to-student relationships as well. This chapter presents analyses of the outcome experiences from two waves of discharge cohorts: 919 students during school years 1999–2000 and 2000–2001 and 858 during 2001–2002 and 2002–2003. Outcome measures include program completion rates, changes in self-esteem and anti-social attitudes, and the relationship between the length of program participation and post-release recidivism rates after controlling for individual risk factors. Recidivism rates were significantly related to length of program participation.

Restorative *justice* practice has become one of the most thoroughly researched criminal justice reform efforts outside of rehabilitation theory. From its inception in the early 1970s, most programs have included some

---

Restorative Justice: From Theory to Practice
Sociology of Crime, Law and Deviance, Volume 11, 99–137
Copyright © 2008 by Emerald Group Publishing Limited
All rights of reproduction in any form reserved
ISSN: 1521-6136/doi:10.1016/S1521-6136(08)00405-3

evaluation component (McCold, 2006). Initial findings have been replicated in a number of different locations on different types of offenses and offenders. These individual program evaluations have been augmented by numerous surveys of the research (Latimer & Kleinknecht, 2000; Daly, 2001a; Braithwaite, 2002; McCold, 2003a; Aertsen, Mackay, Pelikan, Wright, & Wilemsens, 2004; Daly & Hayes, 2005), including at least five meta-analyses (Latimer, Dowden, & Muise, 2001; McCold & Wachtel, 2002; Rowe, 2002; Williams-Hayes, 2002; Nugent, Umbreit, & Williams, 2004) and at least eleven randomized controlled trials (McCold & Wachtel, 1998; McGarrell, Olivares, Crawford, & Kroovand, 2000; Walker, 2002; McCold, 2003b; Sherman et al., 2004). By the turn of the millennium, a substantial body of empirical evidence had been accumulated (Williams-Hayes, 2003).

Evaluations from a variety of settings in a multitude of jurisdictions and social cultures across a variety of offense and offender types have shown remarkably consistent results. Restorative practices are well received by those participating (McCold & Wachtel, 2002), provide substantial emotional relief to distressed crime victims (Strang, 2002; Angel, 2005; Strang et al., 2006), and are highly supported by the public (Weitekamp, 2002; McCold, 2003a). Results regarding effects on reducing re-offending are mixed, but generally recidivism rates have been found to be comparable to those produced through court-based processes (Bonta, 2003; McCold, 2003a; Aertsen et al., 2004; Sherman & Strang, 2007).

> Arguably, if offenders accept responsibility for their offending, feel involved in the decision about how to deal with that offending, feel that they are treated fairly and with respect, apologise and make amends to their victim and take part in a programme designed to deal with the reasons underlying their offending, then we can at least hypothesize that they will be less likely to offend again in the future. (Crime and Justice Research Centre & Triggs, 2005, Section 10.1)

Latimer and his colleagues at the Canadian Department of Justice conclude the Canadian meta-analysis results were consistent with the other available evidence, that "those individuals who choose to participate in restorative justice programs find the process satisfying, tend to display lower recidivism rates and are more likely to adhere to restitution agreements." (Latimer et al., 2001, p. 17). They estimated a mean effect size of $+0.07$ ($n = 32$), indicating that restorative justice practices produce small average decrease in reoffending rates compared to court comparison samples.

SAMPLE SELECTION AND MORTALITY BIAS

A major limitation on the scientific veracity of the conclusions about formal restorative practices remains the problem of controlling for the effects of subject selection and mortality bias that is inherent in any voluntary program (Campbell & Stanley, 1963). Selection bias is introduced when subjects fail to participate in the treatment assigned to them. If the decision to participate is at all related to the outcome variable, then the comparison and treatment groups are not comparable. Subject mortality is simply the program dropout rate. Subjects drop out of experiments for many reasons. Conclusions cannot be based on the subjects who stay if the characteristics of those who drop out are predictive of reoffending (Lloyd, Mair, & Hough, 1994). With selection bias, the groups are not the same prior to the treatment; with mortality bias, the groups are not the same after the treatment, even if the treatment had no effect other than to screen out some subjects.

Selection bias, especially self-selection bias, is a known problem in restorative justice programs. In their randomized experiment in Bethlehem, PA, McCold and Wachtel (1998) concluded the differences in reoffending rates were primarily determined by the offender's decision to participate. Reoffending for the combined conference and declined-to-participate groups was about the same as the offenders assigned to the control groups. This conclusion was supported by earlier conferencing research (Moore, Forsyth, & O'Connell, 1995) and the results replicated in an evaluation of conferencing program in New South Wales (Trimboli, 2000; Luke & Lind, 2002, 2005). In a major evaluation of a four site voluntary adult conferencing pilot in New Zealand, the reconviction rate was not significantly lower than that predicted after controlling for the risk characteristics of the conferenced offenders (Crime and Justice Research Centre & Triggs, 2005, Section 10.7).

One major attempt to control for the effects of selection bias has been a series of randomized controlled trials being conducted by the Jerry Lee Center of Criminology at the University of Pennsylvania (Sherman et al., 2004; Sherman & Strang, 2007). These studies of restorative conferencing controlled for the self-selection effect by removing it from their samples. Only offenders who agree to participate are randomly assigned to control and treatment groups. Offenders who denied their crimes or who otherwise declined to participate were excluded, thereby "controlling for" the self-selection effect. These experiments are finding a mixed effect from conferencing on offender recidivism, but support the highly positive results for other participants in restorative justice (Angel, 2005; Sherman & Strang, 2007).

Another line of research has been conducted in settings where all juvenile offenders are required to participate in restorative justice. For example, since 1989 New Zealand legislatively mandated a conference for all juveniles prosecuted for the more serious criminal offenses except homicide. Offenders who deny responsibility are provided a court adjudicatory fact-finding hearing and, if found responsible, are court-ordered to participate in a family group conference (Brown, 1995; Morris & Maxwell, 1997). There is no equivalent control group with which to compare outcomes, but neither is there much self-selection occurring. In these settings, researchers conducted multivariate retrospective analyses to look for factors that distinguish those who reoffend from those who do not (Maxwell & Morris, 2000; Hayes & Daly, 2003, 2004; Maxwell et al., 2004; Paulin, Kingi, Huirama, & Lash, 2005; Paulin, Kingi, & Lash, 2005). The conclusion from this line of research is that once prior risk factors are controlled for, offenders who had a memorable conference where they expressed remorse and apologized to their victims had lower reoffending rates than offenders who did not. Unfortunately, those are precisely the characteristics likely to explain who would agree to participate had they been given a choice. Any crime reduction effects of conferencing are commingled with the effect of offender remorse, and the independent effect of each of the variables is unknown. Rather than eliminating the self-selection effect, this approach treats it as evidence of a positive experience, confusing the direction of causality. Are those who experience a positive conference less likely to reoffend; or are those less likely to reoffend more likely to have a good conference experience? Given prior evidence of a strong self-selection effect, it seems prudent to assume the latter.

SINGLE SHOT INTERVENTION

Another limitation in the capacity to evaluate the potential effectiveness of formal restorative practices, whatever their setting, is that mediations, conferencing and circles are usually a single-dose intervention. While formal events like a conference or circle may have a powerful impact on those involved in an incident, it is probably unrealistic to think that any one-time intervention of an hour or so duration could counteract on-going influences of negative social environment and poor life-style choices that constituted the conditions both leading to the current offense and conducive to future offending behavior.

On the other hand, inserting a single restorative encounter into the life of an offending young person, if done well, can help realign their social relationships. Changing the social support structure or marshaling previously dormant social supports actually extends the effects of the intervention well beyond the bounds of the formal conference. In family group decision making (FGDM) follow-up conferences are now regularly arranged as part of the initial conference, extending the intervention by further structuring the family supervision and support systems (Merkel-Holguin, Nixon, & Burford, 2003; Nixon, Burford, Quinn, & Edelbaum, 2004).

Unfortunately, the average restorative justice conference tends to be much more mundane and limited in its on-going impact than this ideal. This is especially likely when conferences are conducted by large organizations engaged in arranging a large number of restorative encounters (Wilcox, Young, & Hoyle, 2004). It is also these interventions that are most likely the target of the more sophisticated of the research designs, especially the randomized controlled experiment where differences in recidivism rates are best detected. Because large numbers of cases are essential to this type of research, the mass production of conferences likely leads to a decrease in their average "restorativeness" and, therefore, the recidivism-reducing potential (Daly, 2001b). The resulting lesser quality of the intervention (diluted dosage) could hardly be expected to produce anything more than a small effect on recidivism rates of offenders at best. Assuming that such an effect actually exists, it will be difficult to detect and require very large samples to produce statistical significance (Sherman & Strang, 2004).

Perhaps the best way to test the recidivism-reduction potential of restorative practices is to increase the dosage. If restorative practices are thought to be effective in small dosages, then in much larger dosages the positive benefits should become more evident and measurable. Restorative practices that integrate both formal and informal restorative approaches in an on-going basis for an extended period of time represent a potential maximum dosage of restorativeness (Wachtel, 2000). Such a setting would be ideal for evaluating the effects of restorative practices on rates of reoffending. The purpose of this research was to do just that: test the effects of a restorative social milieu provided in a day treatment setting upon the future offending of misbehaving young people.

RESEARCH SETTING

The Community Service Foundation (CSF) and Buxmont Academy operate eight school/day treatment programs (abbreviated as "CSF Buxmont schools") in southeastern Pennsylvania. They are non-secure alternative schools and community treatment settings for adjudicated delinquent and at-risk youth (for more information on CSF Buxmont schools go to: http://www.csfbuxmont.org). Additionally, CSF operates three auxiliary programs – the residential, intensive supervision, and home and community programs. The residential program provides small family style group homes for a portion of students attending CSF Buxmont schools. The intensive supervision program provides additional support to youth released from drug treatment facilities. The home and community program provides a variety of family-oriented support services for students experiencing family, emotional, and drug- and alcohol-related crises. Some students attending CSF Buxmont schools participate in multiple programs simultaneously as deemed appropriate by the placement agency and CSF senior staff.

All of these programs utilize what is broadly termed "restorative practices." Restorative practices simultaneously provide high levels of control and high levels of support through counselor initiated group and individual level interventions designed to encourage appropriate behavior (Wachtel & McCold, 2000; McCold & Wachtel, 2002). The philosophy underlying these restorative practices holds that human beings are happier, more productive, and more likely to make positive changes in their behavior when those in positions of authority do things WITH them, rather than TO them or FOR them. This hypothesis maintains that the punitive and authoritarian TO mode and the permissive and paternalistic FOR mode are not as effective in changing behavior as the restorative, participatory, and engaging WITH mode (Wachtel, 2000).

CSF Buxmont has developed a culture in which "restorative" characterizes not only staff interaction with students, but staff-to-staff and student-to-student relationships as well.

> The programs of the Community Service Foundation share several common objectives and a mission that includes building among its clients greater self control, a belief in the capacity of people to change, an appreciation of the value of community, and life-styles in which sobriety is the norm. ... The values of believing in peoples capacity to change, the importance of community, the need for open confrontation and the establishment of a few important rules of behavior dominate the agency's culture. (Harris, Jones, Naiburg, & Washnock, 2000, p. 14)

CSF Buxmont has been operating day treatment alternative schools and group homes in southeastern Pennsylvania since 1977. In 1994, CSF began training their staff to facilitate restorative conferences and adopted an explicitly restorative framework to their practice (Wachtel, 1997). Wachtel (2000) describes restorative practices as a continuum ranging from formal restorative justice conferences to the informal practices of making affective statements and asking restorative questions. He stresses the importance of effects from these informal restorative practices, suggesting that the more we engage in the informal, the less we need the use of the formal.

This researcher has coined the term "restorative milieu" because CSF Buxmont culture is consciously comprised of many restorative techniques and processes and not just isolated restorative interventions.[1] Within this restorative milieu, youth are held accountable for their actions while being given the social encouragement and emotional support necessary to make changes. Restorative practices empower the young person and the group to develop their own behavioral standards and actively confront each other's misbehavior. The young people act as a micro-community of support for each other, facilitated by CSF Buxmont staff, which intentionally builds interdependency and a sense of responsibility to the community.

Staff endeavor to partner with the student and their families to support a plan for changes developed together. In addition to daily general and special group sessions, CSF Buxmont schools provided 397 behavior contracts, 221 family planning sessions, 88 special staff meetings and 31 restorative conferences during the most recent two years of this study. During the two years since the end of the current study, CSF Buxmont has embraced the family group decision-making model (FDGM) (Burford & Hudson, 2000; American Humane Association, 2004) for the families of many of their students. The agency now provides a service to facilitate both FGDM and Real Justice restorative conferences as a service to county agencies as well as providing facilitator training in both (see: www.csfbuxmont.org).

This approach of using groups as the primary vehicle for an intervention is not new. What is new is the framework of restorative practices within which the CSF Buxmont programs operate. The term "therapeutic community" has been used for decades to describe small cohesive communities where patients have a significant involvement in decision-making and the practicalities of running the unit. Based on ideas of collective responsibility, citizenship and empowerment, therapeutic communities are deliberately structured in a way that encourages personal responsibility, creates a culture of belonging and encourages open and honest communication.[2] Most crucial is the concept of "community as method," which stresses the "purposive use of the peer group to facilitate social and psychological change in individuals" (de Leon, 1997, p. 5). The social milieu becomes a climate and atmosphere in which the community encourages participants to function as their own change agents.

"Self-help" becomes the primary "therapeutic tool" (Vandevelde, Broekaert, Yates, & Kooyman, 2004, p. 74). Therapeutic communities and shorter term therapeutic milieus have been used successfully with psychiatric hospital patients, nursing home patients, prison inmates, juvenile delinquents, drug addicts, pregnant women, and the homeless (Bloom, 1997; Lees, Manning, & Rawlings, 1999; De Leon, 2000; Jainchill, Hawke, De Leon, & Yagelka, 2000; Bloom & Norton, 2004a, 2004b; Kennard, 2004; Whitely, 2004). Since the late 1990s in the United States, the correction-based therapeutic community has become one of the most described treatment modalities for substance abuse treatment.[3]

Previous Research

Meta-analyses of therapeutic communities have consistently found positive outcomes when used with substance abusers in an extended residential setting (Garrett, 1985; Andrews et al., 1990; Lipsey, 1992). When properly implemented, therapeutic communities have been effective in reducing both substance abuse and delinquency (Mullen, Arbiter, & Gilder, 1991). Wexler found a rearrest rate two years later to be half that of non-participating offenders (Wexler, DeLeon, Thomas, Kessel, & Peters, 1999).

Lipsey's (1992) meta-analysis of roughly 500 juvenile treatment programs found that the most effective tend to use structured, focused treatment using behavioral, skill-oriented, and multi-model methods. In regard to the most serious juvenile offenders, Lipsey, Wilson, and Cothern (2000) found that the best programs for institutionalized youth were those focused on developing interpersonal skills and family style group homes. However, what they called "milieu therapy" was found to be only effective if provided in community settings rather than in institutions (Andrews et al., 1990; Lipsey, 1992, 2000).

Evaluation of therapeutic communities operating as day treatment programs has been less extensive. Earlier research on the effects of Teacher Effectiveness Training, Reality Therapy, Assertive Discipline, and Adlerian approaches in public schools had found positive effects on teacher perceptions and some effects on teacher behavior, but few effects on student behavior or attitudes (Emmer & Aussiker, 1989). Gottfredson (1989) compared three alternative programs for at-risk youth and found academic achievement increased in all three, delinquent behavior decreased only in the program that also increased students' social involvement and attachment to school. More recently, a meta-analysis of 57 alternative school programs concluded that alternative schools can have a positive effect on school performance, attitudes toward school, and self-esteem, but there was little evidence of an effect on future delinquency (Cox, Davison, & Bynum, 1995), and even these effects might be short-lived (Cox, 1999).

While they have not demonstrated an effect on future behavior, there have been a variety of other positive effects documented from participation in at least one-day-treatment alternative school. A five-year evaluation of the OJJDP alternative school model in nine schools involving 1,900 students found that these students were one-third less likely to drop out of school, were more likely to attend school, complete academic and vocational courses, and apply to college, and to receive more opportunities to set goals and reach academic and professional objectives compared with the control group (Kemple & Snipes, 2000).

The fact that therapeutic communities are multi-dimensional – consisting of a great many "molecular" variables that interact in a complex way – creates difficulties in monitoring the quality and amount of the treatment (Campling, 2001). Another problem for evaluation relates to the difficulty of creating equivalent comparison groups. Random assignment is always difficult and expensive to conduct, and true experiments are generally not possible for normal program evaluations without external funding (Weisburd, 2000).

One alternative to randomized assignment or matched cases comparisons in program evaluation is to relate the strength of the dose of the intervention to the observed outcomes. Students who participated a short time serve as the comparison group for those who had participated over a longer time. When therapeutic communities have been found effective in reducing drug use and criminal behavior, the length of time spent in treatment emerges as an important predictor of client outcomes (Heit, 1991; Martin, Butzin, & Inciardi, 1995; Nemes, Wish, & Messina, 1999; Messina, Wish, & Nemes, 2001), but studies vary considerably in terms of the amount of time they found clients need to stay in treatment to produce those outcomes (Condelli & Hubbard, 1994; McCusker et al., 1995).

There also remains a self-selection bias in these studies because those who participate a short time are not like those who participate longer in important ways. Program retention effects are especially important in evaluating the effects of therapeutic communities because they traditionally have high rates of attrition (Condelli, 1994). As was discussed with the evaluation of restorative justice interventions, the actual effect of therapeutic communities can only be evaluated after controlling for the effects of case attrition (dropouts) on the relationship between the length of treatment and reoffending.

Present Study

CSF Buxmont schools have a reputation for empowering students to make positive changes within an explicitly restorative-based therapeutic milieu. This analysis tests the merit of this reputation by examining the effectiveness of the restorative milieu to reduce future offending among adjudicated delinquent and at-risk youth. The hypothesis tested is that participation in the program leads to lower recidivism. Of course, correlation does not mean causation. Without an equivalent comparison group, there is no benchmark against which to evaluate the observed results.

Establishing an equivalent comparison group is, perhaps, the most complicated part of program evaluation methodology. Random assignment to treatment and control groups in the classical experimental design is deemed to be the only truly reliable method for ruling out a variety of known confounding factors. There are two primary types of threats to validity: (1) the various ways in which the comparison group will differ from the treatment group prior to treatment or (2) something other than the treatment causing the groups to become different during the course of the treatment. Random allocation to group is assumed to distribute all individual characteristics equally between the two groups prior to treatment. However, randomized controlled trials (RCT) remain susceptible to the risk of the second type of threat to validity: of misattributing the cause of the changes observed to the effect of the treatment. RCTs are always complicated to manage and expensive to establish (Lipsey & Cordray, 2000; Sherman & Strang, 2004; Berk, 2005). One alternative to RCTs[4] to test the effectiveness of a program is to compare the differences in the length of the treatment (dosage) to the outcomes observed, controlling for the effect of differential retention and other non-treatment effects known to affect the outcome. This is the logic behind multivariate survival analysis (Allison, 1995). If the time of surviving without offending is correlated with the length of treatment, after controlling for the time of surviving in that treatment and the risk factors known to be related to reoffending, there is good reason to conclude that the treatment was the cause.

To conclude that any observed changes are the result of participation in CSF Buxmont's restorative milieu, four conditions must be met:

(1) Recidivism rates must be negatively related to the length of participation (dosage effect significant).
(2) The dosage effect must remain significant after controlling for the effects of early program discharge (case attrition).

(3) The dosage effect must remain significant after controlling for known risk factors, such as age, gender, race, and prior offending (selection bias).
(4) No other causally prior factor accounts for the relationship between recidivism and the length of participation.

METHODOLOGY

Participants

This analysis evaluates the outcome experiences of 1,636 students discharged from CSF Buxmont schools over the course of four school years from the beginning of September 1999 until the end of August 2003. This represents the universe of all CSF clients who spent some time in CSF Buxmont school/day treatment programs over these years.

Students were referred to CSF Buxmont schools from three sources: county juvenile probation agencies (50%), individual school districts (40%), and county children and youth (C&Y) services (10%). Most of the students were boys (70%). A majority were white (68%), with fewer black (12%) and Latino students (8%). Upon program entry, students ranged from 11 to 19 years old with an average age of 15.5 years.

Girls constituted a majority (55%) of C&Y students, compared to about a quarter of those referred by probation (26%) or schools (29%). White students were three-quarters of those referred by court (77%) and schools (75%), while students referred from C&Y were much more likely to be Latino (24%) than their probation (7%) or school (7%) counterparts. Students referred from probation were older (15.7) than students from schools (15.2) or C&Y (15.1). Finally, while students referred from probation represented 58% (199) of students discharged during school years 1999–2000, their numbers declined to 41% (155) during the final year, while students referred from schools increased from 30% (104) to 47% (179) over the same four years.

MEASURES[5]

Dependent Variables

Recidivism was measured by conducting a manual name search (augmented by birth dates) of all juvenile and adult court records in the three primary counties serviced by CSF Buxmont from January to March 2004. Recidivism was defined as a petition in juvenile court for a new offense or the filing of a charge in adult criminal court. Recidivism rates were computed at 6 months for 1,540 students, 12 months for 1,293, 18 months for 1,192, and 24 months for 908 students.

Control Variables

Limited demographic information were extracted from CSF Buxmont's centralized program billing system for each student in the sample, including gender, race, date of birth, and the reason for discharge. Complete juvenile court histories were recorded for each student from juvenile court records, allowing for the number of prior petitions and the age on first petition to be computed. Most of the sample (69%) had at least one court petition recorded prior to coming to CSF Buxmont. Prior court petitions were located in court files for 95.9% of the probation-referred cases, 40.4% of the school and 40.9% of the C&Y-referred students. All of the probation-referred cases had at least one prior petition resulting in their placement with CSF Buxmont so there was a 4.1% miss rate on the record checks. All probation-placed students who had no identified court record were recoded as having one prior record (32 cases) to correct for this known undercount.

Independent Variables

Program participation data were extracted from CSF Buxmont's centralized program billing system, which tracks the number of days present, tardy, and absent for day treatment and the number of days billed for CSF residential and community supervision programs (Intensive Program, IP and Home and Community, H&C). Participation in CSF Buxmont day-treatment schools ranged from less than a day to just over two years. Additionally, one-in-three of these students (532) spend at least some time in one of CSF's residential group homes, one-in-five (341) some time in CSF's intensive supervision program, and one-in-six (261) some time in CSF's "home & community" program.

Students completing their stay in CSF Buxmont schools participate for differing lengths of time depending on a variety of factors. Most are returned to public school after a few months when their referral source and the CSF Buxmont staff deem that the student's behavior has sufficiently improved. Since the start of a new school year or semester presents minimally disruptive opportunities to return students to public schools, many students are normally discharged at these times. Because CSF Buxmont admits students continuously over the course of the year, some near the end of the school semesters, length of stay varies widely, even for students receiving normal discharges. Others are discharged when they turn 18, graduate, or complete their GED.

Some students are discharged early for a variety of behavioral problems – most within a short period of time, but some after extensive participation. Thus, one primary factor determining the length of participation is type of discharge. Half of the normally discharged students participated at least five months, while half of those discharged for misbehavior occurred within three months (means = 6.1 and 4.0, respectively).

The two discharge types were defined as:

(1) Normal Discharge ($N = 992$) – Students successfully completing the program by returning to public school, graduating or receiving GED, or upon turning 18 years old.
(2) Early Discharge ($N = 624$) – Students discharged prior to completing program for repeated non-compliance with program directives (28%), for an arrest resulting in a new placement (23%), failure to attend (19%), running away (16%), or because they were deemed inappropriate for the program (15%).

PROCEDURES

Factors related to the retention rates and recidivism rates were identified and are first considered in their bivariate and multivariate relationship with program retention rates and then in relationship to recidivism rates. General linear models (GLM) were employed to identify relevant variables that were then confirmed using discriminate analysis, logistic regression and Cox survival analysis. When performed on a dichotomous-dependent variable, general linear regression is called a linear probability model. The predicted value can be interpreted as the probability of completing the program to normal discharge or not, or of surviving the follow-up period without a court petition for a new offense. Use of GLM is not usually recommended in the analysis of dependent variables known to have a non-normal distribution, such as dichotomous variables or survival times, as the statistics produced may be biased. However, results from simple regression are easy to interpret and the GLM of regression has proven remarkably robust under violation of assumptions about distribution of variables (Andersen, McCaffery, McCold, & Kim, 1985). Therefore, the standardized beta weight from GLM was validated using more statistically appropriate methods for the dichotomous measure of retention and the two dichotomous measures of recidivism (12 and 24 months).

Finally, Cox proportional hazards survival analysis was conducted on the survival times in CSF Buxmont schools and the time until court petition/filing for students in the sample. Cox regression is specifically designed for these type of data as it allows for the analysis of censored data. Data is censored when an outcome (early discharge or recidivism) never occurs for a portion of the sample during the treatment or follow-up period. Cox regression therefore controls for different lengths of treatment and follow-up time available for each student. A unique advantage of survival analysis is the entire sample (1,534) can be used to test the significance of variables explaining program dropout and reoffending for up to three years after their discharge date.

Finally, in order to test for effects from participating in CSF auxiliary programs on the likelihood of completing their time to normal discharge, dummy variables were created for these programs. Students' ability to complete the school program predicts, to a large degree, how long they participate. Because the time spent in auxiliary programs is highly related to the time spent in the Buxmont school program, but only trivially so, it is inappropriate to use the interval-level length of stay variables to test their effects on retention rates. Dummy variables for IP, HC, and RC were used here, such that $1 =$ some time in the program and $0 =$ no time in the program.

RESULTS

Factors Affecting Retention Rates

Overall, 61% of the students completed the CSF Buxmont program to normal discharge. Students referred by the probation department were 12% more likely than others to complete (67–56%; $\chi^2 = 22.9$, $p < 0.001$).[6] Additionally, students who participated in Home & Community were 14% more likely (73–59%; $\chi^2 = 16.7$, $p < 0.001$) and students who participated in Intensive Program were 12% more likely to complete to normal discharge than their counterparts (71–59%; $\chi^2 = 16.5$, $p < 0.001$).

Black girls ($n = 63$) were 19% less likely than others to complete the program to normal discharge (43–62%; $\chi^2 = 9.5$, $p < 0.01$). As shown in Fig. 1, black and Latino girls who were not placed by probation were less likely to complete normally (46%), and black girls placed by probation were much less likely to complete (39%) than other gender/ethnic combinations.

Overall, students entering CSF Buxmont with two or more prior petitions were as likely to complete to normal discharge as those with none or one prior (62–60%). However, this difference became statistically significant once referral source was controlled as shown in Fig. 2. Among those not placed by probation, those with multiple prior petitions had completion rates 13% lower than others (44–57%; $\chi^2 = 7.7$, $p < 0.01$). Similarly, among those placed by probation, those with multiple prior petitions had a completion rate 9% lower than others (64–73%; $\chi^2 = 5.6$, $p < 0.05$).

There were seven factors eventually found to be statistically predictive of the retention rate. Only four of these factors directly predict program completion: probation referred students, black girls, and participation in IP or H&C auxiliary programs. As was true of the race/gender interaction, the effect of prior record, participation in CSF residential care and age on admission (demonstrated below) are significantly related to completion rates

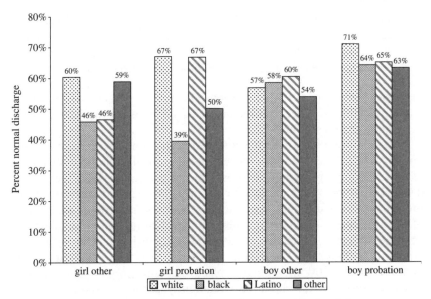

Fig. 1. Completion Rates by Race, Gender and Referral Source.

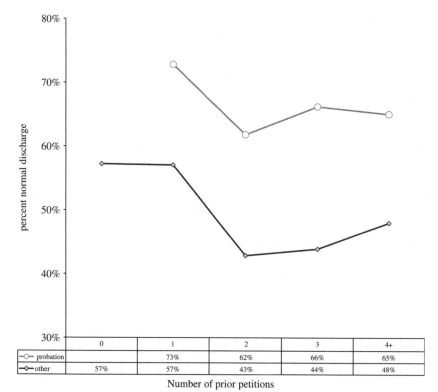

	0	1	2	3	4+
—O— probation		73%	62%	66%	65%
—◆— other	57%	57%	43%	44%	48%

Number of prior petitions

Fig. 2. Retention by Prior Petitions and Referral Source.

only after controlling for other predictive factors. This is, in part, because of the multi-collinearity between the predictor variables, as can be seen in the correlation matrix in Table 1.

A series of multivariate analyses (GLM regression, discriminate, logistic, and survival analysis) were conducted to determine the relative contribution of these factors on program retention and to detect any other factors that distinguish students discharged for misbehavior. Each of these statistical procedures make different assumptions about the underlying distribution of the variables, use different criteria for evaluating goodness of fit, and produce different estimates of regression coefficients. The results are reported in Table 2. The factors of being probation referred, having multiple prior petitions, being a black girl and co-placement in CSF Intensive Program or Home & Community services entered all of the regression equations.

Table 1. Correlation Matrix of Factors Related to Program Retention.

	Complete	2+ Priors	Probation	Black Girl	In CSF IP	In CSF H&C	In CSF RC	Age on Admit
Complete	–	−0.02	0.12	−0.08	0.10	0.10	0.02	0.01
2+ Priors	0.505	–	0.51	−0.07	0.37	0.19	0.24	0.23
Probation	0.000	0.000	–	−0.02	0.46	0.35	0.31	0.19
Black girl	0.002	0.011	0.358	–	−0.09	−0.07	0.03	−0.06
In CSF IP	0.000	0.000	0.000	0.000	–	0.18	0.49	0.28
In CSF H&C	0.000	0.000	0.000	0.005	0.000	–	0.16	0.02
In CSF RC	0.510	0.000	0.000	0.216	0.000	0.000	–	0.09
Age on admit	0.614	0.000	0.000	0.023	0.000	0.423	0.000	–
Number cases	1,596	1,529	1,616	1,616	1,616	1,616	1,616	1,616

Note: Pearson Correlation upper right; Sig. (2-tailed) lower left.

Results from the general linear model (GLM) using least-squared regression are the easiest to interpret. The beta weights are the slope of the relationship between the unique effects of each factor and program completion, measured in units of that factor. For every unit increase in the factor, there is a corresponding one percent increase in the completion rate (or decrease for negative weights). The standardized beta weights are the number of standard deviations that the outcome will change as a result of one standard deviation change in the predictor. Because they are all measured on the same standardized scale, the beta values are directly comparable and indicate the relative importance of each factor (Kerlinger & Pedhauzer, 1973, p. 446).

GLM regression estimates the completion rate is 12% higher for being probation referred, 12% lower for those with multiple priors, 22% lower for black girls, 8% higher for co-placement in Intensive Program, and 7% higher for co-placement in Home & Community program. The more conservative listwise deletion values are within 1% of the values estimated using the mean substitution method except for the effect of being a black girl, in which case it was 4% lower (18%). Both sets of estimates are very close to the bivariate differences observed of 12%, −11%[7], −19%, 12%, and 14%, respectively, as reported above.

The major purpose of discriminate analysis is to predict membership in two or more mutually exclusive groups from a set of predictors. Standardized coefficients are computed by multiplying each raw coefficient by the standard deviation of the corresponding variable. The results are not exactly beta values, but their ranking does reflect relative importance of the regressors in the same way as beta values do. Results of the discriminate analysis support the results produced by the GLM regression; all of the

Table 2. Multivariate Regression Weights Predicting Program Completion.

	Percent Normal Discharge									
	General linear regression				Discriminant		Logistic		Cox	
	Listwise deletion of missing cases		Mean substitute of missing cases		Canonical discriminant function coefficients		Regression coefficients		Proportional survival regression coefficients	
	B	Beta	B	Beta	Raw	Standard	B	Exp(B)−1	B	Exp(B)−1
Probation	0.123	0.126	0.116	0.120	1.257	0.624	0.532	0.703	0.234	0.208
2+ Priors	−0.121	−0.123	−0.117	−0.117	−1.245	−0.617	−0.545	−0.420	−0.433	−0.542
Black girls	−0.222	−0.086	−0.178	−0.071	−2.270	−0.428	−0.926	−0.604	−0.657	−0.929
ln IP	0.090	0.076	0.082	0.069	0.923	0.378	0.415	0.515	0.414	0.339
ln H&C	0.091	0.069	0.083	0.063	0.930	0.345	0.431	0.539	0.498	0.392
ln RC									0.306	0.264
Age at admit									−0.109	−0.115
(Constant)	0.572		0.583		−0.371		0.299	0.348		
Variance explained (%)	3.8		3.2		4.2		5.7		6.5	

Note: Cox proportional hazard regression coefficients were computed and the signs reversed to reflect time to survival rather than time to failure for table consistency.

same variables entered the equation at significant levels with the same order of magnitude: probation and prior record followed by the black girls, followed by CSF auxiliary program effects. However, the estimated standardized coefficients are about five times larger than observed from the bivariate or GLM analyses.

Estimation in logistic regression chooses parameters that maximize the likelihood of observing the sample values. The logistic regression coefficients show the change in the predicted logged odds of having the characteristic of interest for a one-unit change in the independent variables (Pampel, 2000, p. 36). Standardizing this coefficient by subtracting 1 from its exponent produces estimates of the logged odds of completing the program of 0.70 greater for probation referred, 0.42 lower for having two or more prior petitions, 0.60 lower for black girls, and 0.52 and 0.54 higher for those being served by the IP and H&C programs, respectively. These effect estimates are close to those estimated through discriminate analysis, but with a smaller effect attributed to prior record.

The exponent of the Cox regression coefficient, exp(B) in Table 2, is the relative risk of early discharge and, in the case of dichotomous independent variables, is the relative risk of early discharge for an individual with the risk factor present compared with an individual with the risk factor absent, given both individuals are the same on all other covariates. Therefore, probation-referred students were 20% more likely to survive to normal discharges than others, those with two or more prior petitions were 43% and black girls 93% less likely, and students co-placed with IP and H&C programs were 34% and 39% more likely to survive to normal discharge.

Since Cox regression explains the survival rate of students and, therefore, the time in program, two additional variables were statistically significant: whether the students participated in a CSF residential center and their age upon program entry. This latter effect is easily explained by "aging out" of the juvenile system, so that those entering just prior to their 18th birthdays were not staying as long as those with years to go before aging out, controlling for the reason for discharge. For the continuous variable age on admission, the coefficients are exponential. So the risk of program failure increases by 1.12 times (or $+0.12$) for being 13 years old on admission, for being 14 years old the hazard ratio increases by a factor of 1.24 (1.12^2), by a factor of 1.39 for 15 years old, etc. Thus the effect of age on survival risk is much greater than indicated by the unstandardized coefficient.

There was a clear effect from participation in residential care on the probability of surviving to normal discharge. Those who were discharged early participated an average of 10 weeks longer if they also stay in CSF residential care (13–23 weeks). Even those who completed to normal discharge participated longer if they were in residential care (22–29 weeks), as residential placement was highly related to prior record ($r = 0.35$, $p < 0.001$). This variable entered the survival analysis because there was an independent increase in survival time for those participating in residential care after controlling for the proportional hazard functions of the other predictor variables.

Each of the four multivariate models explained only a small percentage of the overall variation in the type of discharge (from 3.2% to 5.7%). While these variables are statistically significant, there remains much that was not explained about why some students complete the program to normal discharge. Still, there is a difference between the percent of variance explained and the slope of a relationship (Blalock, 1979, p. 299). Even though the percentage of the overall variance explained is small, the magnitude of the regression weights and the bivariate relationships already shown indicate that the effects on program completion that these factors do have are actually quite large.

The Cox survival procedure produced larger estimated values, but ones still consistent with the GLM procedure. With the additional effect of participation in residential care, the positive influences are proportionally smaller than the magnitude of the negative factors, and the effect of being a black girl on program retention is greater than prior record, while the reverse was true for GLM. The survival analysis also shows a greatly reduced effect from being probation-placed than was true for GLM. The results of discriminant analysis and the logistic regression had results similar to the survival analysis. Overall, all four methods found similar factors at comparable strengths. Only the GLM procedure produced estimates whose magnitudes were close to the observed bivariate effects. General conclusions about the predictors of program retention were essentially the same for all statistical models.

Factors Affecting Recidivism Rates

Recidivism rates were computed at each month following discharge for those whose follow-up period extended that long. The greater the follow-up period the fewer the cases that had valid values, as shown in Table 3. The follow-up period extended through four months for all 1,549 students, 99.4% at six months, 83.5% at one year, but was reduced to 58.7% at the end of two years. The overall percent of students petitioned in court for a

Table 3.   Recidivism Rates by Type of Discharge and Months
Follow-up.

Months Follow-up	Percent Recidivism			Number of Cases		
	Total	Early	Normal	Total	Early	Normal
0	0	0	0	1,549	597	932
1	4	6	2	1,549	597	932
2	7	10	4	1,549	597	932
3	8	13	5	1,549	597	932
4	11	16	7	1,549	597	932
5	12	17	9	1,544	594	930
6	14	20	11	1,540	593	927
7	17	22	13	1,515	589	906
8	18	23	14	1,399	583	796
9	19	24	16	1,381	566	795
10	21	27	17	1,356	546	790
11	23	28	20	1,324	521	783
12	24	28	21	1,293	507	766
13	25	29	22	1,270	497	753
14	27	31	23	1,251	486	745
15	27	32	24	1,233	472	741
16	28	33	25	1,218	462	736
17	30	34	27	1,197	457	722
18	32	36	29	1,192	455	719
19	33	38	29	1,155	447	690
20	35	40	31	1,022	426	578
21	37	41	32	999	413	570
22	37	42	33	983	402	566
23	38	42	34	959	385	559
24	39	43	35	909	364	530

new offense was 14.5% at six months, 24.1% at 12 months, and 38.5% by two years. Students completing to normal discharge were 8% less likely to be petitioned with two years than those who were discharged early.

To test the magnitude of the effects of those variables that were predictive of students completing the program on the results of recidivism, the correlation matrix of these factors and recidivism at 6, 12, 18, and 24 months were computed as shown in Table 4.

There were moderately strong relationships between completing the CSF Buxmont school program and recidivism at 6, 12, 18, and 24 months, although this factor was strongest at 6 months. Two other variables predictive of program retention were also significantly related to

Table 4. Correlation Matrix of Recidivism Measures and Factors Related to Program Retention.

	Recidivism 6 Months	Recidivism 12 Months	Recidivism 18 Months	Recidivism 24 Months	Complete	Probation	2 + Priors	Black Girl	Age	In IP	In H&C	In RC
Recidivism 6 months	–	0.72	0.60	0.52	-0.12	0.06	0.10	-0.02	-0.01	-0.02	0.01	-0.02
Recidivism 12 months	0.000	–	0.83	0.71	-0.08	0.08	0.12	-0.02	-0.02	0.02	0.01	-0.01
Recidivism 18 months	0.000	0.000	–	0.87	-0.08	0.12	0.17	-0.06	-0.03	0.05	0.02	0.01
Recidivism 24 months	0.000	0.000	0.000	–	-0.08	0.12	0.16	-0.05	-0.07	0.04	0.02	0.04
Complete	0.000	0.003	0.008	0.012	–	0.12	-0.02	-0.08	0.01	0.10	0.10	0.02
Probation	0.015	0.003	0.000	0.001	0.000	–	0.51	-0.02	0.19	0.46	0.35	0.31
2 + Priors	0.000	0.000	0.000	0.000	0.505	0.000	–	-0.07	0.23	0.37	0.19	0.24
Black girl	0.415	0.381	0.033	0.127	0.002	0.358	0.011	–	-0.06	-0.09	-0.07	0.03
Age	0.848	0.491	0.272	0.037	0.614	0.000	0.000	0.023	–	0.28	0.02	0.09
In IP	0.490	0.412	0.111	0.272	0.000	0.000	0.000	0.000	0.000	–	0.18	0.49
In H&C	0.609	0.628	0.524	0.617	0.000	0.000	0.000	0.005	0.423	0.000	–	0.16
In RC	0.496	0.788	0.672	0.260	0.510	0.000	0.000	0.216	0.000	0.000	0.000	–
Number cases	1,540	1,293	1,192	909	1,616	1,636	1,549	1,636	1,616	1,636	1,636	1,636

Note: Pearson correlation upper right; Sig. (2-tailed) lower left.

recidivism – students placed by probation and those having multiple prior petitions. Being a black girl was weakly related to recidivism only at 18 months.

In the multivariate analysis, completing the program to normal discharge continued to be predictive of recidivism even after accounting for the contribution of the specific factors that were predictive of program completion. Once the effect of having multiple prior petitions was taken into account, being probation-placed was no longer related to recidivism. Student age at program admission was only related to recidivism at 24 months, although this relationship remained significant even after controlling for multiple prior petitions ($t = 3.31$, $p < 0.001$). Student participation in CSF auxiliary programs was not directly predictive of recidivism.[8]

The other factors found to be correlated with recidivism rates were the number of prior petitions, gender, being petitioned in court for a new offense while in the program,[9] and the length of time in the program, as shown in the correlation matrix of Table 5. Age on entry was weakly related directly to recidivism only at 24 months. The length of participation directly predicted recidivism throughout the follow-up period, and the interval level measure predicted better than whether students had spent more than four months in the school program. The question is, of course, whether length of participation predicts recidivism after controlling for the other factors. But first, consider the nature of the bivariate correlations.

There was a strong relationship between the number of prior petitions and the recidivism rate after two years of follow-up. Recidivism rates for students with none or one prior court petition (30% and 33%) were much lower than those with two, three or four+ priors (43%, 50%, and 53%) to have a new court petition within 24 months of discharge from CSF Buxmont schools. Every additional prior petition increases the likelihood of a petition within two years of discharge by an average of 6.3%.

Boys were 13% more likely to have a new court petition within two years than girls. Once the effects of gender and prior record were taken into account, no race or race/gender combinations contributed significantly to the prediction of recidivism.

There were 246 (15.9%) students petitioned in court for a new offense while they were in the CSF Buxmont programs. Committing an offense resulting in a new court petition did not necessarily result in a student being discharged from CSF Buxmont schools, but students with one or more petitions for new offenses while in the program were 7% less likely to complete to normal discharge (62–55%; $\chi^2 = 4.6$, $p < 0.05$). However, these

Table 5. Correlation Matrix of Factors Related to Recidivism.

	Recidivism 6 Months	Recidivism 12 Months	Recidivism 18 Months	Recidivism 24 Months	Complete	Prior Petitions	Boys	In-Program Petition	Age on Entry	Weeks in Program	In Program >4 Months
Recidivism 6 months	–	0.72	0.60	0.52	-0.12	0.10	0.09	0.06	-0.01	-0.11	-0.07
Recidivism 12 months	0.000	–	0.83	0.71	-0.08	0.12	0.12	0.11	-0.02	-0.09	-0.07
Recidivism 18 months	0.000	0.000	–	0.87	-0.08	0.18	0.15	0.14	-0.03	-0.09	-0.07
Recidivism 24 months	0.000	0.000	0.000	–	-0.08	0.17	0.15	0.13	-0.06	-0.11	-0.09
Complete	0.000	0.003	0.008	0.012	–	0.02	0.05	-0.06	0.02	0.24	0.17
Prior petitions	0.000	0.000	0.000	0.000	0.463	–	0.20	0.05	0.26	-0.05	-0.04
Boys	0.001	0.000	0.000	0.000	0.041	0.000	–	0.05	0.07	-0.07	-0.07
In-program petition	0.012	0.000	0.000	0.000	0.032	0.042	0.033	–	-0.09	0.16	0.11
Age on entry	0.816	0.557	0.329	0.055	0.474	0.000	0.009	0.000	–	-0.16	-0.13
Weeks in program	0.000	0.001	0.001	0.001	0.000	0.059	0.004	0.000	0.000	–	0.80
In program >4 months	0.005	0.013	0.015	0.005	0.000	0.144	0.004	0.000	0.000	0.000	–
Number cases	1,538	1,291	1,190	907	1,614	1,547	1,634	1,547	1,616	1,634	1,634

Note: Pearson Correlation upper right; Sig. (2-tailed) lower left.

students were 13% and 17% more likely than other students to recidivate at 12 and 24 months, respectively ($\chi^2 = 14.9$ and 15.0, both $p < 0.001$).[10]

Lastly, the two measures of the length of participation in CSF Buxmont schools were predictive of recidivism. The length of participation in CSF Buxmont schools ranged from 65 students participating less than a month to 4 students with stays exceeding two years. The mean length of participation in program was 5.42 months (median = 5). As shown in Fig. 3, the length of participation was negatively correlated with recidivism rates at both one- and two-year follow-up periods. The longer the participation, the greater the benefits of participation. There was no dramatic turning point or critical length of stay evident in these data, as was found in our earlier report (see McCold, 2002).

The differences in recidivism trends between short-stay and longer-stay students demonstrates the hypothesized effect of the CSF Buxmont restorative milieu on recidivism. Controlling for type of discharge, the 24-month recidivism rates are dramatically reduced throughout the 24-month follow-up

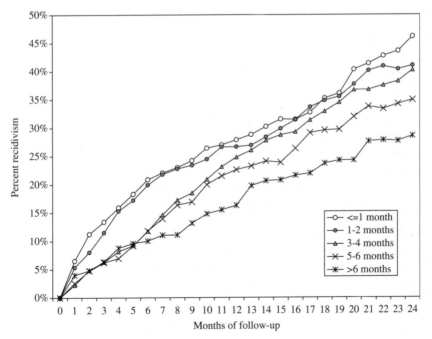

Fig. 3. Percent Recidivism by Months Follow-up for Differing Lengths of Stay.

period. Students with early discharges had 6% lower recidivism rates if they participated more than four months (38–45%). Students discharged normally had recidivism rates 11% lower after 24 months, if they had participated for more than four months (28–39%).

All of the risk variables related to recidivism at 12 months or 24 months were entered into the multivariate analyses without the treatment variable. As shown in Table 6, the number of prior petitions, student gender, the presence of in-program petitions, and retention in the program to completion were all statistically significant predictors of recidivism at both 12 and 24 months. Predicting recidivism at 24 months, age also entered the equations for all models, and program completion fell below statistical significance in the discriminate analysis.

After the other variables entered the equation, the significance of the treatment variable was tested for entry into the models. Weeks in the program, entered at both 12 months and 2 years, contributed significant predictive power to all five statistical models. The statistics were $t = -3.0$, $p < 0.001$ and $t = -3.4$, $p < 0.001$ for listwise GLM at 12 and 24 months, respectively; $t = -2.8$, $p < 0.001$ and $t = -3.3$, $p < 0.001$ for meansub GLM, Wilk's Lambda 12.1 and 16.9, both $p < 0.001$ for discriminant; Wald 9.1, $p < 0.01$ and 11.6, $p < 0.001$ for the logistic models. Cox regression controls for censored data, so produces the hazard coefficients over the entire range of the follow-up period. Again, after the other variables had entered the model, the number of weeks in the program added significant predictive power to the model (Wald $= 11.1$, $p < 0.001$).

Comparing the zero-order relationships between the predictor variables and recidivism to the estimates obtained from the GLM regression equations demonstrates the degree to which these variables are explaining the same part of the variance or are explaining relatively unique parts of the variance of recidivism. Bivariate estimates of the effects were changed for prior petitions from $r = 0.174$ to 0.169, for gender from $r = 0.152$ to 0.121, for in-program petitions from 0.128 to 0.108, and for normal program completion from -0.084 to -0.060. Age on entry went from $+0.018$ to -0.111. Finally, weeks in program went from -0.113 to -0.114 after entering the other predictive variables. Other variables related bivariately to recidivism at 24 months became non-significant once the predictive variables entered the equations, that is being probation-placed, being a black girl, having multiple priors, and participation in the three CSF auxiliary programs.

Although the total variance explained by the complete models seems small (3.5–11.8%), the large sample size in the current study limits the amount of

Table 6. Multivariate Regression Weights Predicting Recidivism.

| | Reneral Linear Regression | | | | Discriminant | | Logistic | | Cox | |
| | Listwise deletion of missing cases | | Mean substitute of missing cases | | Canonical discriminant function coefficients | | Regression coefficients | | Proportional hazard regression coefficients | |
	B	Beta	B	Beta	Raw	Standard	B	Exp(B)−1	B	Exp(B)−1
Petitioned at 12 months										
# of priors	0.028	0.091	0.025	0.089	0.316	0.433	0.157	0.170		
Boys	0.088	0.094	0.065	0.079	0.982	0.446	−0.554	−0.425		
In-program petition	0.119	0.102	0.105	0.098	1.331	0.485	−0.626	−0.465		
Complete	−0.057	−0.065	−0.045	−0.057	−0.637	−0.311	0.312	0.367		
Weeks in program	−0.002	−0.087	−0.002	−0.073	−0.026	−0.411	−0.015	−0.015		
(Constant)	0.198		0.203		−0.473		−0.591	−0.446		
Variance explained (%)	4.2		3.5		4.6		6.9			
Petitioned at 2 years										
# of priors	0.062	0.173	0.036	0.131	0.450	0.605	0.277	0.320	0.198	0.219
Boys	0.130	0.120	0.066	0.083	0.916	0.407	−0.627	−0.466	0.691	0.996
In-program petition	0.139	0.106	0.094	0.092	1.086	0.401	−0.620	−0.462	0.450	0.569
Age at admit	−0.041	−0.112	−0.024	−0.090	−0.308	−0.411	−0.191	−0.173	−0.108	−0.103
Complete	−0.060	−0.061	−0.032	−0.042	—		0.271	0.311	−0.280	−0.244
Weeks in program	−0.004	−0.116	−0.002	−0.084	−0.032	−0.482	−0.019	−0.018	−0.010	−0.010
(Constant)	0.921		0.707		3.896		2.983	18.757		
Variance explained (%)	8.1		4.5		8.4		11.8		9.4	

variance that can be explained. This is why small correlation coefficients (e.g., 0.06) are statistically significant. Once sample sizes exceed 500, the magnitude of regression parameters are on a different scale than for samples below 100 cases (Renninger & Hidi, 1992, p. 199). Nonetheless, there remains a large amount of variation in recidivism rates that remained unexplained.

The results confirm the hypothesis that the length of participation in the CSF Buxmont milieu was significantly related to reduced reoffending, and this relationship held after controlling for the known risk factors. The null hypothesis was that length of participation had no effect on recidivism is rejected. The null hypothesis that whatever relationship existed was due to other risk variables rather than program participation is also rejected.

The results presented satisfy three of the four criteria for causality. There was a significant dosage effect; it held after controlling for case attrition, and it held after controlling for the risk factors of prior offending, in-program offending, gender, and age. The fourth condition for causality was that there are no other variables that explain the relationship between length of participation and the recidivism rates. If this were true, than the residuals of the regression equation would be unrelated to the observed recidivism rate. That is, if the variance not explained by the regression equations is randomly distributed, then there is no more systematic variance to explain. If, however, the residual is correlated, then there exists the possibility that some unknown and unmeasured variable is the real cause of the reduced recidivism. An examination of the residuals from each of the five prediction models found there was a significant correlation between the residual variation and the measure of recidivism. Thus, one cannot rule out the possibility of unmeasured and unknown variables that are causally prior to both.

Discussion

The CSF Buxmont schools and their associated support programs provide a restorative milieu in which students are encouraged to begin to take adult responsibility for their lives. This milieu works together to set and enforce high behavioral expectations while simultaneously providing the emotional and social support necessary for at-risk students to make the positive changes necessary to lead successful lives. This restorative milieu, including supported classroom instruction and daily group processes, is provided at least five days a week for an average of 18 weeks. As an intervention, it represents a much higher dosage of restorativeness than is possible for a single family group conference. Had this research not been able to demonstrate a reduction in recidivism as a result of such a large dosage, there would be no hope that lesser intensive interventions could expect to have a measurable effect.

Prior record, gender, and age are all well-recognized risk factors for juvenile delinquency (Braithwaite, 1989). Once prior record is taken into account, race no longer was predictive in this sample. Once these factors were accounted for, the success of the student in CSF Buxmont schools was still predictive of future delinquency. The remaining differences in recidivism were attributable to the dose response effect of the length of exposure to the restorative milieu. Any improvements from participation in CSF's intensive, residential care, and home and community programs contributed indirectly to increasing a student's odds of completing the day treatment school program.

The comparison of four different multivariate regression procedures revealed that the simple generalized least-squares model (GLM) produced the least-biased estimates, in spite of the violation of the distributional assumptions required by the procedure. The results were nearly identical in terms of the factors that were found to be significant and relative importance. The Cox proportional hazards survival analysis proved to be most sensitive of the procedures, as it allowed for the statistical control of two additional factors related to recidivism. Participation in CSF Buxmont schools was found to significantly reduce recidivism under all four of the statistical procedures tested.

It is never possible to validate a research finding to absolute scientific certainty. Program evaluations are inevitably fraught with threats to the validity of a significant finding, especially given the built-in bias in favor of falsely finding a positive program effect due to selective participant dropouts. This problem can be minimized by maximizing the program retention rate, but very high retention rates are unrealistic for most programs. The more pragmatic approach to program evaluation is to account for and statistically control for the "sample mortality" effect in the interpretation of the results.

Evaluating the results of a program that is based upon a new paradigm (restorative) on the basis of the criteria of an old paradigm (deterrence) is not wholly appropriate. Restorative practices are intended for the benefit of the victim, the offender, and the "community." Even if it were conclusively demonstrated that restorative practices had no effect on the future behavior of offenders, there would still be valid and socially useful reasons for preferring it whenever possible.[11]

Another limitation on the present study is the degree to which the results are generalizable to other students, other settings or other approaches. "One does not really care about the results of a study unless its conclusions can be used to guide future decisions. Generalization is a prerequisite for that guidance" (Berk, 2005, p. 15). There are several kinds of generalization that might be desirable: to different subjects, to different settings, to different times, to related interventions, and to related outcomes. These results should generalize to other day-treatment alternative school programs treating delinquent and at-risk teens, but it becomes a problem of program implementation. Whether the results can be expected to apply to students in public schools, is yet to be determined though early indications are positive (Preston, 2002; Mirsky, 2007).

Formal use of restorative practices in the criminal justice setting have also spawned a multitude of applications in settings other than in response to criminal wrongdoing, including organizational management, family rela-tionships, child protection services (Merkel-Holguin et al., 2003), and, most obviously, schools (Riestenberg, 1997; Braithwaite, 2000; Cameron & Thorsborne, 2001; Karp & Breslin, 2001; Braithwaite, Morrison, Ahmed, & Reinhart, 2003; Ierley & Claassen-Wilson, 2003; Morrison, 2003; Claassen & Claassen, 2004; Hopkins, 2004; Blood & Thorsborne, 2005; Youth Justice Board, 2005).

The question resolved here is that restorative practices can reduce recidivism among delinquent and at-risk youth. What remains an open question is whether these results are generalizable to public school settings for normal student populations. Can public schools produce a significant amount of the culture of restorative milieu? If so, would this produce a measurable improvement in the behavior of students who are not at risk of delinquency?

CONCLUSIONS

The CSF Buxmont restorative milieu produced positive results in all three performance measures: program completion, student attitudes, and offend-ing following discharge. The majority of youth successfully completed the program with rates of 66% for probation referrals, 53% for school referrals, and 57% for referrals from children and youth. These rates are very high when compared to programs serving similar populations. The average completion rate for programs serving youth placed by Philadelphia Juvenile Court is estimated at 35% for community-based programs and 55% for non-community-based programs excluding boot camps (Jones, Harris, Grubstein, & Fader, 2000). About 33% of non-adjudicated youth in Philadelphia's delinquency prevention programs complete their program and 40% simply stopped attending (Jones, Harris, Poulin, & Moss, 2001). Thus, the completion rates for CSF Buxmont schools are very respectable for a community-based program. These high completion rates are especially significant because CSF Buxmont schools have a very open referral policy and accept youth with a wide range of offense seriousness and related risk factors (Harris et al., 2000).

In the prior research, McCold (2002) found that, rather than screening out high-need students, CSF Buxmont's restorative milieu tends to retain them. Students with the lowest social values and self-esteem scores upon entry were retained longer than others. It was these students that showed the greatest improvements. This is especially impressive in light of the fact that the proportion of students receiving a behavioral discharge did not differ by age, gender, race, prior offending, or other risk factors.

Offending during the six months following discharge was reduced by 58% for those students who completed the program successfully with more than three months participation. Youth in all risk categories were less likely to offend following discharge, including those discharged unsuccessfully, if they participated in the program for more than three months. Finally, the greatest reduction in offending occurred among students with the highest risk factors for offending (McCold, 2002).

Absent random assignment, no program evaluation can rule out possible unmeasured and unknown variables rendering relationships spurious. If such effects exist, they are not obvious. Thus, these results present sufficient empirical evidence to conclude that changes in attitudes and behavior of students were the result of participating in CSF's restorative milieu causing a reduction in recidivism detectable for up to three years following discharge, because:

(1) Recidivism rates were negatively related to the length of participation (dosage effect significant).
(2) The dosage effect remained significant after controlling for the effects of early program discharge (case attrition).
(3) The dosage effect remained significant after controlling for known risk factors, such as age, gender, race, and prior offending (selection bias).

These results provide sufficient empirical support to conclude that restorative practices are effective; that youth in a restorative milieu are supported and encouraged to become more positive in their social values and develop an improved self-image; and that these changes help ensure that at-risk young people are less likely to offend in the future. Certainly, these results should encourage the development and evaluation of additional programs like CSF Buxmont in different settings with similar populations. These results should encourage the further development and evaluation of restorative practices in traditional school setting to retain troubled students in the first place.

The methodology used in this study allowed for a comparison of the capacity of different multivariate techniques to detect changes in recidivism related to the length of participation. All four regression models easily detected the recidivism reduction effect after taking account of the standard control variables. While all models produced beta weights of similar magnitude, survival analysis proved to be more sensitive in the detection of program effects than general linear, discriminant, or logistic regression. Post-hoc multivariate analysis of program effects was shown to be a viable methodology for delinquency prevention program evaluation.

NOTES

1. Others have connected the idea of restorative justice to the operation of prisons. For example, Cullen, Wozniak, and Sundt (2001) call for developing a "virtuous prison" to use offenders' time of incarceration to cultivate moral awareness by creating a "virtuous milieu."

2. The idea of a social milieu as the mechanism of therapy began as a way to treat psychologically traumatized soldiers in the UK during WW2 (Jones, 1952). Therapeutic communities have since been established in prisons, schools, community homes for those with mental illnesses, and secure psychiatric units (Campling, 2001).

3. "The origins and development of the therapeutic community have been traced back to two independent traditions: the American hierarchical concept-based TC and the British democratic Maxwell Jones-type TC. Both branches have developed independently, targeting different people and tackling diverse problems ... The hierarchical approach was modeled on Synanon, founded by Charles Dederich. It developed as a self-help movement for the treatment of substance abusers, primarily using behavioral modification techniques. The democratic approach is most commonly associated with Maxwell Jones. It developed as a professional group work method to treat people suffering from a range of psychiatric difficulties, primarily using social learning principles" (Vandevelde et al., 2004, pp. 66–67). Despite their success in prison settings, many of these innovative programs were terminated during the 1970s on fictitious grounds of "cost-effectiveness" (Vandevelde et al., 2004).

4. Another important underutilized alternative is the single group time series design, which has fewer threats to validity than true experimental designs (Campbell & Stanley, 1963).

5. Data collected for the present study were part of a larger evaluation conducted during the four years reported here. For a description of the other measures gathered for this larger study, see McCold (2002).

6. This evidence of a court-order incentive to participate is consistent with findings from evaluations of therapeutic communities (Messina et al., 2001, p. 44).

7. Weighted average of 13% for 755 non-court and 9% for 774 court placed students is 10.8%.

8. This was true for both the dummy variables and the interval level lengths of stay. These programs indirectly affect recidivism by contributing to an increased retention rate.

9. In-program petitions were not included in the predictors of retention rates since they are confounded with the dependent variable (i.e., rearrest was one reason for early discharge).

10. Care was taken not to confuse a petition resulting in a discharge from petitions occurring after discharge. Those with petition dates within three days of discharge were assumed to be petitioned in program, those occurring four or more days afterwards were counted as recidivist events.

11. It is not intended to suggest that restorative justice is a sufficient response to the needs of crime victims (see, Herman, 2004).

REFERENCES

Aertsen, I., Mackay, R., Pelikan, C., Wright, M., & Wilemsens, J. (2004). *Rebuilding community connections: Mediation and restorative justice.* Strasbourg: Council of Europe.

Allison, P. (1995). *Survival analysis using the SAS system: A practical guide.* Gary, NC: SAS Institute, Inc.

American Humane Association. (2004). FGDM programs around the world. [Online] National Center on Family Group Decision Making. Available at http://www.americanhumane. org/site/PageServer?pagename = pc_fgdm_programs. Retrieved on January 4, 2005.

Andersen, D., McCaffery, D., McCold, P., & Kim, D. (1985). Modelling complexity: Using dynamic simulation to link regression and case studies. *Journal of Policy Analysis and Management, 4*(2), 196–216.

Andrews, D., Zinger, I., Hoge, D., Bonta, J., Gendreau, P., & Cullen, F. (1990). Does correctional treatment work? A clinically-relevant and psychologically-informed meta-analysis. *Criminology, 28*(3), 369–404.

Angel, C. (2005). *Crime victims meet their offenders: Testing the impact of restorative justice conferences on victims' post-traumatic stress symptoms.* Unpublished Doctoral dissertation, Nursing and Criminology Faculties, University of Pennsylvania.

Berk, R. (2005). Randomized experiments as the bronze standard. Paper presented at the Fifth Annual Jerry Lee Crime Prevention Symposium, Adelphi, Maryland, May.

Blalock, H. (1979). *Social statistics* (Revised 2nd ed.). New York: McGraw-Hill.

Blood, P., & Thorsborne, M. (2005). The challenge of culture change: Embedding restorative practice in schools. Paper presented at the 6th International Conference on Conferencing, Circles, and other Restorative Practices, Sydney, Australia, March.

Bloom, S. (1997). Creating sanctuary: Toward the evolution of sane societies. [Online] Available at http://www.sanctuaryweb.com/main/therapeutic_communikty.htm. Retrieved on September 29, 2005.

Bloom, S., & Norton, K. (2004a). Introduction special section: The therapeutic community in the 21st century. *Psychiatric Quarterly*, *75*(3), 229–232.

Bloom, S., & Norton, K. (2004b). The art and challenge of long-term and short-term democratic therapeutic communities. *Psychiatric Quarterly*, *75*(3), 249–263.

Bonta, J. (2003). Restorative justice and recidivism research: Summary, *Corrections Research and Development*, *8*(1). Ottawa, Canada: Department of Public Safety and Emergency Preparedness. Available at http://www.psepc-sppcc.gc.ca/publications/corrections/200301_e.asp. Retrieved on October 10, 2005.

Braithwaite, J. (1989). *Crime, shame and reintegration*. Cambridge, UK: Cambridge University Press.

Braithwaite, J. (2002). *Restorative justice and responsive regulation*. Cambridge, UK: Cambridge University Press.

Braithwaite, V. (2000). Values and restorative justice in schools. In: H. Strang & J. Braithwaite (Eds), *Restorative justice: Philosophy to practice* (pp. 121–144). Burlington, VT: Ashgate Publishing.

Braithwaite, V., Morrison, B., Ahmed, E., & Reinhart, M. (2003). Researching the prospects for restorative justice practice in schools: The 'Life at School Survey' 1996–99. In: L. Walgrave (Ed.), *Repositioning restorative justice* (pp. 169–190). Devon: Willan Publishing.

Brown, M. (1995). Background paper on New Zealand youth justice process Paper presented at International Bar Association Judges' Forum, Section on General Practice. Edinburgh, June. Available at http://www.restorativepractices.org/library/NZ.html. Retrieved on October 10, 2005.

Burford, G., & Hudson, J. (Eds). (2000). *Family group conferencing: New directions in community-centered child and family practice*. New York: Aldine de Gruyter.

Cameron, L., & Thorsborne, M. (2001). Restorative justice and school discipline: Mutually exclusive?. In: H. Strang & J. Braithwaite (Eds), *Restorative justice and civil society* (pp. 180–194). Cambridge, UK: Cambridge University Press.

Campbell, D., & Stanley, J. (1963). *Experimental and quasi-experimental designs for research.* Chicago: Rand McNally.

Campling, P. (2001). Therapeutic communities. *Advances in Psychiatric Treatment*, *2001*(7), 365–372. Available online at http://apt.rcpsych.org/cgi/reprint/7/5/365.pdf

Claassen, R., & Claassen, R. (2004). Creating a restorative discipline system: Restorative justice in schools. *The Fourth R: Newsletter of the Education Section* (Association for Conflict Resolution). Winter, pp. 9–12.

Condelli, W. (1994). Domains of variables for understanding and improving retention in therapeutic communities. *International Journal of Addiction*, *29*(5), 593–607.

Condelli, W., & Hubbard, R. (1994). Relationship between time spent in treatment and client outcomes from therapeutic communities. *Journal of Substance Abuse Treatment*, *11*(1), 25–33.

Cox, S. (1999). An assessment of an alternative education program for at-risk delinquent youth. *Journal of Research in Crime and Delinquency*, *36*(3), 323–336.

Cox, S., Davison, W., & Bynum, T. (1995). A meta-analytic assessment of delinquency-related outcomes of alternative education programs. *Crime and Delinquency*, *41*(2), 219–234.

Crime and Justice Research Centre & Triggs, S. (2005). *Evaluation of the court-referred restorative justice pilot: Evaluation.* Wellington: Victoria University of Wellington and Ministry of Justice. Available at http://www.justice.govt.nz/pubs/reports/2005/nz-court-referred-restorative-justice-pilot-evaluation/index.html. Retrieved on October 10.

Cullen, F., Wozniak, J., & Sundt, J. (2001). Virtuous prison: Toward a restorative rehabilitation. In: H. Pontell & D. Shichor (Eds), *Contemporary issues in crime and criminal justice: Essays in honor of Gilbert Geis* (pp. 265–286). Upper Saddle River: Prentice Hall.

Daly, K. (2001a). Conferencing in Australia and New Zealand: Variations, research findings, and prospects. In: A. Morris & G. Maxwell (Eds), *Restorative justice for juveniles: Conferencing, mediation and circles* (pp. 59–83). Oxford: Hart Publishing.

Daly, K. (2001b). Mind the gap: restorative justice in theory and practice. Paper presented to Cambridge Seminar on Restorative Justice, Toronto, May. Available at http://www.aic.gov.au/rjustice/sajj/index.html. Retrieved on October 10, 2005.

Daly, K., & Hayes, H. (2005). Restorative justice and conferencing. In: A. Graycar & P. Grabosky (Eds), *Handbook of Australian criminology* (pp. 294–311). Cambridge, UK: Cambridge University Press.

De Leon, G. (1997). *Community as method: Therapeutic communities for special populations and special settings.* Westport, CT: Praeger/Greenwood.

De Leon, G. (2000). *The therapeutic community: Theory, model, and method.* New York: Springer.

Emmer, E. T., & Aussiker, A. (1989). School and classroom discipline programs: How well do they work?. In: O. C. Moles (Ed.), *Strategies to reduce student misbehavior* (pp. 105–142). Washington, DC: Office of Educational Research and Improvement (ED 311 608).

Garrett, C. (1985). Effects of residential treatment of adjudicated delinquents: A meta-analysis. *Journal of Research in Crime and Delinquency, 22*(4), 287–308.

Gottfredson, D. (1989). Developing effective organizations to reduce school disorder. In: O. C. Moles (Ed.), *Strategies to reduce student misbehavior* (pp. 87–104). Washington, DC: Office of Educational Research and Improvement (ED 311 608).

Harris, P., Jones, P., Naiburg, J., & Washnock, J. (2000). *Objectives and outcomes of Community Service Foundation programs: Results of the evaluability assessment study.* Philadelphia: Crime and Justice Research Institute.

Hayes, H., & Daly, K. (2003). Youth justice conferencing and re-offending. *Justice Quarterly, 20*(4), 725–764.

Hayes, H., & Daly, K. (2004). Conferencing and re-offending in Queensland. *The Australian and New Zealand Journal of Criminology, 37*(2), 167–191. Available at http://www.aic.gov.au/rjustice/docs/hayes.pdf. Retrieved on October 10, 2005.

Heit, D. (1991). The therapeutic community in America today. Paper presented at the 14th World Conference of Therapeutic Communities, Montreal, Canada, September.

Herman, S. (2004). Is restorative justice possible without a parallel system for victims? In: H. Zehr & B. Toews (Eds), *Critical issues in restorative justice* (pp. 75–83). Monsey, NY: Criminal Justice Press.

Hopkins, B. (2004). *Just schools: A whole school approach to restorative justice.* London: Jessica Kingsley Publishers.

Ierley, A., & Claassen-Wilson, D. (2003). Making things right: Restorative justice for school communities. In: T. S. Jones & R. Compton (Eds), *Kids working it out: Stories and strategies for making peace in our schools* (pp. 199–209). San Francisco: Jossey-Bass.

Jainchill, N., Hawke, J., De Leon, G., & Yagelka, J. (2000). Adolescents in therapeutic communities: One-year post-treatment outcomes. *Journal of Psychoactive Drugs, 32*(1), 81–94.

Jones, M. (1952). *Social psychiatry: A study of therapeutic communities.* London: Tavistock Publications.

134   PAUL McCOLD

Jones, P., Harris, P., Grubstein, L., & Fader, J. (2000). *Juvenile Justice Trends and Projections. Program Development and Evaluation System.* Philadelphia, PA: Crime and Justice Research Institute.

Jones, P., Harris, P., Poulin, M., & Moss, M. (2001). *Delinquency Prevention Program Trends and Projections. Prevention Outcome Monitoring Information System (PROMIS).* Philadelphia, PA: Crime and Justice Research Institute.

Karp, D., & Breslin, B. (2001). Restorative justice in school communities. *Youth & Society,* *33*(2), 249–272.

Kemple, J., & Snipes, J. (2000). *Career academies: Impacts on students' engagement and performance in high school.* San Francisco: Manpower Demonstration Research Corporation.

Kennard, D. (2004). The therapeutic community as an adaptable treatment modality across different settings. *Psychiatric Quarterly, 75*(3), 295–307.

Kerlinger, F., & Pedhauzer, E. (1973). *Multiple regression in behavioral research.* New York: Holt, Rinehart and Winston.

Latimer, J., Dowden, C., & Muise, D. (2001). *The effectiveness of restorative justice practices: A meta-analysis.* Ottawa: Department of Justice Canada.

Latimer, J., & Kleinknecht, S. (2000). *The effects of restorative justice programming: A review of the empirical.* Ottawa: Department of Justice Canada.

Lees, J., Manning, N., & Rawlings, B. (1999). Therapeutic community effectiveness. A systematic international review of therapeutic community treatment for people with personality disorders and mentally disordered offenders. New York: NHS Centre for Reviews and Dissemination. Available at http://www.pettarchiv.org.uk/atc-briefingpaper.htm. Retrieved on October 10, 2005.

Lipsey, M. (1992). Juvenile delinquency treatment: A meta-analytic inquiry into the variability of effects. In: T. Cook, H. Cooper, D. Cordray, H. Hartmann, L. Hedges, R. Light, T. Louis & F. Mosteller (Eds), *Meta-analysis for explanation: A casebook.* New York: Russell Sage Foundation.

Lipsey, M. (2000). What 500 intervention studies show about the effects of intervention on the recidivism of juvenile offenders. Paper presented at the Annual Conference on Criminal Justice Research and Evaluation, Washington, DC, July.

Lipsey, M., & Cordray, D. (2000). Evaluation methods of social intervention. *Annual Review of Psychology, 51,* 345–375.

Lipsey, M., Wilson, D., & Cothern, L. (2000). Effective intervention for serious juvenile offenders. *Juvenile Justice Bulletin.* Washington, DC: Office of Juvenile Justice and Delinquency Prevention.

Lloyd, C., Mair, G., & Hough, M. (1994). Explaining reconviction rates: A critical analysis. *Research Findings* [No. 12]. London: Home Office Research and Statistics Department.

Luke, G., & Lind, B. (2002). Reducing juvenile crime: Conferencing versus court. *Crime and Justice Bulletin: Contemporary Issues in Crime and Justice.* Sydney: New South Wales Bureau of Crime Statistics and Research.

Luke, G., & Lind, B. (2005). Comparing reoffending. In: J. Chan (Ed.), *Reshaping juvenile justice* (pp. 141–169). Sydney: The institute of Criminology.

Martin, S., Butzin, C., & Inciardi, J. (1995). Assessment of a multistage therapeutic community for drug-involved offenders. *Journal of Psychoactive Drugs, 27,* 109–116.

Maxwell, G., Kingi, V., Robertson, J., Morris, A., Cunningham, C., & Lash, B. (2004). Achieving effective outcomes in Youth Justice Research Project. Final report to the Ministry of Social Development, Ministry of Social Development, Wellington.

Maxwell, G., & Morris, A. (2000). Restorative justice and re-offending. In: H. Strang & J. Braithwaite (Eds), *Restorative justice: Philosophy to practice* (pp. 93–103). Aldershot, England: Ashgate/Dartmouth.

McCold, P. (2002). Evaluation of a restorative milieu: CSF Buxmont School/Day Treatment programs 1999–2001 evaluation outcome technical report. Paper presented at the American Society of Criminology Annual Meeting, Chicago, Illinois, November. Available at http://www.iirp.org/Pages/erm.html. Retrieved on October 4, 2007.

McCold, P. (2003a). A survey of assessment research on mediation and conferencing. In: L. Walgrave (Ed.), *Repositioning restorative justice* (pp. 67–120). Devon, UK: Willan Publishing.

McCold, P. (2003b). An experiment in police-based restorative justice: The Bethlehem (PA) Project. *Police Practice and Research, 4*(4), 371–382.

McCold, P. (2006). The recent history of restorative justice: Mediation, circles, and conferencing. In: D. Sullivan & L. Tifft (Eds), *Handbook of restorative justice: A global perspective*. New York: Routledge.

McCold, P., & Wachtel, B. (1998). *Restorative policing experiment: The Bethlehem Pennsylvania police family group conferencing project*. (Final Report) U.S. Dept. of Justice, National Institute of Justice. Washington, DC: National Criminal Justice Reference Service. [NCJ177564]. Available at http://fp.enter.net/restorativepractices/BPD.pdf. Retrieved on October 23, 2006.

McCold, P., & Wachtel, T. (2002). Restorative justice theory validation. In: E. Weitekamp & H.-J. Kerner (Eds), *Restorative justice: Theoretical foundations* (pp. 110–142). Devon, UK: Willan Publishing.

McCusker, J., Vickers-Lahti, M., Stoddard, A., Hindi, R., Bigelow, C., Zorn, M., Garfield, F., Frost, R., Love, C., & Lewis, B. (1995). The effectiveness of alternative planned durations of residential drug abuse treatment. *American Journal of Public Health, 10*, 1426–1429.

McGarrell, E., Olivares, K., Crawford, K., & Kroovand, N. (2000). *Returning justice to the community: The Indianapolis juvenile restorative justice experiment*. Indianapolis: Hudson Institute. Available at http://www.hudson.org/files/publications/Restoring_Justice_Report.pdf. Retrieved on October 10, 2005.

Merkel-Holguin, L., Nixon, P., & Burford, G. (2003). Learning with families: A synopsis of FGDM research and evaluation in child welfare. *Protecting Children, 18*(1–2), 2–11. Available at http://www.americanhumane.org/site/DocServer/FGDM_Research_intro.pdf?doc. Retrieved on October 10, 2005.

Messina, N., Wish, E., & Nemes, S. (2001). Therapeutic community treatment may reduce future incarceration: A research note. *Federal Probation, 65*(3), 40–45.

Mirsky, L. (2007). SaferSanerSchools: Transforming school cultures with restorative practices. *Reclaiming Children and Youth, 16*(2), 5–12.

Moore, D., Forsyth, L., & O'Connell, T. (1995). A new approach to juvenile justice: An evaluation of family conferencing in Wagga Wagga. Centre for Rural Social Research, Charles Sturt University-Riverina, Australia. Available at http://www.aic.gov.au/crc/reports/moore/. Retrieved on October 4, 2007.

Morris, A., & Maxwell, G. (1997). Re-forming juvenile justice: The New Zealand experiment. *Prison Journal, 77*(2), 125–134.

Morrison, B. (2003). Regulating safe school communities: Being responsive and restorative. *Journal of Educational Administration, 41*(6), 689–704.

Mullen, R., Arbiter, N., & Gilder, P. (1991). Comprehensive therapeutic community approach for chronic substance abusing juvenile offenders. The Amity model. In: T. Armstrong (Ed.), *Intensive interventions with high risk youths*. Monsey, NY: Willow Tree Press.

Nemes, S., Wish, E., & Messina, N. (1999). Comparing the impact of standard and abbreviated treatment in a therapeutic community: Findings from the District of Columbia treatment initiative experiment. *Journal of Substance Abuse Treatment, 17*(3&4), 339–347.

Nixon, P., Burford, G., Quinn, A., & Edelbaum, J. (2004). A survey of international practices, policy and research on family group conferencing and related practices. Paper presented at the American Humane Conference on Family Group Decision Making, Long Beach, California, June. Available at http://www.americanhumane.org/site/DocServer/FGDM_www_survey.pdf?docID=2841. Retrieved on October 10, 2005.

Nugent, W., Umbreit, M., & Williams, M. (2004). Participation in victim-offender mediation and the prevalence of subsequent delinquent behavior: A meta-analysis. *Research on Social Work Practice, 14*(6), 408–416.

Pampel, F. (2000). *Logistic regression: A primer*. Thousand Oaks, CA: Sage Publications.

Paulin, J., Kingi, V., Huirama, T., & Lash, B. (2005). *The Wanganui Community-Managed Restorative Justice Programme: An evaluation*. Wellington, NZ: Ministry of Justice.

Paulin, J., Kingi, V., & Lash, B. (2005). *The Rotorua second chance restorative justice programme: An evaluation*. Wellington, NZ: Ministry of Justice.

Preston, N. (2002). *Restorative justice: A new school of thought? Introducing restorative justice into the school setting*. Chilton, England: Thames Valley Partnership.

Renninger, K. A., & Hidi, S. (1992). *The role of interesting learning and development*. Hillsdale, NJ: Lawrence Erlbaum Associates.

Riestenberg, N. (1997). Changing the paradigm: Restorative justice in Minnesota schools. *The ICCA Journal, 3*(August), 17–1928.

Rowe, W. (2002). *A meta-analysis of six Washington state restorative justice projects for July 2000-June 2001*. Olympia, WA: Governor's Juvenile Justice Advisory Committee, Office of Juvenile Justice. Available at http://www.juvenilejustice.dshs.wa.gov/pdf/Misc.%20Reports/Community%20Justice%20Final%20ReportFINAL%201-24-02.pdf. Retrieved on October 10, 2005.

Sherman, L., Barnes, G., Strang, H., Woods, D., Inkpen, N., Newbury-Birch, D., et al. (2004). Restorative justice: What we know and how we know it. Working Paper # 1, University of Pennsylvania, Lee Center of Criminology, Philadelphia. Available at http://www.sas.upenn.edu/jerrylee/rjWorkingPaper1.pdf. Retrieved on October 10, 2005.

Sherman, L., & Strang, H. (2004). Verdicts or inventions? Interpreting results from randomized controlled experiments in criminology. *American Behavioral Scientist, 47*(5), 575–607.

Sherman, L., & Strang, H. (2007). *Restorative justice: The evidence*. London: The Smith Institute.

Strang, H. (2002). *Repair or revenge: Victims and restorative justice*. Oxford: Oxford University Press.

Strang, H., Sherman, L., Angel, C., Woods, D., Bennett, S., Newbury-Birch, D., & Inkpen, N. (2006). Victim evaluations of face-to-face restorative justice conferences: A quasi-experimental analysis. *Journal of Social Issues, 62*(2), 281–306.

Trimboli, L. (2000). *An evaluation of the NSW youth justice conferencing scheme*. Sydney: New South Wales Bureau of Crime Statistics and Research.

Vandevelde, S., Broekaert, E., Yates, R., & Kooyman, M. (2004). The development of the therapeutic community in correctional establishments: A comparative retrospective account of the 'democratic' Maxwell Jones TC and the hierarchical concept-based TC in prison. *International Journal of Social Psychiatry, 50*(1), 66–79.

Wachtel, T. (1997). *Real justice*. Pipersville, PA: Piper's Press.

Wachtel, T. (2000). Restorative practices with high-risk youth. In: G. Buford & J. Hudson (Eds), *Family group conferencing: New directions in community centered child and family practice* (pp. 86–92). Hawthorne, NY: Aldine de Gruyter.

Wachtel, T., & McCold, P. (2000). Restorative justice in everyday life. In: J. Braithwaite & H. Strang (Eds), *Restorative justice in civil society* (pp. 117–125). New York: Cambridge University Press.

Walker, L. (2002). Conferencing: A new approach for juvenile justice in Honolulu. *Federal Probation Journal, 66*(1), 38–43.

Weisburd, D. (2000). Randomized experiments in criminal justice policy: Prospects and problems. *Crime and Delinquency, 46*(2), 181–193.

Weitekamp, E. (2002). Restorative justice: Present prospects and future directions. In: E. Weitekamp & H.-J. Kerner (Eds), *Restorative justice: Theoretical foundations* (pp. 322–338). Devon, UK: Willan Publishing.

Wexler, H., DeLeon, G., Thomas, G., Kessel, D., & Peters, J. (1999). The Amity Prison TC evaluation. *Criminal Justice and Behavior, 26*(2), 147–167.

Whitely, S. (2004). The evolution of the therapeutic community. *Psychiatric Quarterly, 75*(3), 223–248.

Wilcox, A., Young, R., & Hoyle, C. (2004). Two-year resanctioning study: A comparison of restorative and traditional cautions. *Home Office Online Report* 57/04. London: Home Office. Available at http://www.homeoffice.gov.uk/rds/pdfs04/rdsolr5704.pdf. Retrieved on October 10, 2005.

Williams-Hayes, M. (2002). *The effectiveness of victim-offender mediation and family group conferencing: A meta-analysis*. Unpublished Doctoral Dissertation, University of Tennessee, Knoxville.

Williams-Hayes, M. (2003). What the literature seems to suggest about restorative justice effectiveness: An overview of a meta-analysis. *Social Policy Times, 3*(2) [Online]. Research Center on Societal and Social Policy. Available at http://www.rcssp.org/sp32williams.htm. Retrieved on October 10, 2005.

Youth Justice Board. (2005). *National evaluation of the restorative justice in schools programme*. London: Youth Justice Board. Available at http://www.yjb.gov.uk/Publications/Scripts/prodView.asp?idproduct = 207. Retrieved on September 24, 2007.

FAITH-BASED MENTORING AND RESTORATIVE JUSTICE: OVERLAPPING THEORETICAL, EMPIRICAL, AND PHILOSOPHICAL BACKGROUND [☆]

Ronald L. Akers, Jodi Lane and Lonn Lanza-Kaduce

ABSTRACT

This chapter focuses on restorative/rehabilitative faith-based programs, in particular, a youth mentoring program conducted by the Florida Department of Juvenile Justice. We begin with a brief description of a faith- and community-based juvenile mentoring program of the Florida Department of Juvenile Justice (which we are in the process of evaluating) intended to provide community reintegration and restoration of adjudicated delinquents released from state juvenile correctional facilities. Then we move to the overlapping theoretical, philosophical, and empirical backgrounds of restorative justice, faith-based rehabilitative/restorative, and mentoring programs. We conclude with a review of programmatic and empirical issues in faith-based mentoring programs.

[☆]Revision of a paper presented at the annual meetings of the Southern Sociological Society, Atlanta, 2007.

Restorative Justice: From Theory to Practice
Sociology of Crime, Law and Deviance, Volume 11, 139–165
Copyright © 2008 by Emerald Group Publishing Limited
All rights of reproduction in any form reserved
ISSN: 1521-6136/doi:10.1016/S1521-6136(08)00406-5

THE FLORIDA FAITH- AND COMMUNITY-BASED DELINQUENCY TREATMENT INITIATIVE

Both the promise and the problems of faith-based programs as well as the challenges of evaluation are found in the mentoring program initiated by the Department of Juvenile Justice in Florida – *the Florida Faith- and Community-Based Delinquency Treatment Initiative* (*FCBDTI*). The program and the process and outcome evaluation research project that the authors are conducting are funded by the Office of Juvenile Justice and Delinquency Prevention (OJJDP). This program originally involved five residential juvenile facilities receiving the program (two for girls and three for boys), which included mentoring, and four comparison facilities without the mentoring program (all operated by DJJ). This is a program in which faith- and community-based adult mentors are recruited (from within a 50-mile radius of each facility), trained, and assigned to adjudicated delinquents (who choose to take part in the program and have parental or guardian permission to do so). The mentoring is supposed to begin when the adjudicated delinquents first arrive at the juvenile facility and continue for a year after their release back to the community. The mentors are expected to provide positive role models, spend time with the youth, engage in various activities with the youth (homework, recreation, sports, movies), and talk with them about any issues about which the youth wants to have conversations. The mentors are expected to develop a good relationship with the youth and attempt to facilitate their reintegration into the community. They are instructed not to raise questions of faith on their own but to be open and responsive to any such questions raised by the youth. The youth in all of the facilities have the same in-facility programming except those in the comparison facilities did not participate in the faith-based services, including the mentoring program (for additional description of the program see Lane & Lanza-Kaduce, 2007; Lanza-Kaduce & Lane, 2007; Schrage, Lane, Lanza-Kaduce, Perry, & Akers, 2007).

Our research task is to assess the process of implementing the program, the fidelity of that implementation to the program design, and the effects of the program on youth behavior, attitudes, and recidivism (compared to a group of youth released from the facilities which did not take part in the FCBDTI). We have encountered problems at each of these tasks including closing of facilities, staff turnover, difficulty of getting accurate and timely data on program participants, and attrition of sample (our targeted sample of youth was 240, and we have been able to obtain data from 160).

At this point we have collected data from a self-report interview schedule with most of the youth and some of the staff. We have made observational visits to the facilities. We have a self-report survey instrument for mentors, but as of yet we have no data from the mentors. Also, we do not yet have any recidivism data on the youth to report at this time. The main task here, therefore, is our analysis of the theoretical and philosophical assumptions and linkages relevant to such a program. We do not imply that this is the body of knowledge and analysis that actually was self-consciously used by the DJJ in the design and implementation of the FCBDTI.

THEORY AND RESEARCH ON THE EFFECTS OF RELIGIOSITY ON DELINQUENCY

Radical or fanatical adherents of any ideology or belief system – whether political, religious, economic, or cultural – commit terrorist and criminal acts as expressions of commitment to extreme beliefs and groups (Barlow, 2007). Conflict theory (Vold, 1958) expects such behavior toward members of outgroups, and the use of radical ideology as rationalization and justification for violence is consistent with the concept of "definitions favorable" to crime in social learning theory (Akers & Silverman, 2004). Extreme religious beliefs sometimes provide motivation or justification for crime (Miller, 2006). Except for these cases of religious extremism, however, common sense and virtually all theoretical perspectives on crime and delinquency expect that those who adhere to recognized and established religious faith and practices would be less likely to be delinquent or criminal offenders than others. The expectation is that religion as an institution generally supports conventional social and legal norms in society and that individuals' beliefs, involvement in religious activity, and adherence to religious doctrine act against violation of those norms. Certain Christian doctrines, for instance, teach respect and obedience to both secular and spiritual authorities (see Romans 13:1–2; I Peter 2:13–17), and Christians are expected to follow Jesus' admonition, "if you love me, keep my commandments" (John 14:15) to "love one another," "do unto others as you would have them do unto you," and "love your neighbor as yourself." Faithful adherence to such religious beliefs is bound to have a preventive, protective, or corrective effect on criminal, delinquent, or deviant behavior.

There is theoretical reason to predict an inverse relationship between religion and offending against the law and society. Although Hirschi (1969) downplayed the significance of religion, the logic of his social bonding theory, for instance, would apply to religious beliefs as one form of endorsement of conventional values, to adherence to religious faith and practice as commitment to conformity and involvement in conventional activities, and to the integration in a body of believers as attachment to others. All of these are social bonds to society that the theory predicts have a negative effect on delinquency. Social learning theory (Akers, 1973, 1998) would make the same prediction of a negative relationship between religiosity and delinquency because it views religious beliefs as general, and in some cases as specific, "definitions unfavorable" to delinquency, and more involvement with others in worship and other religious activities as greater "differential association" with conforming than with deviant peers and adults. The theory would also see such activities as providing greater exposure to conforming behavioral and role models and "differential social reinforcement" for conforming more than delinquent behavior. General strain theory (Agnew, 2006) would see religiosity as countering or directing individuals away from deviant adaptations to stresses and strains. In fact, one is hard pressed to find any contemporary criminological theory that would hypothesize anything to the contrary about the negative relationship between non-extremist religiosity and law violation, either as an indirect or direct effect.

Moreover, these doctrinal and theoretical expectations about the negative relationship between religion and delinquency tend to be supported by research evidence. Early research by Hirschi and Stark (1969) found attachment to religion to be unrelated to delinquency, and others reported mixed findings, but the preponderance of evidence from a large body of subsequent research supports the hypothesis that the more adolescents hold to religious beliefs and regularly participate in religious practices and activities, the less likely they are to engage in delinquency, substance use, and violence (see Cochran & Akers, 1989; Ross, 1994; Evans, Cullen, Dunaway, & Burton, 1995; Johnson, Larson, De Li, & Jang, 2000a; Johnson, De Li, Larson, & McCullough, 2000b; Johnson, Jang, Larson, & De Li, 2001; Baier & Wright, 2001; Benda, 2002; Regnerus, Smith, & Fritsch, 2003; NSDUH, 2004; Smith, Rizzo, & Empie, 2005; Welch, Tittle, & Grasmick, 2006). A common conclusion in the literature is that "[M]ost research confirms the ability of individual religiosity to predict adherence to the law, absence of alcohol and drug abuse, and obedience to other social norms such as school-based rules and mandates for appropriate juvenile conduct" (Welch et al., 2006, p. 1605). Johnson et al. (2000b) reported that all but one of the 40 studies they reviewed found the expected negative effect of religion on delinquency, and in 35 of the studies, that effect was statistically significant. Baier and Wright (2001) found in their meta-analysis of data on the effects of religion on delinquency and crime reported in 60 research articles that

> The mean reported effect size was $r = -.12$ (SD $= .09$), and the median was $-.11$. About two-thirds of the effects fell between $-.05$ and $-.20$, and, significantly, *none of them was positive*. A test of the null hypothesis that the mean effect for religion on crime equals zero was strongly rejected at $t = -11.9$. These findings show that religious behavior and beliefs exert a significant, moderate deterrent effect on individuals' criminal behavior. (Baier & Wright, 2001, p. 14, emphasis added)

In short, the conclusion from research is that the more faith and religious activities, the less delinquency. The more methodologically sound the study, the more likely it is to have found that religious belief and observance operate as significant protective social factors against delinquent involvement.

THEORETICAL AND PHILOSOPHICAL UNDERPINNINGS OF RESTORATIVE JUSTICE AND FAITH-BASED PROGRAMS

If doctrine, common sense, criminological theory, and research evidence all point to the religious factor as having at least a moderate constraining effect on crime and delinquency, then it is reasonable to expect that at least some of the applied efforts to prevent, treat, or deter law violations would include actions designed to promote or enhance faith and religious activities. This assumption was behind the early penitentiary reform movement of the nineteenth century, continued to inform prison ministries over the generations, and underlies much of the current faith-based initiatives in the juvenile justice, criminal justice, and private systems. *All* state and federal prison systems have long provided and continue to provide funding, space, and time for chaplaincy, religious counseling, worship services, and faith instruction (Editors of Corrections Compendium, 2003; Mears, Roman, Wolff, & Buck, 2006). The state and federal provision for religious expression by juvenile and adult inmates today is predicated and justified on human and constitutional rights for prisoners, but in the background lies the continuing hope that staying or getting close to God will have positive effects on inmate attitude and behavior while incarcerated and after release (remorse, seeking forgiveness and redemption, attempting to make amends to victims and society, obeying the law, etc.). This hope is in the forefront of efforts such as visitations by ministers and others with those in custody in jail, juvenile facilities, and prisons and church ministries that provide help in community reintegration, housing, job seeking, and education (with attendant faith-related instruction and counseling) to ex-offenders who have been released into the community. Although the history of reform and rehabilitation in both the juvenile and adult systems does not leave much ground for believing that high hopes will be realized, some prevention and rehabilitation efforts have made a difference (Lattimore, 2006).

These efforts from the faith-based community and efforts by secular reform and rehabilitation groups fit into current theoretical and policy developments in criminology and the criminal justice system, most notably the "restorative justice" movement (Van Ness & Strong, 2006; Braithwaite, 2002). Long-standing and recent faith-based prison and community programs reflect many of the same principles undergirding restorative justice policies, and advocates from faith-based backgrounds and organizations were among the earliest, and remain among the most persistent, major proponents of the restorative justice movement (Van Ness & Strong, 1997, 2006).

> Faith communities have the potential to be agents for reintegration for both victims and offenders ... the church's strong and extensive *history of involvement* with those in need, its *traditions* that speak of both the call and the resources to undertake such a task, and its *presence* in virtually every part of the world make it a promising agent for reintegration. (Van Ness & Strong, 2006, p. 107, emphasis in original)

Religiously based rehabilitation and self-help programs run by inmate groups, local and national prison ministry organizations (such as Prison Fellowship and Justice Fellowship), and other groups have long flourished both inside correctional institutions and in the community (Johnson, Larson, & Pitts, 1997; Van Ness & Strong, 2006; O'Connor & Perreyclear, 2002). They provide individual and group-based spiritual counseling, Bible study, worship service, and other ways of helping and reforming prisoners by inculcating and strengthening faith and values of decency, kindness, honesty, responsibility, and consideration toward others. They teach spiritual growth, repentance, seeking forgiveness, and attempting to reconcile with those one has harmed. They also advocate a broader concern for fairness, rehabilitation, and reintegration in the community and help for victims and their families as well as aiding the families of offenders. Similarly, programs of Bible study, faith-centered activities, spiritual guidance, and family and vocational counseling for ex-convicts through halfway houses and groups in the local community can be found all over the country.

Many programs that would easily fit under the rubric of restorative justice predate the movement self-consciously identified as restorative justice. Historical traditions of reconciliation and customary dispute resolution and a variety of activities such as victim advocacy, conflict resolution, mediation, and community service have long been incorporated formally into criminal justice policies or practiced informally in the community and anticipated many of the within-institution and community programs now identified as restorative justice (Van Ness & Strong, 2006; Braithwaite, 2002).

These restorative justice policies and practices may be based on a number of theoretical concepts. However, they are most likely to be linked in the literature to Braithwaite's reintegrative shaming theory, although most predate Braithwaite's first book and he did not himself explicitly link restorative justice to his theory until later (Van Ness & Strong, 2006; see also Bazemore & Day, 1996; Bazemore & Umbreit, 1998; Schiff, 1998; Bazemore & Schiff, 2001; Braithwaite, 2002; Braithwaite, Ahmed, & Braithwaite, 2006).

> Reintegrative shaming has been a motivating framework for only some restorative justice programs. However the theory does specifically predict that this kind of intervention will reduce crime regardless of whether those implementing it have any discursive consciousness of the theory of reintegrative shaming. The theoretically relevant features of restorative justice are confrontation of the offender in a respectful way with the consequences of the crime (shaming without degradation), explicit efforts to avert stigmatization, (e.g. opportunities to counter accusations that the offender is a bad person with testimonials from loved ones that she is a good person) and explicit commitment to ritual reintegration (e.g. maximizing opportunities for repair, restoring relationships, apology and forgiveness that are viewed as sincere). (Braithwaite et al., 2006, p. 408)

In Braithwaite's (1989) theory, stigmatizing punishment and shaming of offenders hypothesized to produce greater risk of recidivism is contrasted with reintegrative shaming in which sanctions and public shaming are done to produce remorse and repentance in a communitarian context of acceptance and forgiveness that reintegrates the offender into the community and reduces the risk of recidivism. Hopefully restorative justice practices will provide the right amount of shame and remorse in a context of community acceptance so that offenders do not do harm in the future. It is with regard to this goal of changing the attitudes and behavior of offenders that restorative justice is linked to treatment and rehabilitation programs and to other criminological theories, beyond reintegrative shaming, on which those programs are based (Cullen, Sundt, & Wozniak, 2001).

The mechanisms by which restorative justice programs may affect values, beliefs, and behavior of offenders reflect the concepts, variables, and social cognitive processes proposed in social bonding theory (Hirschi, 1969) and social learning theory (Akers, 1998). The cognitive-behavioral principles in social learning theory, for instance, are applicable to a range of correctional, treatment, rehabilitation, and prevention programs (Triplett & Payne, 2004), and programs predicated on these principles have been shown to be more effective than those based on alternative approaches (Andrews & Bonta, 2003). If faith-based approaches produce the desired spiritual and faith changes in individuals the result should be the same pro-social changes in patterns of interaction, thinking/attitudes, and behavioral tendencies to which secular cognitive-behavioral strategies are directed. Therefore, as Hall (2003) argues, there should be some compatibility between social behavioral and faith-based treatment approaches:

> A cognitive-behavioral approach seems to be quite compatible with pastoral counseling and education aimed at treating criminal thinking patterns. This approach assumes a relationship between events, thoughts, feelings, and behaviors ... [C]ognitive therapy techniques and Christian ideas can be blended to provide an effective healing environment. (Hall, 2003, pp. 108–109)

Similarly, O'Connor and Perreyclear (2002) saw reflections of both social learning and social bonding theory in their findings on the salutary effect of religious involvement by prison inmates on their in-prison behavior. Clear and Sumter (2002) report similar findings that psychological adjustment to prison and fewer disciplinary infractions are related to higher levels of religious commitment by inmates. Mears et al. (2006, p. 354) maintain that the underlying logic of, and mechanisms involved in, "how faith-based prisoner reentry programs are supposed to work – that is identifying what it is that makes them effective – is largely unknown." I have pointed here to some of that logic, and Sumter and Clear (2005) also refer to possible mechanisms by which faith may have an impact. They suggest that social learning and spiritual processes may be intertwined in faith-based programs in that the faith component may foster change among offenders through (1) socialization into pro-social values and conduct, (2) differential association wherein positive interactions in religious groups replace antisocial associations, and (3) "transcendence" in which "religion might transform the individual spiritually from a worldly person concerned with self to a devout person concerned with inward, sacred matters" (Sumter & Clear, 2005, p. 106). The social learning/differential association mechanisms would be among the "indirect" effects to which Mears et al. (2006) refer, and transcendence would seem to relate, at least in part, to what Mears et al. (2006) mean by a possible "threshold" effect, in which a "sufficient dose" of faith produces an inner change or "epiphany" that runs counter to continued criminal involvement.

As is true for all social policies and practices, the restorative justice movement not only reflects testable theories of criminal and delinquent behavior, it is also grounded on political, religious, and moral philosophy (Akers & Sellers, 2004). Restorative justice proponents contend that the morally right response to crime is to hold offenders responsible for law violations but at the same time to restore both them and their victims to the community (Schiff, 1998). It is a "value-based vision" of justice that seeks "to rebuild the capacity of citizens and community groups to mobilize informal social control and socialization processes." It downplays deterrence, incapacitation, retribution, treatment, and formal criminal justice efforts. There is a clear preference for informal, non-adversarial, decision-making that holds "lawbreakers accountable for the harm caused ... in ways that 'make things right' ... to include victim, offender, and community in developing a plan for repairing this harm" (Bazemore & Schiff, 2001, pp. 4–8).

The same reference to moral values must be made in regard to programs that are self-consciously rehabilitative, whether or not their proponents view them as part of the restorative justice movement.

> But rehabilitation is, at its core, a moral enterprise. It depends on the existence of social consensus about shared values – about what is right and what is wrong. It is morally judgmental; it accepts a standard for moral and legal behavior and defines those not meeting this standard as in need of adjustment ... progressive scholars, recognize the *importance of talking about virtue or morality* in formulating correctional policy in prisons." (Cullen et al., 2001, p. 269, emphasis in original)

The moral philosophy underlying restorative justice is well articulated by Braithwaite's (1989, 1995, 1997, 2002) "normative theory" (Braithwaite & Drahos, 2002). The "master political value is republican freedom, or freedom as non-domination ... [through] virtuous control ... respect for the person, humility by the controller" (Braithwaite, 1997, p. 89). Braithwaite (2002) rejects moral and cultural relativism by endorsing respect for human rights, dignity, good citizenship, and political and religious freedom as universally applicable values. He proposes that these values along with respectful listening, mercy, apology, and forgiveness on the part of everyone are central components of restorative justice philosophy. This is not to say that coercion and punishment have no place in restorative justice; they are needed to prevent those who do not endorse these values from opting out of the restorative processes (Braithwaite, 2002).

The values expressed in Braithwaite's self-consciously secular approach are essentially the same as those that undergird faith-based programs (Van Ness & Strong, 1997, 2006). But, by definition, such a program adds an open emphasis on spiritual values. It teaches "biblical standards of justice, principles of confession, repentance, forgiveness, and reconciliation, and provides offenders with a better understanding of the effects crime has on individual families and communities" (Eisenberg & Trusty, 2002, p. 5) and other positive values that have been claimed by the restorative justice movement. Braithwaite's normative theory is a secularized, political version of religious philosophy found in the Biblical tradition that rejects retribution and revenge and teaches that one should "turn the other cheek," "forgive one another," "bless them that curse you, do good to them that hate you" (see Matthew 5:38–39, 43–44; 6:14). Reintegration of released offenders into conforming society as law-abiding citizens has long been the goal of correctional, rehabilitation, diversion, community control, and other criminal justice policies and programs. Now, the terms "redemption" (Lattimore, 2006) and "self-redemption" (Braithwaite et al., 2006) are being used by some in the restorative justice movement with reference to community reentry and reintegration even for offenders released from prison. Redemption is "the opportunity for offenders to turn their lives around ... [and] requires action not only by the offender, but by society taking steps to facilitate and allow an offender to reclaim a 'straight' life" (Lattimore, 2006, p. 3). Although defined in secular terms, this concept of "redemption" is transparently rooted in central faith-based tenets. "The Judeo-Christian tradition teaches care for the outcast, relief for those in need, and the intrinsic value of human beings as created and loved by God. Biblical tradition and stories show God's desire that all should be redeemed" (Van Ness & Strong, 2006, p. 109). The "spiritual roots" of restorative justice concepts and practices can be found not only in the Biblical tradition to which Van Ness and Strong refer, but in Buddhism, Hinduism, aboriginal spirituality, Islam and other faith traditions to which Hadley and contributors refer (Hadley, 2001).

"Peacekeeping criminology" (Pepinsky & Quinney, 1991) advocates policies similar to restorative justice and has both recognized and unrecognized links to faith and spiritual issues. In Quinney's view, the criminal justice system must operate on the principles of love and non-violence. "When our hearts are filled with love and our minds with willingness to serve, we will know what has to be done and how it is to be done. Such is the basis of a nonviolent criminology" (Quinney, 1991, p. 12). Others take more secular approaches to peacemaking criminology, but Quinney's is based on an admixture of Christian and Buddhist beliefs. Later advocates also explicitly recognize religious (as well as secular) traditions in peacemaking criminology (Fuller & Wozniak, 2006).

Faith-based programs, however, add an explicit emphasis on the traditional goals of rehabilitation and personal reform leading to lower probability of recidivism that is often missing in other restorative justice and peacemaking programs (Cullen et al., 2001). Cullen et al. (2001) believe this fusion of the rehabilitative and restorative ideals provides a foundation for building what they call the "virtuous prison" in which "restorative rehabilitation" would be practiced to engage prisoners in restorative activities and to foster inmate contact with "virtuous people" from the community, "including those religiously-inspired ... to mentor inmates, and to visit and socialize with inmates ... [because] such volunteers are modeling the very kind of pro-social, virtuous behavior that we wish inmates to learn"(Cullen et al., 2001, pp. 279–280).

Cullen et al. (2001) recognize that the faith impetus behind rehabilitative and restorative justice today is the same impetus behind much of the ameliorative correctional reform movements of the past. They refer particularly to the late nineteenth century reformatory movement led by reformers such as Zebulon Brockway that was intended to provide alternatives to the harsh, degrading conditions of many penitentiaries of the time (which it should be remembered originated as alternatives to earlier practices of direct and brutal physical punishments):

> But if the dawn of Christianity has reached us, if we have learned the lesson that *evil is to be overcome with good*, then *let prisons and prison systems be lighted by this law of love.* Let us leave for the present, the thought of inflicting punishment upon prisoners to satisfy so-called justice, and turn toward the two grand divisions of our subject, the real objects of the system, vis., *the protection of society by the prevention of crime and reformation of criminals.* (Brockway, 1871, p. 42, as cited in Cullen et al., 2001, emphasis in the original)

Some of the faith-based programs, in particular, clearly include among their restorative and reintegrative goals of reconciliation and personal reformation the same goal of reducing recidivism found in any correctional, treatment, or rehabilitation program. Cullen et al.'s (2001) argument for the integration of restorative justice and rehabilitative ideals is directly linked to recidivism reduction, although there is mixed evidence to support the recidivism-reduction of faith-based in-prison treatment programs (Johnson et al., 1997; Clear & Sumter, 2002; Johnson & Larson, 2003; Johnson, 2004).

The expectation is that even the best programs will have modest success in achieving restoration and reintegration, but "effective interventions [that] are rooted in behavioral or cognitive-behavioral models of treatment" will be more effective than those programs that do not follow sound principles of rehabilitation (Levrant, Cullen, Fulton, & Wozniak, 1999). There have been no programs for incarcerated youth similar to those for adult inmates, and therefore there is no research on the effectiveness of institutional faith-based programs for juvenile offenders. However, cost-effective volunteer outreach and services for disadvantaged, at-risk youth in urban community by churches and faith-based ministries has a long and successful history that compares favorably to secular, publicly funded programs (DiIulio, 2004; Hockensmith, 2003). In addition, national programs such as Teen Challenge has a long history as the largest privately funded "faith-saturated" organization providing rehabilitation for substance-abusing adolescents. These local and national programs do more than their share of rescuing troubled youth while operating on budgets funded at only a fraction of the budgets of government-supported secular groups. They are effective in many ways, but so far there is only "spotty evidence" on how well they do in reducing post-treatment relapse rates compared to alternative "secular treatment programs that serve the same populations," and the high percentage of success claimed by Teen Challenge does not take into account the high percentage of dropouts (presumably the highest risk youth) experienced by the program (DiIulio, 2004, p. 81).

As Cullen and Sundt (2003) point out, the practical outcome of faith-based programs can be assessed by the same standard, namely effectiveness in modifying behavior, as secular programs. This pragmatic argument resonates well with the stance taken by Byron Johnson.

> Correctional leaders must set a priority for collecting data on the forgotten "faith factor" in corrections. Minimally, mechanisms should be put in place to assess and study religious variables, whether in terms of programs, adjustment, infractions or other key prison outcome measures ... Until such steps take place, it will remain difficult to determine the effectiveness of these volunteers and religious programs. If such steps are not taken, religion, a potentially beneficial factor, will remain a neglected, forgotten piece of the criminal justice puzzle. (Johnson, 1998, p. 112)

It is adherence to the kind of faith-imbued values mentioned above that both provides religious motivation for volunteers to give of themselves in service to others and, if incorporated into one's belief system, provides cognitive and attitudinal changes that foster prevention of delinquency and rehabilitation/reintegration of offenders. However noble the motivations and intentions of those who lead and work in faith-based programs, we must still ask the question of effectiveness in achieving program goals and ultimately in the prevention of delinquency and/or reduction in recidivism. We turn now to these issues of faith, prevention, rehabilitation, and program evaluation with regard specifically to youth mentoring programs.

FAITH- AND COMMUNITY-BASED MENTORING PROGRAMS FOR JUVENILES

A large portion of restorative justice programs are directed toward adjudicated juvenile delinquents, and virtually all mentoring programs are directed toward youth. In spite of this common focus on juveniles, mentoring programs are not typically described, or self-consciously identified, as types of restorative justice programs. This is partly because the bulk of mentoring programs are aimed at "at-risk" youth with a goal of preventing future offending rather than reconciling or restoring identified offenders and their victims. It is also partly because many of the activities (victim–offender meetings, reparative probation, restitution, sentencing councils, and so on) carried out in the name of restorative justice are not central to mentoring programs (even though they be part of the court's dispensation of youthful offenders who also have been matched with mentors). Nevertheless, there is clear overlap, and the issues related to faith-based mentoring programs apply to faith-based restorative justice programs of any type. "Restorative justice can be characterized by dialogue (i.e. among a victim, an offender, and community members), relationship building, and *the communication of moral values*" (Rodriquez, 2005, p. 104, emphasis added). The assumption in mentoring programs is that moral values will be transmitted in the mentoring relationship. This concept of mentors as models acting as moral guides is not confined to Western society, but is very similar to Asian (Confucian) concepts of mentoring in which correctional or probation staff are expected to act as mentors establishing emotional ties juvenile delinquents to affect change in the youth's life. Moreover, mentoring programs in which the mentors are matched to delinquents under custody and continue with the relationship after the juveniles' release share the goal of community reintegration with the restorative justice philosophy. Further, as we have seen, assumptions of remorse, repentance, forgiveness, change of attitude, and view of life identified specifically with Judeo-Christian and other faith traditions or their secularized, cultural versions are core philosophical components of the restorative justice movement. These same values undergird faith-based youth mentoring programs.

The practice of a somewhat older and more accomplished person guiding, teaching, and providing learning situations for a younger protégé or apprentice is an ancient one that has long been institutionalized in academic, occupational, professional, religious, and other endeavors. Parents, uncles, older siblings and friends, and other adults who aid, guide, befriend, and socialize children and young into adulthood, of course, is as old as society itself. In these naturally occurring relationships, the role of the mentor is as a positive role model, teacher by example and word, a source of anticipatory socialization, and a friend and personal resource for the younger learner. Although not always explicitly defined, the designed and deliberate matching and facilitation of mentoring (the type that MENTOR, 2007, refers to as "formal" mentoring) that takes place in a delinquency prevention or treatment program is more or less based on this model of informal mentoring. It is intended to be a specific relationship between older teens or adults and children or youth who because of family, economic, educational, neighborhood, or other life contexts are deemed to be disadvantaged or "at-risk" of failure, antisocial behavior, or delinquency. It seems to be almost self-evident that such a relationship would have beneficial pro-social and restorative outcomes for the youngster and for the mentor as well. There are programmatic issues, however, about mentoring that revolve around finding ways to recruit volunteers and to create, develop, and facilitate mentoring relationships in the community and juvenile justice system in cost-efficient and outcome-effective ways.

The most common approach to these goals is for agency staff or funded project staff to recruit and train volunteer mentors from the community, both from secular and faith-based backgrounds, so that they may be matched with youth (also on a voluntary basis) identified as potentially benefiting from such a relationship. With some exceptions (Eells, 2003), these mentors are not professionally trained therapists or juvenile justice workers, but are recruited from among the general population. These efforts have a fairly long history, and the past decade has seen the development of national overviews of mentoring activities in the United States. MENTOR has conducted a national survey of mentors in 2002, again in 2005, and plans to conduct a survey every two years. MENTOR is self-described as "leading the national movement to connect young Americans with caring adult mentors. As a national advocate and expert resource for mentoring, MENTOR delivers the research, policy recommendations and practical performance tools needed to help make quality mentoring a reality for more of America's young people" (MENTOR, 2007, p. 15). The surveys have found mentoring to be widespread with 3 million adult volunteers (about equally divided among community-based, school-based, and faith-based settings) serving as mentors to youth in 2005 (an increase of 19% from 2002). But even with this many involved adults there is still a sizeable "mentoring gap" with only about 2.5 million youth in mentoring programs with an estimated unserved 15 million at-risk youth identified as eligible for and in need of mentoring. Mentoring occurs on both an individual and group basis, with the average mentoring relationship lasting nine months. Less than a third of mentoring is "formal," with mentors having been recruited, trained, and supported by an organization; the rest are "informal," more or less operating on their own. Will the designed mentoring relationships actually prevent, delay, or modify delinquent behavior in the targeted youth? How well does faith-based mentoring fare compared to general community-based mentoring? How well does mentoring do compared to non-mentoring delinquency prevention and treatment programs? Unfortunately, research to date does not provide much of an answer to these and related questions.

Nevertheless, one often sees statements in the literature that the evidence unequivocally shows effectiveness of the mentoring relationship:

> Research shows that youth who participate in mentoring relationships experience a number of positive benefits. These benefits include better attendance and attitude toward school, less drug and alcohol use, improved social attitudes and relationships, more trusting relationships and better communication with parents and a better chance of going on to higher education. (MENTOR, 2007, p. 1)

MENTOR cites no research data for this statement, and its survey does not track outcomes of mentoring. Rather its research is on the characteristics of mentors and mentoring process. There has been research on the success of mentoring in achieving various outcomes, but very little of it focuses on the effects on delinquent behavior. There is little research on mentoring among samples of adjudicated or incarcerated delinquents, and essentially nothing on the effectiveness of faith-based versus community-based mentoring or comparison of mentoring programs with family, school, or other prevention/treatment programs. This is shown in the DuBois, Holloway, Valentine, and Cooper (2002) meta-analysis of 55 evaluation studies of mentoring programs. None of the projects in the study is identified as faith-based, and, although the terms "at-risk" and "high risk" are used for the meta-analysis, only one of the studies used delinquent behavior as the outcome measure. Rather, 44 different types of outcomes were identified as the dependent variables in the studies, and these were collapsed into five general categories of emotional/psychological well-being, problem or high-risk behavior, social competence, academic/educational, and career/employment. Nevertheless, the meta-analysis produced findings and conclusions that may be relevant to evaluation of programs that are faith-based specific and delinquency specific. In general, Dubois et al. (2002) found that mentoring has beneficial effects on youth, but the effects are modest or small (average d-index effect size of .14 or .18). They point out that the effectiveness of a program is directly related to the quality of program design and implementation that can promote or undercut the success of mentoring, among the most important of which are recruitment of mentors, length of the mentoring relationship, and the regularity and quality of contact between the youth and the mentor.

Grossman and Rhodes (2002) report similar findings on the importance of length of mentorship from a random assignment study of urban adolescents in the Big Brother/Big Sister (BB/BS) program compared to a non-mentored control group. The authors expected that data collected in the 18-month follow-up would "provide evidence of positive influences on adolescent development outcomes, including improvements in academic achievement, self-concept, prosocial behavior, and interpersonal relationships" (Grossman & Rhodes, 2002, p. 200). They found that mentor relationships lasting less than a year do not have these desired outcomes. Youth who continued with a mentor for more than a year showed better results than non-mentored youth in self-worth, perceived social acceptance, skipping school, school grades, quality of parental relationships, hitting someone, and frequency of substance use.

Jones-Brown and Henriques (1997) compared the "carrot" of assignment to a mentor with the "stick" dispositions of commitment to a juvenile boot camp or waiver to adult court for juvenile court adjudicated delinquents aged 15–18 in Newark. The mentors were recruited from local colleges, the university, professional organizations, churches, and other community groups. During the 14 months in which the mentor program was in operation, 40 different males were recruited and were assigned 51 youth to mentor. The mentoring activities included going to movies, recreational and sports activities, attending sports events, involvement in community service projects, and informal tutoring. Jones-Brown and Henriques provide no systematic recidivism data (and indeed seemed to be opposed to using recidivism rates as measures of success of the program). Nonetheless, "the authors believe that ... mentoring represents a community-oriented, cost-efficient, and safe means of handling and helping some delinquent youths"

(Jones-Brown & Henriques, 1997, p. 224). If this is the promise of mentoring, the pitfalls include not having enough volunteer mentors, limited time of mentors, resistance of some youth to being mentored, difficulty of holding youth and mentors accountable for time and activity commitments, and lack of monitoring the relationship by the juvenile justice staff.

The major organization, with funding support from the U.S. Justice Department's OJJDP, in developing, supporting, and doing research on mentoring and other programs is Public/Private Ventures (P/PV), with a particular focus on faith-based programs in its National Faith-Based Initiative (NFBI). P/PV provides guidelines, literature, and research on mentoring in various settings and groups (Sipe, 1996; Trulear, 2000; Ericson, 2001; Bauldry & Hartmann, 2004; P/PV, 2007). The OJJDP began federal funding of mentoring programs for "at-risk" and adjudicated juveniles and other mentoring-related activities of public and private groups in 1992, and in 1994 started its JUMP (Juvenile Mentoring Program) funding program (Novotney, Mertinko, Lange, & Baker, 2000). Other federal agencies such as the Department of Health and Human Services also have funded various kinds of mentoring programs in Florida and elsewhere (see for instance, Hands on Broward Partners programs for children of incarcerated parents at http://www.handsonbroward.org/index.html).

JUMP defines mentoring as matching a "responsible and caring" adult who is willing to give extra time and effort (4–6 hours a month) to being a friend with a youth in need of academic help, social skills, and emotional support (MENTOR, 2007). Essentially this same definition guides other programs that want to match "qualified caring adults with youth to provide mentoring, friendship, and support" (Hands on Broward Partners, 2000). This is a fairly non-specific definition and leaves open the question of what mentors actually do with and for their "mentees." It appears to have come directly from the BB/BS organization which (although not itself directed specifically to delinquency) has provided the foremost model on which almost all mentoring programs, including those for delinquency prevention and treatment, have been based. BB/BS was founded in 1904 and is not only the oldest, but the largest mentoring endeavor in the United States involving 470 agencies in 5,000 communities with mentors matched to 225,000 youngsters aged 5–18 (BB/BS, 2007). BB/BS claims that

Research and anecdotal evidence show specifically that BBBS one-to-one mentoring helps at-risk youth overcome the many challenges they face. Little Brothers and Sisters

156 RONALD L. AKERS ET AL.

are less likely to begin using illegal drugs, consume alcohol, skip school and classes, or engage in acts of violence. They have greater self-esteem, confidence in their schoolwork performance, and are able to get along better with their friends and families.

One of the first efforts of P/PV in this area was evaluation research to see if such claims hold true. The research was conduced over a period of years that eventually included 15 BB/BS programs, six "Campus Compact," four programs at Temple University, and two projects in the juvenile justice system (Sipe, 1996). These provided different settings, volunteers (e.g. college students, senior citizens, working professionals), and youth (e.g. juvenile offenders, at-risk middle school youth, youth in single-parent homes). All of the programs shared "a common definition of mentoring – one-to-one relationships in which an adult volunteer and youth meet frequently over a period of several months or years. In these programs, mentors are expected primarily to offer support and friendship, rather than to try changing youth's behavior" (Sipe, 1996, p. 3).

Even though mentors were restrained from trying to have a direct impact on the youth's behavior, P/PV wanted to learn whether mentoring programs could nonetheless actually change attitudes and behavior of at-risk youth. Only one BB/BS study reported findings on differences between mentored and non-mentored youth (10–15 years old), and those differences favored the mentored youth. The P/PV research also examined what characterizes meaningful and effective mentoring relationships and found, not surprisingly, that the motivation of volunteers is of prime importance. Further, those "who take the time to develop trusting relationships with youth are much more likely to foster the changes that other volunteers pursue" (Sipe, 1996, p. 7). Good screening, orientation and training, ongoing supervision, and support of mentors by project staff are "critical infrastructure" elements in good mentoring.

Two of the evaluated programs were involved with youth in the juvenile justice system, but neither program provided adequate resources, supervision of mentors was simply added to the already existing job tasks of the juvenile justice staff, and the staff felt they had no real "authority" over the volunteers to get them to meet their agreed upon mentoring commitments. Needless to say, these mentoring programs were not successful. The bottom line question that confronts any youth mentoring endeavor is "Are there large enough numbers of adults with time and resources to take on mentoring of at-risk youth?" The answer from the P/PV evaluation is "not really." BB/BS seems to be able to enlist large numbers of adult volunteer mentors, but even in that program, the number of youth identified as in need of a mentor is always larger than the number of mentors available.

In any given year, about one-third of the youth applying get matched with a mentor, another one-third of the mentors are rejected, and one-third was still in process (see also MENTOR, 2007).

Almost all of the mentoring efforts, faith-based and secular, and research found in the literature have been focused on disadvantaged or troubled youth in general or youth deemed to be at-risk of delinquency, with very little direct attention to mentoring of adjudicated or incarcerated delinquents. "In 1997 P/PV began to investigate the extent to which faith-based institutions serve high-risk youth; by high-risk youth we mean youth who are already involved in criminal and violent activities or who have been deemed likely candidates for such behavior by neighborhood residents, law enforcement and juvenile justice agencies, school officials or community leaders ..." (Trulear, 2000, p. 1, emphasis added; see also Bauldry & Hartmann, 2004). Fifteen sites were selected by P/PV and invited to submit applications for participation in a demonstration project, NFBI, designed to provide information on faith-based programs for youth around the country intended to counter delinquency and drug use while increasing educational achievement and preparing youth for legitimate employment (Trulear, 2000).

Observations of the demonstration projects indicated the importance of forging genuine relationships of mentors with youth and making available the necessary resources and services (Ericson, 2001). Evaluation of the NFBI projects explored "whether a mentoring program run by a faith-based organization is a viable intervention for high-risk youth" (Bauldry & Hartmann, 2004, p. 2). There were 12 participating sites in NFBI, but the evaluation study was a survey of volunteers at only four of the sites (Bronx, Brooklyn, Philadelphia, and Baton Rouge). These were community-based programs. None of the four programs included institutionalized or incarcerated youth, but a high proportion were involved in law violations and drug use, and one program (Bronx) had some youth who had been referred from Juvenile Probation. The commitment by mentors and youth (mean age of 15) was for two hours a week for one year (Bauldry & Hartmann, 2004).

Five elements were identified as necessary for effective mentoring: (1) good screening of volunteers by staff and understanding by the volunteers of the demands of mentoring; (2) training of mentors in the mentoring relationship and how to meet challenges as they come up; (3) care in matching mentors and youth; (4) ongoing training and supervision; and (5) flexibility to modify program as needed. The value of recruiting from faith organizations lies in the level of commitment and dedication that characterizes people of faith who are actively involved in their churches that can be expected to carry over into their work as volunteer youth mentors. "Programs often struggle to find volunteers. P/PV hypothesized that faith-based organizations could fill this void because the mentors would be motivated by their religious faith and would receive support from their organizations" (Bauldry & Hartmann, 2004, p. 23).

NFBI relies on faith motivation to recruit mentors and faith commitment of mentors to carry through, in each site, but there was a worry at each site that the very faith commitment that drew the volunteers into the programs would lead to the volunteers proselytizing youth:

> Site operators also tried to gauge a volunteer's desire to proselytize, explaining that proselytizing was not a program goal. However, the subject was sensitive because the sites were using faith to recruit volunteers and all sites needed more mentors. While the staff members screened out volunteers with a clear desire to proselytize, they accepted some volunteers with a more subtle sense of faith-sharing into their mentoring programs. (Bauldry & Hartmann, 2004, p. 16)

> Volunteers found the distinction [between proselytizing and sharing of faith] more difficult to make. They were recruited through their church, volunteering on their personal time – time normally devoted to the church and often met with the young person at the church. From their perspective, their volunteer work was an extension of their involvement in church. (Bauldry & Hartmann, 2004, p. 19)

Eventually an on-going accommodation was worked out that allowed mentors to show their faith by example and to involve youth in church and church-related events as part of the mentoring activities. And it turned out that the worries were misplaced because, "Despite staff members' concerns, youth felt the mentors were respectful of their limits and did not 'push' faith on them" (Bauldry & Hartmann, 2004, p. 38).

The evidence that mentors did not "push" their faith inappropriately is not surprising, and there is no research evidence from any faith-based mentoring program that youth have been forced or pressured into conversion by the mentor from one religious faith (or no faith) to another. There is, of course, legitimate concern about placing vulnerable and perhaps immature youngsters in situations in which they may be exposed to certain beliefs, under public auspices or funding, to which they may not otherwise have been, or to which their parents or guardians would not want them to be, exposed. But as noted above the assumption is that moral values as modeled by the mentor's behavior and in the mentor's conversation will be passed on to the youth in a way sufficient to have a pro-social effect on his or her attitudes and behavior. To what extent is the "transcendence" mechanism (Sumter & Clear, 2005) mentioned above operative in the influence of the faith-based mentor? On the one hand, the volunteers are recruited by deliberate appeal to their faith commitment to serve and help troubled youth; on the other, they are cautioned not to rely too much on their faith sharing in order to have a positive effect on the youth.

This worry over proselytizing and instructions to staff to limit faith sharing by mentors while at the same time leaning heavily on recruiting volunteers from faith communities is a potential source of conflict and perhaps ineffectiveness in achieving the restorative and reintegrative values and goals of faith-based programs. Do the rules, regulations, and stipulations about not proselytizing by volunteer mentors lean too far in the direction of concern over the establishment of religion clause in the U.S. Constitution at the expense of protecting rights of religious people to express their faith under the Free Exercise Clause? Justice Stewart's concurring opinion in *Sherbert v. Verner* (1963) warned that "there are many situations where legitimate claims under the Free Exercise Clause will run into head-on collision with the Court's insensitive and sterile construction of the Establishment Clause."

Given First Amendment and common sense issue of fairness, finding the right balance of religious establishment and free exercise, is an unavoidable issue in faith-based programs. The way in which the NFBI sites handled it would seem to be reasonable and perhaps represents the right balance. That is, ask for restraint in direct or overbearing proselytizing but allow faith sharing by example, inviting mentees to worship services, and involving them in church-related youth activities. If the mentored youth accept those invitations and thereby become exposed to the proselytizing and religious influence that comes from other youth and adults who may share the gospel and witness of their faith that is inherent in those church activities, then that is a normal part of free exercise of religious participation. This is similar to the balance found in the "open-forum" model of the FCBDTI which "avoid(s) viewpoint discrimination ... [and provides a forum in which] youth can develop their beliefs, but it does not pressure them about their beliefs (including rejecting religion)" (Lanza-Kaduce & Lane, 2007, p. 145).

For the Christian volunteers, who comprise the vast majority of volunteers in faith-based programs, mentoring is an expression of *agape* (unconditional) love and their commitment to the teachings of Christ. For volunteers from other faith communities, such as the Jewish and Muslim volunteers in the Brooklyn program, participation is an expression of their religious principles and values emphasizing help to those in need. Over 90% of the mentors in the NFBI were members of church congregations, and almost all of them (85%) had been church members for more than five years. Moreover, they were currently deeply involved in prayer, youth ministry, choir, and other activities in their respective churches and had previous experience as a volunteer in other causes. Two-thirds were female. Their length of service as a mentor averaged 20 months. "These mentors came forward despite multiple constraints on their time – most were employed and most volunteered in other areas ... Faith-based organizations that foster close relationships with congregations would seem to enjoy a built-in recruitment base not typically available to other mentoring programs" (Bauldry & Hartmann, 2004, pp. 27–28). Even with this faith motivation advantage, NFBI learned that it is still difficult to get large enough numbers of volunteers.

For the four sites, the effort was made to get commitment from mentors for two hours a week for a year, but the average length of mentoring was eight months (ranging from 7 to 11 months), which would seem to be insufficient for significant benefits of the program. Also, there were several other elements of the program to which the youth were exposed besides the mentoring component. "All of the participants in the NFBI programs received services other than mentoring, and, as such, were involved in the overall program longer than they were matched with mentors" (Bauldry & Hartmann, 2004, p. 44). The effects of the NFBI programs are yet to be determined, but this intermingling of mentoring with other components and the mixing of faith-based and non-faith services and treatment suggests that if the programs are found to be effective, it will be difficult to ferret out any effects uniquely attributable to the faith-based mentoring component.

CONCLUDING OBSERVATIONS

Faith assumptions underlie many restorative justice and rehabilitation efforts. There are similar theoretical and philosophical principles for restorative justice and faith-based programs of all kinds, including mentoring initiatives. The preponderance of empirical evidence shows significant (albeit moderate) effects of religious belief and practice on delinquent and criminal behavior. It is reasonable to expect, therefore, that faith-based mentoring (or any other restorative justice, prevention, or treatment program that effectively fosters faith commitment) will have the desired effect of preventing or reducing delinquent involvement of the youth participated in the program. There is some evidence that faith-based rehabilitation can be at least modestly effective in reducing recidivism. But empirical verification of the positive effects of mentoring depends on proper design and implementation of a quality mentoring program, and programs often fall short of these standards. There is a body of research on the characteristics and effects of mentors and mentoring programs, but there is a paucity of research evidence on how effective such programs (faith-based or otherwise) are in prevention or treatment of delinquency. A central value of establishing faith-based initiatives in mentoring and restorative justice programs is that they are able to draw directly from and rely on the faith-based motivation and service ethic of the volunteers to give unselfishly of themselves, their time, and efforts. Another positive value may be found in renewal or finding of faith-based motivation on the part of the youthful (or older) offenders to adapt their attitudes and behavior in the pro-social direction. The challenge of mentoring programs of any kind is to recruit and train mentors with strong motivation, accomplish good matching of mentors and youth, and mentoring relationship with the right mix of activities, learning, and modeling as well as the continuation of that relationship over a sufficiently long enough time to be effective. Faith-based programs face the additional challenge of achieving a proper balance of relying on the faith motivation and moral values of the volunteers, while at the same time ensuring that the exercise of that faith in the mentoring relationship is done appropriately (see Lanza-Kaduce & Lane, 2007).

REFERENCES

Agnew, R. (2006). *Pressured into crime: An overview of general strain theory.* Los Angeles: Roxbury Publishing.

Akers, R. L. (1973). *Deviant behavior: A social learning approach.* Belmont, CA: Wadsworth.

Akers, R. L. (1998). *Social learning and social structure: A general theory of crime and deviance.* Boston: Northeastern University Press.

Akers, R. L., & Sellers, C. S. (2004). *Criminological theories: Introduction, evaluation, and application.* Los Angeles: Roxbury Publishing Company.

Akers, R. L., & Silverman, A. (2004). Toward a social learning model of violence and terrorism. In: M. A. Zahn, H. H. Brownstein & S. L. Jackson (Eds), *Violence: From theory to research* (pp. 19–35). Cincinnati, OH: Anderson Publishing.

Andrews, D. A., & Bonta, J. (2003). *The psychology of criminal conduct* (3rd ed.). Cincinnati, OH: Anderson Publishing.

Baier, C. J., & Wright, B. R. E. (2001). If you love me, keep my commandments: A meta-analysis of the effect of religion on crime. *Journal of Research in Crime Delinquency, 38*, 3–21.

Barlow, H. (2007). *Dead for good: Martyrdom and the rise of the suicide bomber.* Boulder: Paradigm Publishers.

Bauldry, S., & Hartmann, T. A. (2004). *The promise and challenge of mentoring high-risk youth: Findings from the national faith-based initiative.* Philadelphia: Public/Private Ventures. Available at http://www.ppv.org

Bazemore, G., & Day, S. E. (1996). Restoring the balance: Juvenile and community justice. *Juvenile Justice, 3*, 3–14.

Bazemore, G., & Schiff, M. (Eds). (2001). *Restorative community justice: Repairing harm and transforming communities.* Cincinnati, OH: Anderson Publishing.

Bazemore, G., & Umbreit, M. (1998). *Guide for implementing the balanced and restorative justice model.* Washington, DC: U.S. Department of Justice, Office of Juvenile Justice and Delinquency Prevention.

BB/BS. (2007). Big Brothers Big Sisters. Available at www.bbbs.org

Benda, B. B. (2002). Religion and violent offenders in boot camp: A structural equation model. *The Journal of Research in Crime and Delinquency, 39*(1), 91–123.

Braithwaite, J. (1989). *Crime, shame, and reintegration.* Cambridge: Cambridge University Press.

Braithwaite, J. (1995). Reintegrative shaming, republicanism, and policy. In: H. Barlow (Ed.), *Crime and public policy: Putting theory to work* (pp. 191–204). Boulder, CO: Westview Press.

Braithwaite, J. (1997). Charles Tittle's control balance and criminological theory. *Theoretical Criminology, 1*, 77–97.

Braithwaite, J. (2002). *Restorative justice and responsive regulation.* New York: Oxford University Press.

Braithwaite, J., Ahmed, E., & Braithwaite, V. (2006). Shame, restorative justice, and crime. In: T. C. Francis, J. P. Wright & K. R. Blevins (Eds), *Taking stock: The status of criminological theory. Advances in criminological theory* (Vol. 15, pp. 397–412). New Brunswick, NJ: Transaction Publishers.

Braithwaite, J., & Drahos, P. (2002). Zero tolerance, naming and shaming: Is there a case for it with crimes of the powerful? *Australian and New Zealand Journal of Criminology, 35*, 269–288.

Brockway, Z. R. (1871). The ideal of a true prison system for a state. In: E. C. Wines (Ed.), *Transactions of the national congress on penitentiary and reformatory discipline* (pp. 38–65). Albany, NY: Weed, Parsons & Co.

Clear, T. R., & Sumter, M. T. (2002). Prisoners, prison and religion: Religion and adjustment to prison. *Journal of Offender Rehabilitation, 35*(3/4), 127–166.

Cochran, J. K., & Akers, R. L. (1989). Beyond hellfire: An exploration of the variable effects of religiosity on adolescent marijuana and alcohol use. *Journal of Research in Crime and Delinquency, 26*, 198–225.

Cullen, F. T., & Sundt, J. L. (2003). Reaffirming evidence-based corrections. *Criminology and Public Policy, 2*(2), 353.

Cullen, F. T., Sundt, J. L., & Wozniak, J. F. (2001). The virtuous prison: Toward a restorative rehabilitation. In: H. N. Pontell & D. Shichor (Eds), *Contemporary issues in crime and criminal justice: Essays in honor of Gilbert Geis* (pp. 265–286). Saddle River, NJ: Prentice-Hall.

DiIulio, J. J. (2004). Getting faith-based programs right. *Public Interest, 155*, 75–88.

DuBois, D., Holloway, L. B. E., Valentine, J. C., & Cooper, H. (2002). Effectiveness of mentoring programs for youth: A meta-analytic review. *American Journal of Community Psychology, 30*, 157–197.

Editors of Corrections Compendium. (2003). Faith-based programming. *Corrections Compendium, 28*(8), 8.

Eells, S. (2003). The girls' assets program: Providing therapeutic mentoring. *Corrections Today*, *65*(6), 20–22.

Eisenberg, M., & Trusty, B. (2002). *Overview of the innerchange freedom initiative: The faith-based prison program within the texas department of criminal justice*. Austin: Criminal Justice Policy Council. Available at http://www.cjpc.state.tx.us/reports/alphalist/IFI.pdf

Ericson, N. (2001). Public/Private Ventures' evaluation of faith-based programs. OJJDP Fact Sheet #38.

Evans, T. D., Cullen, F. T., Dunaway, R. G., & Burton, V. S. (1995). Religion and crime reexamined: The impact of religion, secular controls, and social ecology on adult criminality. *Criminology*, *33*, 195–224.

Fuller, J. R., & Wozniak, J. F. (2006). Peacemaking criminology: Past, present, and future. In: F. T. Cullen, J. P. Wright & K. R. Blevins (Eds), *Taking stock: The status of criminological theory. Advances in criminological theory* (Vol. 15, pp. 251–273). New Brunswick, NJ: Transaction Publishers.

Grossman, J. B., & Rhodes, J. E. (2002). The test of time: Predictors and effects of duration in youth mentoring relationships. *American Journal of Community Psychology*, *30*, 199–219.

Hadley, M. L. (Ed.) (2001). *The spiritual roots of restorative justice*. Albany, NY: SUNY Press.

Hall, S. T. I. (2003). Faith-based cognitive programs in corrections. *Corrections Today*, *65*, 108–137.

Hands on Broward Partners. (2000). Available at http://www.handsonbroward.org/index.html

Hirschi, T. (1969). *Causes of delinquency*. Berkeley, CA: University of California Press.

Hirschi, T., & Stark, R. (1969). Hellfire and delinquency. *Social Problems*, *17*, 202–213.

Hockensmith, C. (2003). *Improving juvenile delinquency through faith-based services*. Washington, DC: Office of Juvenile Justice and Delinquency Prevention.

Johnson, B. R. (1998). The faith factor: Studies show religion is linked to the mental and physical health of inmates. *Corrections Today*, *60*, 106–114.

Johnson, B. R. (2004). Religious programs and recidivism among former inmates in prison fellowship programs: A long-term follow-up study. *Justice Quarterly*, *21*(2), 329–354.

Johnson, B. R., De Li, S., Larson, B., & McCullough, M. (2000b). A systematic review of the religiosity and delinquency literature. *Journal of Contemporary Criminal Justice*, *16*, 32–52.

Johnson, B. R., Jang, S. J., Larson, D. B., & De Li, S. (2001). Does adolescent religious commitment matter? A reexamination of the effects of religiosity in delinquency. *Journal of Research in Crime and Delinquency*, *38*, 22–44.

Johnson, B. R., & Larson, D. B. (2003). *The innerchange freedom initiative: A preliminary evaluation of a faith-based prison experiment*. Philadelphia: Center for Research on Religion and Urban Civil Society.

Johnson, B. R., Larson, D. B., De Li, S., & Jang, S. J. (2000a). Escaping from the crime of inner cities: Church attendance and religious salience among disadvantaged youth. *Justice Quarterly*, *17*, 377–391.

Johnson, B. R., Larson, D. B., & Pitts, T. C. (1997). Religious programs, institutional adjustment, and recidivism among former inmates in prison fellowship. *Justice Quarterly*, *14*, 145–166.

Jones-Brown, D., & Henriques, Z. W. (1997). Promises and pitfalls of mentoring as a juvenile justice strategy. *Social Justice*, *24*, 212–233.

Lane, J., & Lanza-Kaduce, L. (2007). Before you open the doors: Ten lessons from Florida's faith and community-based delinquency treatment initiative. *Evaluation Review*, *31*, 121–152.

Lanza-Kaduce, L., & Lane, J. (2007). Initiating faith-based juvenile corrections: Exercising without establishing religion. In: M. D. McShane & F. P. Williams III (Eds), *Youth violence and delinquency: Monsters and myths* (pp. 131–148). Westport, CN: Praeger.

Lattimore, P. K. (2006). Reentry, reintegration, rehabilitation, recidivism, and redemption. *The Criminologist, 31*(May/June), 1–6.

Levrant, S., Cullen, F. T., Fulton, B., & Wozniak, J. F. (1999). Reconsidering restorative justice: The corruption of benevolence revisited? *Crime and Delinquency, 45*, 3–27.

Mears, D. P., Roman, C. G., Wolff, A., & Buck, J. (2006). Faith-based efforts to improve prisoner reentry: Assessing the logic and evidence. *Journal of Criminal Justice, 34*, 351–367.

MENTOR. (2007). Mentoring in America 2005: A snapshot of the current state of mentoring. National Mentoring Partnership. Available at www.mentoring.org

Miller, M. K. (2006). *Religion in criminal justice*. New York: LFB Scholarly Publishing.

Novotney, L. C., Mertinko, E., Lange, J., & Baker, T. K. (2000). Juvenile mentoring program: A progress review. *Juvenile Justice Bulletin*. Washington, DC: OJJDP.

NSDUH (National Survey on Drugs and Health). (2004). The NSDUH Report. Office of Applied Studies, Substance Abuse and Mental Health Services Administration, January 30. Available at http://www.DrugAbuseStatistics.samsha.gov

O'Connor, T. P., & Perreyclear, M. (2002). Prison religion in action and its influence on offender rehabilitation. *Journal of Offender Rehabilitation, 35*(3/4), 11.

Pepinsky, H. E., & Quinney, R. (Eds). (1991). *Criminology as peacemaking*. Bloomington, IN: Indiana University Press.

P/PV. (2007). Public/Private Ventures. Available at www.ppv.org

Quinney, R. (1991). The way of peace: On crime, suffering, and service. In: H. E. Pepinsky & R. Quinney (Eds), *Criminology as peacemaking* (pp. 3–13). Bloomington, IN: Indiana University Press.

Regnerus, M., Smith, C., & Fritsch, M. (2003). *Religion in the lives of American adolescents: A review of the literature*. A Research Report of the National Study of Youth and Religion Number 3. National Study of Youth and Religion, Chapel Hill.

Rodriquez, N. (2005). Restorative justice: Communities and delinquency: Whom do we reintegrate. *Criminology and Public Policy, 4*, 103–130.

Ross, L. (1994). Religion and deviance: Exploring the impact of social control elements. *Sociological Spectrum, 14*, 65–86.

Schiff, M. F. (1998). Restorative justice interventions for juvenile offenders: A research agenda for the next decade. *Western Criminological Review 1*(1). [Online]. Available at http://scr.sonoma.edu./v1n1/schiff.html

Schrage, C., Lane, J., Lanza-Kaduce, L., Perry, J., & Akers, R. L. (2007). Religious beliefs among youths in Florida's faith and community-based delinquency treatment initiative. Paper presented at the annual meetings of the Academy of Criminal Justice Sciences, March, Seattle.

Sipe, C. (1996). *Mentoring: A synthesis of P/PV research 1988–1995*. Philadelphia: Public/Private Ventures.

Smith, T. R., Rizzo, E., & Empie, K. M. (2005). Yielding to deviant temptation: A quasi-experimental examination of the inhibiting power of intrinsic religious motivation. *Deviant Behavior, 26*, 463–482.

Sumter, M. T., & Clear, T. R. (2005). Religion in the correctional setting. In: R. Muraskin (Ed.), *Key correctional issues* (pp. 86–119). Upper Saddle River, NJ: Pearson Prentice Hall.

Triplett, R., & Payne, B. (2004). Problem solving as reinforcement in adolescent drug use: Implications for theory and policy. *Journal of Criminal Justice, 32*, 617–630.

Trulear, H. D. (2000). *Faith-based institutions and high-risk youth: First report to the field.* Philadelpia: Public/Private Ventures.

Van Ness, D., & Strong, K. H. (1997). *Restoring justice.* Cincinnati, OH: Anderson Publishing.

Van Ness, D., & Strong, K. H. (2006). *Restoring justice: An introduction to restorative justice.* Cincinnati, OH: Anderson Publishing.

Vold, G. B. (1958). *Theoretical criminology.* New York: Oxford University Press.

Welch, M. R., Tittle, C. R., & Grasmick, H. G. (2006). Christian religiosity, self-control, and social conformity. *Social Forces, 84*, 1605–1624.

CASES CITED

Sherbert v. Verner, 374 U.S. 398 (1963).

LOCALIZING RESTORATIVE JUSTICE: AN IN-DEPTH LOOK AT A DENVER PUBLIC SCHOOL PROGRAM ☆

Wesley G. Jennings, Angela R. Gover and Diane M. Hitchcock

ABSTRACT

Although the research literature has been expanding on restorative justice inquiries in the last few decades, there are only a few U.S.-based studies that have focused on restorative justice programming within public schools. Specifically, research is even more scant on the implementation concerns surrounding school-based restorative justice initiatives. Discussions of the effectiveness of these approaches for reducing school disciplinary problems resulting in suspensions, expulsions, and arrests are also rather limited. This chapter presents an in-depth examination into these issues by providing a thorough description of a restorative justice program in its early implementation stages in several Denver,

☆The authors wish to express their gratitude to Benjamin Cairns and Jeremy Simons, RJ Coordinators at North High School, Denver, Colorado, for their assistance with the development of this manuscript.

Restorative Justice: From Theory to Practice
Sociology of Crime, Law and Deviance, Volume 11, 167–187
Copyright © 2008 by Emerald Group Publishing Limited
All rights of reproduction in any form reserved
ISSN: 1521-6136/doi:10.1016/S1521-6136(08)00407-7

Colorado public schools. The chapter concludes with a discussion of preliminary program evaluation findings and focuses on the overall feasibility of incorporating restorative justice programming in schools.

INTRODUCTION

While various philosophies of punishment have a long-standing history in the United States (i.e., retributive justice, just deserts), restorative justice as a philosophy, policy, and practice has only recently been gaining attention in modern day criminological literature and criminal justice programming. At the fundamental level, restorative justice is a multi-pronged approach that essentially focuses on the interrelations of the victim, the offender, and the community (Bazemore, 1992; Braithwaite, 1989; Johnstone, 2002; Morris, 2002; Zehr, 2002). More specifically, the underlying assumption of restorative justice is that when an individual commits a delinquent, criminal, or disciplinary infraction at school their behavior breaches the proverbial social contract that exists between them and the community (or the school). Thus, it is ultimately the school community's responsibility to ensure that the offender is held accountable in order to correct or restore the harm caused (Dorne, 2008).

Although the term "restorative justice" as applied to modern day criminological thought has only been developing over the last several decades and scholars who have been examining the restorative philosophy have emphasized the difficulty in defining restorative justice (see Bazemore & Schiff, 2004; Bonta, Wallace-Capretta, Rooney, & McAnoy, 2002; Braithwaite, 1989; Harris, 2004; Hayes & Daly, 2004; Karp, 2004; McCold, 2004; Presser & Van Voorhis, 2002; Strang, 2004; Zehr, 2002), its origin can actually be traced to the ancient vengeance-related concept of *lex talionis* or an "eye for an eye" or a "tooth for a tooth" (Dorne, 2008). The reasoning behind this punishment-oriented thinking was that the offender should be giving something back to those whom they have harmed in order to make things whole again. This early practice mirrors the core tenet of restorative justice today, which is its emphasis on restitution or the practice of requiring an offender to provide money or a service either directly to the victim(s) and the community or to the victim(s) and the school as discussed in this chapter.

While a number of studies have focused on restorative justice programs in general (see Zehr, 2002), there has been considerably less research on restorative justice programs operating in the United States overall. Still, there have been even fewer studies that examine restorative justice programs in schools (see Stinchcomb, Bazemore, & Riestenberg, 2006). Therefore, in this chapter we provide an in-depth exploration into one such program that has recently been implemented in several participating schools from the public school system in Denver, Colorado.

CONCEPTUALIZING RESTORATIVE JUSTICE

The primary goal behind a restorative justice-based program is to restore the status quo, and to place less emphasis on punishment and more on offender responsibility and accountability. These practices include various reparation and reengagement tasks in order to repair the broken trust that has resulted from the offender's decision to engage in misconduct and harm the victim, which subsequently may harm the school community. Oftentimes, the offenders are required to write formal letters of apology to the victims and in some instances, offenders have face-to-face meetings with their victims (Forgays & DeMilio, 2005). Bazemore and Umbreit (2001) also stress the issue of offender accountability in their balanced restorative justice model, along with discussing the importance of increasing the offender's competencies and protecting the public by encouraging victims, offenders, and school community members to be actively involved in the restoration process. Or stated differently, "restorative justice is the process to involve, to the extent possible, those who have a stake in a specific offense and to collectively identify and address harms, needs, and obligations, in order to heal and put things as right as possible" (Zehr, 2002, p. 37).

Restorative justice as a philosophy hinges on several critical yet debatable assumptions. First, the philosophical ideals behind restorative justice assume that most (if not all) offenders have a conscience and that they do or can feel guilt and remorse. This assumption certainly makes offenders with anti-social personality disorders unlikely candidates for a restorative justice-based program. However, just because an offender may be able to feel guilt over their offending, they may not necessarily wish to be forgiven by their victim and reintegrated back into the community as a socially accepted individual. A more plausible assumption is that offenders are perhaps at the very least more likely to prefer participating in a restorative justice program in lieu of being sent to jail or prison, or be suspended or expelled from school for their behavior. Second, restorative justice assumes that the victim is a true and innocent individual that can benefit from being provided an opportunity to realize their empowerment over their victimization experience and the perpetrator. Therefore, in many cases when there is not a clear or identifiable victim such as in drug dealing, prostitution, and other forms of vice crimes, a restorative justice program may not necessarily apply.

Finally, restorative justice, as applied in policy and practice, is heavily dependent on the ability of the program to be accepted as a viable supplement to traditional juvenile justice or criminal justice system processing. Or in the case of a school-based restorative justice approach, the program must have organizational and administrative support as a reasonable alternative to the established disciplinary procedures. In either case, if the program is not inherently linked or housed within traditional agencies (i.e., schools, police, courts, or corrections), then its likelihood of garnering continued support over time among criminal justice personnel, politicians, policymakers, school administrators and officials, and the community will be tested (Dorne, 2008).

While Roach (2006, p. 168) has argued that restorative justice "means different things to different people," there is a growing amount of literature that has consistently found that those that have participated in restorative justice-based programs report a high level of satisfaction with the entire restorative process and the outcomes (see Hayes & Daly, 2004; Latimer, Dowden, & Muise, 2001; McGarrell, 2001; Miers et al., 2001; Morris, 2002; Presser & Van Voorhis, 2002; Umbreit, Coates, & Vos, 2001). Specifically, research has shown that victims who participate in these programs report feeling safer and less fearful of crime afterwards, now that they are aware of the offender's motives and explanation for the offense (Hayes & Daly, 2003; Johnstone, 2002). The offenders also report feeling more fairly treated than they would compared with traditional criminal justice or school system processing because they are able to learn and recognize the extent of the harm they caused and they are able to get an impression of what individuals in their school or community will not accept as tolerable behavior (Hayes & Daly, 2003). One recent meta-analysis of thirty-five restorative justice studies indicated that the victims and offenders that participated in restorative justice programs were significantly more satisfied with the program compared with other juvenile or criminal justice system alternatives (see Latimer et al., 2001).

In addition, prior scholars have argued that the school/community plays a vital role in the restorative justice process (Braithwaite, 1989) and that restorative justice can strengthen the school/community as a whole (Bazemore, 2005). For instance, the school/community can have an effect on the ability of an offender to successfully reintegrate back into the community by reducing the offender's feeling of stigmatization and giving them a sense of worth. Including residents of the community or other students and school employees in the restorative justice process also enables individuals to have a voice in determining what values and norms they wish to emphasize in their own school/community, along with making recommendations and offering solutions for managing offenders or disciplinary infractions (Clear & Karp, 1999, 2000; Karp, 2001). However, the school/community may also impede the reintegration process by ostracizing rather than accepting the offender's attempt to "right the wrong" they have done (see Bazemore, 2005; Braithwaite, 1989; Clear & Karp, 1999; Rodriguez, 2005).

INCORPORATING RESTORATIVE JUSTICE IN SCHOOLS

In light of increasing school violence across the nation, many educational systems have implemented discipline strategies that not only sanction offenders, but increase the safety of students. Similarly, a number of school systems since the 1990s have instituted zero-tolerance policies with the assumption that removing the student with the discipline issue will "fix" the problem as well. Zero-tolerance policies vary among school systems, but the main goal is to enact swift punishment for violating disciplinary rules. The use of these policies has been particularly supported in incidents where students' safety is threatened, such as the carrying of weapons to school (Stinchcomb et al., 2006).

Although these policies were enacted with the intent of decreasing school violence, their unforeseen effect has been an increase in the number of school suspensions and expulsions, and zero-tolerance policies have been shown to have little, if any, effect on school safety. In fact, the National Center for Education Statistics reports that schools with zero-tolerance policies are no more safe, and in fact less safe, than those without them (Skiba & Peterson, 1999). In addition, studies have shown that students in schools with less harsh discipline policies report feeling safer than those in schools with more strict punishment (McNeely, Nonnemaker, & Blum, 2002).

Given the recent research denouncing zero-tolerance policies, school systems have been investigating alternative disciplinary action to hold offenders accountable and at the same time increase the safety of the school environment. In response to these efforts, restorative justice practices have been gaining popularity in educational settings in an attempt to reduce violence, disciplinary infractions, school suspensions, and expulsions. The ultimate goal of such programs is to transform the culture and climate of the school in order to influence and promote positive behavioral change rather than to alienate and stigmatize wayward adolescents (Stinchcomb et al., 2006).

Similar to restorative justice programs in general (see Zehr, 2002), restorative justice programs in school settings use varying models of mediation and intervention between the offender and victim to encourage accountability and remorse as well as facilitating understanding and forgiveness. The central tenet of these school-based programs is to repair the relationship between the students involved in a dispute. Additionally, guided by the assumption that crime affects the victim, the offender, and those around them, restorative justice attempts to address the harm done at an individual level and also at a larger social level within the school. Thus, mediation techniques are used to reintegrate the offender back into the school community, rather than to alienate him or her with punitive measures. The ultimate goal of school-based restorative justice is for all individuals involved in the conflict and those in the larger community to recognize and understand the wrongfulness of the behavior and to prevent its reoccurrence in the future (Stinchcomb et al., 2006).

The recent incorporation of restorative justice programming in schools has taken different forms. Some of the more common uses of restorative justice in educational environments are victim-offender mediation (VOM), which involves group, family, or circle conferencing geared toward conflict resolution. In VOM, a trained mediator facilitates discussions between the victim and offender. The goal of the VOM approach is to open up dialogue between the two parties so that feelings can be expressed and heard, recognition and understanding of behavior can begin, and a collective decision can be made about how to repair the harm incurred (Bazemore, 2001).

Comparatively, in family and group conferencing, members of the school community and family members of those involved are invited to participate in the process. In this restorative practice, the aim is to include input from not only the victim and offender, but from everyone involved in the incident or conflict, so that a greater understanding of the situation can be realized. This practice is also beneficial when determining the appropriate sanction for the offender, as it provides all stakeholders an opportunity to come to a consensus of how best to repair the harm done (Bazemore, 2001).

Similar to family and group conferencing in schools and community-based restorative justice circles in general (Coates, Umbreit, & Vos, 2003) circle conferencing within schools typically includes the students directly harmed by the offense and additional students, teachers, parents, coaches, administrators, and any other member(s) of the school community who may have been involved in, or indirectly harmed by, the school infraction (Drewery, 2004). However, rather than handing down punishment and further alienating the offender and victim, circle conferencing allows for a consensus to be reached as to the appropriate resolution. Or in other words, Drewery (2004) refers to circle conferencing as a restorative justice approach where "they all meet together to decide what should happen next, rather than to have a decision imposed on them" (p. 337). Overall, this process empowers the parties involved and provides a forum for everyone to converse and agree on a resolution to the problem. In following the principles of restorative justice, those affected are heard, and the offender is held accountable for his or her behavior, but also returns to the school community, ideally with the harmed relationship repaired. Thus, instead of a retributive action that typically would occur in traditional school disciplinary polices, circle conferences allow students to return and reintegrate back into their school environment, rather than be abandoned or stigmatized.

Implementation Issues Surrounding Restorative Justice in Schools

Preliminary evidence suggests that school-based restorative justice programs are effective, yet they often can be difficult to implement. Karp and Breslin (2001) identify three areas in particular that make the creation of restorative justice programs in school settings problematic. First, the authors suggest that administrators express concern over the amount of time it takes for restorative practices to develop and have an impact. For example, time is needed to appropriately train school faculty and staff. There is also typically a one- to three-year period before the culture or the climate of the school can change and have an impact on overall student behavior. Therefore, in contrast to many current school disciplinary policies, the process of restorative justice is time-consuming. No longer are the administrators or school officials simply punishing the student for his or her behavior and enacting immediate sanctions, such as detention or suspension. Instead, they are now referring the student to a restorative justice-based practice, which calls for mediation, conferencing, and/or a number of other procedures depending on the particular program the school has decided to utilize. Thus, many administrators and school officials may have trouble recognizing the benefit of restorative justice as it prolongs the overall disciplinary process for the student (Karp & Breslin, 2001).

In addition to the time-consuming efforts associated with the implementation of restorative justice programs, developing these programs in educational settings can be difficult because of the already existing retributive practices. It can be complicated to integrate a new policy when the one currently being used is inherently different. For example, in contrast to zero-tolerance policies, where a student would simply be suspended and removed from school for an infraction, with restorative practices, the student would remain in school and partake in a mediation session. While administrators oftentimes opt for an either/or approach of retributive or restorative discipline, it is possible for them to be used in conjunction with each other (Karp & Breslin, 2001; Stinchcomb et al., 2006). Thus, if a swift sanction such as a suspension is needed for safety reasons, then the student could participate in a restorative justice program after returning to school.

Also noted by Karp and Breslin (2001), another restorative justice program implementation issue is that the culture of the school is often so ingrained in retributive practices that even with a full system of restorative justice, school personnel and students have long been socialized to use other modes of discipline. Therefore, it can be difficult to implement the either/or approach. In recognition of this, and in following with the idea that an all or nothing attitude is often not the best solution to resolve a school-based incident, it has been argued that a discipline policy that uses both retributive sanctions and restorative practices simultaneously may be the most effective way to incorporate new policies in school settings (Karp & Breslin, 2001; Stinchcomb et al., 2006).

In developing a policy that incorporates both traditional disciplinary action and restorative principles, Braithwaite (2002) suggests a pyramid method. Wherein, 5–10% of the most serious offenders may need to continue to be dealt with using punitive measures, and as the pyramid widens, encompassing the remaining students, restorative justice can be used as an appropriate approach for disciplinary action. The combination of the two will make the implementation of restorative justice practices smoother, as well as satisfying the existing administrative culture (Stinchcomb et al., 2006).

Effectiveness of Restorative Justice in Schools

While a handful of studies have begun to provide evidence that restorative justice programs are effective in reducing recidivism among juveniles in general (see De Bues & Rodriguez, 2007), there is less empirical evidence directly related to whether or not school-based restorative justice programs have desired program impacts. However, restorative justice programs have been shown to have lasting effects on the culture of the institution, and subsequent student behavior (Karp & Breslin, 2001; Stinchcomb et al., 2006).

For instance, McNeely et al. (2002), using data from a nationally representative sample of students in grades seven through twelve, found evidence indicating that classroom management policies promoting school connectedness and self-discipline resulted in a 30–100% reduction in the number of referrals to the principal for acting out, fighting, and assaults. As McNeely et al. (2002) suggest, such classroom management strategies that improve student behavior are those that allow for student autonomy, provide care and support from adults, and promote acceptance from peers. The use of restorative justice in schools is aimed at increasing the responsibility of students as well as promoting acceptance from peers to reintegrate them back into the school community (Forgays & DeMilio, 2005). Given the relationship with school connectedness and discipline, as discussed by McNeely et al. (2002), it is not surprising that many schools are now adopting restorative justice practices.

More recently, Stinchcomb et al. (2006) discussed the implementation of restorative justice programs in South Saint Paul, Minnesota elementary schools. The schools were encouraged to adapt a restorative program appropriate to their particular needs, but most schools chose to use circle conferencing methods (Stinchcomb et al., 2006; Coates et al., 2003). Focusing on one school as an example, acts of physical aggression dropped from 773 to 153, the number of out-of-school suspensions declined from 30 to 11, and the number of behavioral referrals decreased from 1,143 to 407. Thus, it appears that the use of restorative practices in the school setting has the ability to not only repair the situation, but also to transform the environment by establishing a new culture and climate that discourages disrespectful and disruptive behavior.

THE DENVER PUBLIC SCHOOL RESTORATIVE JUSTICE PROGRAM

Background

According to the Colorado Department of Education (CDE), the number of in-school and out-of-school suspensions in the Denver Public School System

(DPS) increased at alarming rates between 2000–2001 and 2004–2005 school years.[1] In addition to the increase in suspensions, the DPS system also experienced an increase in the number of incidents occurring at school that required police intervention for either issuing a ticket or making an arrest. Tickets and arrests were made for a range of student behavior, including the destruction of property, bullying, minor fighting, carrying dangerous weapons, and drug violations.[2] DPS staff suggest that the DPS system has been known for their overreliance on out-of-school suspension as a disciplinary tactic, given that they had the highest rate of out-of-school suspensions among all large school districts in Colorado (B. Cairns and J. Simons, personal communication, October 12, 2007).

Since the DPS system serves a diverse community of students, the fact that the school administrators and staff advocated for a student discipline policy highlights the importance of incorporating culturally competent programming within the learning environment in an effort to achieve racial, ethnic, and cultural equity. Specifically, the student discipline policy and accompanying procedures are intended to help DPS eliminate racial and ethnic disparities. During the 2004–2005 academic year, a disproportionate number of in-school and out-of-school suspensions, tickets, and arrests involved Latino and African-American students, compared with their make-up in the general student population. For example, African-American students made up 19% of the student population but comprised 33% of the out-of-school suspensions and 35% of all expulsions for the 2004–2005 academic year. Similarly, while Latinos made up 57% of the total student population they represented 70% of all tickets issued to students for misconduct in 2004–2005.

DPS responded to the increase in disciplinary problems and racial disparities in school discipline by applying for and receiving an "Expelled and At-Risk Student Services (EARSS)" grant from the Colorado Department of Education in 2006. The grant provided funding for the implementation of a three-year Restorative Justice (RJ) program within one high school and the three middle schools that feed into the high school. It was anticipated that exposing students to the restorative justice philosophy within an academic environment during middle school would increase the likelihood that the restorative school culture would set the tone for the high school environment.

The overall goal of the DPS RJ Program is to address student conflict and misbehavior by keeping students in school and requiring them to be accountable for their actions. The RJ program promotes the resolution of disciplinary matters at the lowest level possible while reserving the most severe discipline (out-of-school suspension and extended out-of-school suspension, expulsion, and referral to law enforcement) for misbehavior that most seriously disrupts the school environment or endangers other students or school staff. By using this unique approach to discipline, DPS anticipates that the numbers of students who are suspended, expelled, and/or require police intervention would decline.

Program Design

The implementation of a comprehensive RJ strategy recognizes the importance of the community-at-large as a component of the educational community. The DPS RJ program is unique in its collaboration with three community groups in their delivery of services. These groups have established their restorative justice mission within the Denver community and have worked with various public schools to integrate RJ practices within their educational practices. The *Victims Offenders Reconciliation Program* (VORP) of Denver is a small non-profit organization that operated out the basement of the Denver First Mennonite Church. The program consisted of two part-time staff that coordinated volunteer mediators to respond to referrals from the city's juvenile misdemeanor court. VORP provided assistance to the DPS RJ program by providing volunteer mediators for assistance in the restorative process. *Padres y Jovenes Unidos* is a community-based organization that was initially formed by parents who were concerned about low academic achievement and low graduation rates. As a multi-generational organization led by people of color, *Padres* strives for educational justice and equality and racial justice for youth. *Padres* also connect schools and communities by providing outreach services. The third organization that collaborated with the DPS RP program is *Restorative Solutions, LLC.* This organization is recognized in Denver for pioneering restorative justice in government, schools, community organizations, faith communities, and within individuals. This organization collaborated with the DPS RJ program by providing training and ongoing consultation about the RJ philosophy within schools and peer mediation to program staff on an ongoing basis. All three community organizations assist the DPS RJ program with their efforts to conduct outreach to parents and other members in the community.

In addition to the involvement of community groups, the RJ program emphasizes the importance of family involvement in their delivery of services. Family members are encouraged to be part of the RJ process because parental involvement and support are commonly recognized risk factors for delinquency (Lipsey & Derzon, 1998; Resnick, Ireland, & Borowsky, 2004). In addition, the RJ philosophy strives to involve all relevant stakeholders in the process, which includes the offending student's parents or other influential family members. Parental involvement is important so that the offending student feels that they have external support for their participation in the program and to serve as an additional check of the student's accountability in a positive way. By participating in the process, parents have an opportunity to express their feelings about their child's behavior while keeping them in school and out of the court system. By being included in the RJ process, parents assist in the creation of a learning opportunity for their child. Furthermore, students are less likely to minimize the harm their actions caused when a parent is involved in the reparation process, so the RJ program recognizes that parents serve a relevant role as an effective moral influence on their children.

The Process

The RJ program operates during regular school hours in each school and is overseen by a full-time RJ Coordinator (although two part-time individuals share the Coordinator position in one of the schools). Meetings are convened biweekly for RJ Coordinators, other relevant school representatives, and partnering community groups. The RJ Coordinators are responsible for serving as the liaison between their program and teachers, administrators, and parents within their school community.

The RJ Program provides an alternative to student suspension and expulsion by incorporating key restorative justice concepts within the school system's existing discipline strategies. Students may be referred to the program by a school staff member, such as the Dean, student advisor, teacher, or students may self-refer to the program.

There are three phases to the RJ Program: (1) Pre-conference; (2) Joint meeting; and (3) Follow-up. The pre-conference involves a thorough investigation of incident records by the RJ Coordinator, individual meetings between the RJ Coordinator and each party involved to explain the expectations and process of the RJ program, and a determination of the willingness of each party to engage in the process. During the individual meetings, each offending student is required to complete a "Restorative Action Plan" which assists in determining how the offender's behavior will be addressed. The offending student is also required to put in writing their commitment to mediation.

The RJ Coordinator listens carefully to each party's account of the event(s) in question to determine whether a joint meeting should be held. Parents are also contacted during this phase to discuss the RJ process and to request permission for participation. Parents are usually always invited to participate in the process. In developing rapport with parents the RJ Coordinator expresses their overall concern and safety for the student's well-being and academic success. According to DPS Coordinators, the program works best when parents are involved in the process, which is not consistent with typical disciplinary practices in public schools (B. Cairns and J. Simons, personal communication, October 12, 2007).

The second phase involves a joint meeting with all parties involved. During this meeting the group discusses the incident in question, the harm caused by the offending student's actions, how the harm will be repaired, and strategies to prevent similar events from reoccurring in the future. All parties involved are given the opportunity to explain the full impact of the situation on them, an approach that shows that the school community is requiring the offending student to accept responsibility for his or her actions. Punishment, according to the RJ philosophy, requires consideration of the harm caused. Expulsion from school does not allow the offending student to immediately address the harm caused by their actions because they are removed from school grounds. The goal of this phase is to end the meeting with the action plan signed by all individuals involved.

The third phase is the follow-up period in which the RJ Coordinator will convey the final, agreed upon action plan to all parties involved, including the source of the RJ program referral and parents. The RJ Coordinator then monitors the situation to oversee that the plan is appropriately implemented. If the action plan is not followed, the RJ Coordinator is responsible for implementing contingency consequences. In sum, the RJ process teaches students how to use critical thinking skills to understand the consequences of their actions by promoting empathy, responsibility, and accountability. The restorative process enables the school system to address misbehavior and conflict while keeping students in school to stay focused on their academic efforts.

Approach to Discipline

According to the DPS student discipline policy, the goal of student discipline is to teach students behavior that contributes to their academic achievement and success in school, and to create an educational environment that fosters respect and responsibility among students and staff. The DPS discipline policy attempts to maximize the amount of time students spend in school learning and minimize the disruption caused by students that would typically result in their removal from the classroom. The policy recognizes that effective school discipline occurs when misbehavior is prevented and when effective interventions are used when misbehavior does occur.

While the student discipline policy identifies three types of school discipline intervention strategies (Administrative, Restorative, and Skill Based/Therapeutic), RJ principles are explicitly incorporated into the overall DPS student discipline policy. For example, the policy states that the DPS system of discipline is built on personal accountability, which is defined as: (1) recognizing that misbehavior damages relationships between the person or persons who misbehave, the person harmed by the behavior, and the community as a whole; (2) having an opportunity to repair harm done and restore relationships whenever possible, as opposed to excluding the person who misbehaved; and (3) building personal responsibility by helping individuals develop empathy, self-control, and motivation. The final section of this chapter discusses the incorporation of a restorative student discipline policy within four public schools. Preliminary process and outcome evaluation findings are discussed that document the implementation of the RJ program.

Participating Schools

The RJ program was incorporated in four schools in the DPS system. These schools consisted of one high school (North) and the three "feeder" middle schools for the high school in Denver (Skinner, Horace, & Lake), all of which were targeted because of their high rates of suspensions, tickets, and arrests.

Known for their strong and long-time community support, North High School (NHS) had a student population of 1,354 and was one of nine public high schools in the Denver metropolitan area (excluding the charter and alternative schools) when the restorative justice program was implemented.

Eighty-six percent of the student population at NHS was reported to have been Latino and 3% were African-American. During the 2004–2005 school year, 288 students at NHS received out-of-school suspensions, 5 students were expelled, and 68 students received tickets or were arrested for misconduct. Skinner Middle School had a student population of 633. Eighty-five percent of the student population was reported as being Latino and 3% were African-American. During the 2004–2005 school year, 350 students received out-of-school suspensions, 4 students were expelled, and 72 students received tickets or were arrested. Horace Mann Middle School had the lowest student population of the three middle schools and served 448 sixth, seventh, and eight graders. Nearly all students attending Horace Mann were reported as being Latino (92%) and 4% were African-American. During the 2004–2005 school year, 220 students received out-of-school suspensions, 3 students were expelled, and 22 students either received tickets or were arrested for misbehavior. The student population at Lake Middle School was 697 with 89% of the student population reported as being Latino and 4% were African-American. In the 2004–2005 school year, 288 students received out-of-school suspensions, 5 students were expelled, and 58 students either received tickets or were arrested.

Preliminary Findings

The Denver Public School system contracted with Outcomes, Inc., of Denver, to conduct external process and outcome evaluations of the DPS RJ program. The information presented here represents findings presented in the DPS Restorative Justice Disciplinary Program Report 2006–2007, which was submitted to DPS in September 2007 (Baker, 2007). At present, outcomes have been assessed for the program's first year of operation (the 2006–2007 school year).

The process evaluation indicated that the three middle schools did not have their programs implemented during the entire school year because RJ Program Coordinators were not hired until March 2007. Therefore, outcome evaluation findings are limited in terms of the total number of cases referred. Comparatively, the program was fully implemented in NHS during the entire school year, in part because this school was the site of the pilot project for the grant. Therefore, the summary of the findings presented here are considered to be exploratory in nature, and second year process and outcome evaluation data (2007–2008) are anticipated to show a more accurate assessment of program success.

During the first year of the RJ program (school year 2006–2007) a total of 213 students participated in the RJ program across the four schools (grades 6 though 12). Approximately half of these students attended NHS ($n = 109$) and the remaining students attended one of the three middle schools. The majority of the RJ participants were male (63%) and Latino (84%).

Of the 213 students who participated in the RJ program, nearly half of the students were referred because of "interpersonal conflicts," which typically consisted of non-physical, verbal disagreements between students. An additional 20% of the students were referred for "verbal harassment," which was behavior that was considered to be slightly more serious than interpersonal conflicts and included behaviors such as racial slurs and personal insults. Twenty-five percent of the students were referred because of physical altercations, such as pushing and shoving, and the remaining students were referred for damaging property or theft.

Many family members, teachers, and other staff members participated in the restorative justice process during the program's first year. Phone contacts about the restorative process were made with over one hundred parents ($n = 111$) and an additional 48 family members (41 parents and 7 other family members) participated in the process itself. Conference participation was also seen by 44 teachers and other staff members, 77 non-referred students, and 43 community volunteers. Of all cases referred to the restorative program, nearly half of them (51%) resulted in a "*restorative agreement*" and another 11% resulted in a "*handshake agreement.*" Sixteen percent of all cases referred resulted in a restorative group conference that consisted of at least four individuals who represented the school community (other students, teachers, administrators, or community members). Twelve percent of the cases referred only participated in the process up to the meeting with the RJ Program Coordinator ("*preconference assessment*"). Finally, a very small proportion of the referred cases did not continue with the process and an even smaller proportion (2%) resulted in a "*restorative family agreement.*"

The process evaluation assessed the implementation of key restorative justice principles into the DPS program. Students, staff members, community members, and family members who participated in the process were surveyed after the medication was completed to assess perceptions of the process fairness and overall satisfaction with the process. Survey results indicated a high degree of support for the RJ program. For example, 90% of the participating individuals surveyed agreed with the statement: "I had the chance to explain my feelings," 86% agreed with the statement: "The RJ agreement was fair to all," and 87% agreed with the statement: "Meeting with the other person was helpful." Data also indicated that the majority of the participants received answers to their questions, thought that the other person understood them better, would recommend the RJ program, and were satisfied with the outcome of the process. Survey data with parents and teachers who participated in the process indicated strong support for the program. Overall, parent and teacher participants felt that students who participated in the process expressed their feelings in an appropriate manner, showed that they understood the feelings of others, and showed respect for others in the restorative circle.

In terms of school-wide disciplinary outcomes, opposite findings were reported for the middle schools compared with the high school. The high school experienced an increase in out-of-school suspensions and expulsions while all three middle schools experienced a decrease in these outcomes compared with rates from the 2005 to 2006 school year. An examination of changes in rates for tickets and arrests was not possible due to data collection issues, therefore overall law enforcement referral rates were compared in terms of changes between the 2005–2006 and the 2006–2007 school years. Similar to the other school-wide disciplinary measures, reductions were seen in rates in the middle schools and an increase was seen at NHS. The increase in rates for NHS was attributed to systemic changes in the school's administration because the school experienced turnover in the principal and assistant principal positions during the year the RJ program was implemented. Evaluators suspected that second-year evaluation findings will be more indicative of program impact due to stability in the school's leadership and support for the program.

Follow-up data were collected from 80% of the students who participated in the RJ program to assess the student's completion with the RJ agreement. Overall, the majority of students surveyed indicated that their relationship with the other party improved as a result of the RJ program. Agreements were reported to be completed by 72% of students surveyed. An additional 63% reported that the other party involved in the conflict completed their part of the agreement.

Overall some of the findings from the evaluation of the first year of the implementation of the RJ program are positive. However, the evaluator noted that it may not be reasonable to expect *immediate* results from the implementation of the RJ program because accurate assessments of outcomes may require a shift in the overall school climate and culture. In other words, enough time may not have passed at the time of the first year evaluation to capture the overall incorporation of the RJ philosophy into the DPS schools examined.

CONCLUSION

This chapter sought out to provide a detailed description of one particular school-based restorative justice program recently implemented in several participating schools from the Denver public school system. We readily acknowledge that the findings are preliminary at best and that this approach may not necessarily be the optimal alternative to traditional school disciplinary procedures in other school systems in other parts of the United States. However, in terms of the DPS RJ program, we and the present evaluators suspect that the evaluation findings from the second and third year of program operation should provide a better indication of the effectiveness of the program. This expectation is certainly consistent with Karp and Breslin's (2001) argument regarding restorative justice program-ming in schools where they suggest that it typically takes anywhere from one to three years before the culture or the climate of the school can effectively change and have an impact on overall student behavior.

Nevertheless, the early evidence has at least suggested that the majority of those individuals involved or processed through the DPS RJ initiative report being satisfied with this alternative compared with the traditional school disciplinary procedures such as suspension, expulsion, ticketing, or arrest. These findings are also consistent with a growing amount of literature that has found that individuals who participate in restorative justice programs generally report greater levels of satisfaction with the entire process and the outcome (see Hayes & Daly, 2004; Latimer et al., 2001; McGarrell, 2001; Miers et al., 2001; Morris, 2002; Presser & Van Voorhis, 2002; Umbreit et al., 2001).

Thus, in light of the seeming "epidemic" of violence in schools, it is important that students, school administrators and staff, and the commu-nity become aware that there are definitely alternative approaches for managing wayward adolescent behavior compared with the traditional punitive response. Perhaps if all of these individuals and actors come to understand the benefits that can be provided by restorative justice initiatives such as the one currently operating in several of the schools in the Denver public school system, then the offending adolescents may learn to comprehend and understand the errors and inappropriateness of their behavior early on, and the community can take part in facilitating reintegration. Furthermore, by focusing on the restorative justice-based efforts of the schools such as the recognition of the importance of peers in reintegrating youth back into the school community, these approaches may further insulate the adolescents that may only be "acting out" from continuing down the spiraling path toward delinquency and crime.

NOTES

1. Colorado Department of Education. Safety and Discipline Indicator Reports, 2000–2001 school year to 2004–2005.
2. Denver Public Schools, 2003–2004. DPA Suspension Types Categorized by CDE Types.

REFERENCES

Baker, M. (2007). *Restorative justice disciplinary program report 2006–2007*. Report submitted to the Denver Public School System on September 20, 2007, by Outcomes, Inc., of Denver, Colorado.

Bazemore, G. (1992). On mission statements and reform in juvenile justice: The case of the "balanced approach". *Federal Probation, 56*, 64–70.

Bazemore, G. (2001). Young people, trouble, and crime: Restorative justice as a normative theory of informal social control and social support. *Youth and Society, 33*(2), 199–226.

Bazemore, G. (2005). Whom and how do we reintegrate? Finding community in restorative justice. *Criminology and Public Policy, 4*, 901–918.

Bazemore, G., & Schiff, M. (2004). Paradigm muddle or paradigm paralysis? The wide and narrow roads to restorative justice reform. *Contemporary Justice Review, 7*, 37–57.

Bazemore, G., & Umbreit, M. (2001). *A comparison of four restorative conferencing models*. Washington, DC: U.S. Department of Justice, Office of Juvenile Justice and Delinquency Prevention.

Bonta, J., Wallace-Capretta, S., Rooney, J., & McAnoy, K. (2002). An outcome evaluation of a restorative justice alternative to incarceration. *Contemporary Justice Review, 5*, 319–338.

Braithwaite, J. (1989). *Crime, shame, and reintegration*. Cambridge, UK: Cambridge University Press.

Braithwaite, J. (2002). *Restorative justice and responsive regulation*. New York: Oxford University Press.

Clear, T., & Karp, D. (1999). *The community justice ideal*. Boulder, CO: Westview Press.

Clear, T., & Karp, D. (2000). Toward the ideal of community justice. *National Institute of Justice Journal*, 21–27. Office of Justice Programs, U.S. Department of Justice.

Coates, R. B., Umbreit, M., & Vos, B. (2003). Restorative justice circles: An exploratory study. *Contemporary Justice Review, 6*(3), 265–278.

De Bues, K., & Rodriguez, N. (2007). Restorative justice practice: An examination of program completion and recidivism. *Journal of Criminal Justice, 35*, 337–347.

Dorne, C. K. (2008). *Restorative justice in the United States.* Upper Saddle River, New Jersey: Prentice Hall.

Drewery, W. (2004). Conferencing in schools: Punishment, restorative justice, and the productive importance of the process of conversation. *Journal of Community and Applied Social Psychology, 14*, 332–344.

Forgays, D. K., & DeMilio, L. (2005). Is teen court effective for repeat offenders? A test of the restorative justice approach. *International Journal of Offender Therapy and Comparative Criminology, 49*, 107–118.

Harris, M. (2004). An expansive and transformative view of restorative justice. *Contemporary Justice Review, 7*, 117–141.

Hayes, H., & Daly, K. (2003). Youth justice conferencing and reoffending. *Justice Quarterly, 20*, 725–760.

Hayes, H., & Daly, K. (2004). Conferencing and re-offending in Queensland. *Australian and New Zealand Journal of Criminology, 37*, 167–191.

Johnstone, G. (2002). *Restorative justice: Ideas, values, debates.* Portland, OR: Willan.

Karp, D. (2001). Harm and repair: Observing restorative justice in Vermont. *Justice Quarterly, 18*, 727–757.

Karp, D. (2004). Birds of a feather: A response to the McCold critique of community justice. *Contemporary Justice Review, 7*, 59–67.

Karp, D. R., & Breslin, B. (2001). Restorative justice in school communities. *Youth and Society, 33*, 249–272.

Latimer, J., Dowden, C., & Muise, D. (2001). *The effectiveness of restorative justice practices: A meta-analysis.* Ottawa, Ontario: Department of Justice, Research and Statistics Division.

Lipsey, M. W., & Derzon, J. H. (1998). Predictors of violent and serious delinquency in adolescence and early adulthood: A synthesis of longitudinal research. In: R. Loeber & D. P. Farrington (Eds), *Serious and violent juvenile offenders: Risk factors and successful interventions* (pp. 86–105). Thousand Oaks, CA: Sage.

McCold, P. (2004). Paradigm muddle: The threat to restorative justice posed by its merger with community justice. *Contemporary Justice Review, 7*, 13–35.

McGarrell, E. (2001). *Restorative justice conferences as an early response to young offenders.* Washington, DC: U.S. Department of Justice, Office of Juvenile Justice and Delinquency Prevention.

McNeely, C. A., Nonnemaker, J. M., & Blum, R. W. (2002). Promoting school connectedness: Evidence from the national longitudinal study of adolescent health. *Journal of School Health, 72*, 138–146.

Miers, D., Maguire, M., Goldie, S., Sharpe, K., Hale, C., Netten, A., Uglow, S., Doolin, K., Hallam, A., Enterkin, J., & Newburn, T. (2001). *An exploratory evaluation of restorative justice schemes.* Available at http://www.homeoffice.gov.uk/rds/prgpdfs/crrs09.pdf.

Morris, A. (2002). Critiquing the critics: A brief response to critics of restorative justice. *British Journal of Criminology, 42*, 596–615.

Presser, L., & Van Voorhis, P. (2002). Values and evaluations: Assessing processes and outcomes of restorative justice programs. *Crime and Delinquency, 48*, 162–188.

Resnick, M. D., Ireland, M., & Borowsky, I. (2004). Youth violence perpetration: What protects? What predicts? Findings from the National Longitudinal Study of Adolescent Health. *Journal of Adolescent Health, 35*(424), e1–e10.

Roach, K. (2006). The institutionalization of restorative justice in Canada: Effective reform or limited and limiting add-on? In: I. Aertsen, T. Daems & L. Robert (Eds), *Institutionalizing restorative justice* (pp. 167–193). Portland, OR: Willan.

Rodriguez, N. (2005). Restorative justice, communities, and delinquency: Who do we reintegrate? *Criminology and Public Policy, 4*, 601–629.

Skiba, R., & Peterson, R. (1999). Zap zero tolerance. *Education Digest, 64*, 24–31.

Stinchcomb, J. B., Bazemore, G., & Riestenberg, N. (2006). Beyond zero tolerance: Restoring justice in secondary schools. *Youth Violence and Juvenile Justice, 4*, 123–147.

Strang, H. (2004). The threat to restorative justice posed by the merger of community justice: A paradigm muddle. *Contemporary Justice Review, 7*, 75–79.

Umbreit, M., Coates, R., & Vos, B. (2001). The impact of victim offender mediation: Two decades of research. *Federal Probation, 65*, 99–112.

Zehr, H. (2002). *The little book of restorative justice*. Intecourse, PA: Good Books.

RESTORATIVE JUSTICE AND YOUTH COURTS: A NEW APPROACH TO DELINQUENCY PREVENTION

Holly Ventura Miller

ABSTRACT

This study presents findings from the South Carolina Youth Court Initiative, a statewide community corrections approach to delinquency prevention. The national youth court movement, its restorative justice theoretical underpinnings, and a brief history of youth courts in South Carolina are reviewed as a context for the present study. A mixed-methodological design utilizing a survey, costs–benefits analysis, site visits, and interviewing was employed to analyze the entire study population (N = 21). Findings are presented which call into question the value of youth court performance in terms of effectiveness and expenditure.

As juvenile correctional populations have increased considerably (Puzzanchera, Stahl, Finnegan, Tierney, & Snyder, 2004), so too has the need for developing viable alternatives to incarceration. Diversion from confinement is a common

Restorative Justice: From Theory to Practice
Sociology of Crime, Law and Deviance, Volume 11, 189–205
Copyright © 2008 by Emerald Group Publishing Limited
All rights of reproduction in any form reserved
ISSN: 1521-6136/doi:10.1016/S1521-6136(08)00408-9

objective of both the criminal and juvenile justice systems, reflected in the plethora of probationary and intermediate sanction programming popular today (MacKenzie, 2000; Petersilia, Lurigio, & Byrne, 1992; Petersilia & Turner, 1993; Tonry, 1998). Youth court, also referred to as teen or peer court, is one leading diversionary programmatic approach representing two general justice system movements – the proliferation of specialty courts to enhance individualized treatment and community-based corrections. Specialty courts emerged and quickly grew in popularity during the late 1980s and early 1990s, first limiting jurisdiction to non-violent drug offenders. Since that time, programs have grown in number and scope to include not only drug courts but also domestic violence and alternative juvenile courts.

Within the juvenile justice system, the emergence of youth court programs across the nation has quickly become a viable alternative to traditional family court-based adjudication and disposition of juvenile delinquency cases (Bazemore & Schiff, 2005; Bush, 2002; Crawford & Newburn, 2002; Pearson & Jurich, 2005). Similar to family court, youth courts remain grounded in *parens patriae* wherein the court acts in the best interests of juveniles. Best interests are determined according to multiple factors specific to offenders and their offenses and, within youth courts, pursued through various models of justice.

In general, youth court programs involve proceedings wherein young people are sentenced by their peers in, typically, either a school or courthouse setting with the cooperation of state agencies such as departments of education and juvenile justice. Nationally, youth court programs have grown by more than 1000% during the last decade to a total of 1,035 programs that are now operative in all but two states (National Youth Court Center (NYCC), 2002; Pearson & Jurich, 2005). The widespread development and implementation of youth courts is, itself, a national justice system movement fueled by the emergence of additional programs at a steady pace.

Not only are youth courts viewed as a viable diversionary program for first time and minor offenders, they also promise a fiscally conservative alternative to the traditional family court process (Hissong, 1991; Miller, Shutt, & Ventura, 2005; Zehner, 1997). Youth courts typically operate with the assistance of school and community volunteers thus allowing for relatively low operating budgets. Claims of efficiency and effectiveness by proponents of the youth court movement have facilitated their development around the nation, however, very few evaluations have been conducted assessing relative impact (see, e.g., Hissong, 1991; Zehner, 1997). This chapter describes an evaluation of all youth courts ($N = 21$) operating within South Carolina and presents findings related to program effectiveness as compared to family court.

BACKGROUND

Fundamental Youth Court Concepts

Although youth courts have received increased attention in the previous decade, some programs have been operational for over 30 years. A recent national evaluation of active programs indicated the earliest youth court appeared in Illinois in 1972 and nearly half of all programs (47%) have been operational for at least six years (Pearson & Jurich, 2005). Youth courts have evolved considerably in the previous three decades, although all share common features and core assumptions.

One of the fundamental concepts guiding the youth court process is the symbolic and actual authority given to youth. Although youth courts assume different structural and operational models, a common theme is *youth authority.* The youth represent and assume the role of contributing actors in the courtroom process including: judge, clerk of the court, bailiff, prosecutor, defense attorney, and jurors. The authority is exercised under strict adult supervision, but is nonetheless real in that youth forge actual sanctions. Through direct participation youth learn to accept responsibility and how to effectively manage and control authority. The utilization of youth authority facilitates multiple goals: (1) civic awareness through familiarization and participation in legal process, (2) peer justice with reintegrative shaming effects that constitute both accountability and deterrence, and (3) pro-social bonding through victim restitution and community involvement.

The concept of peer justice, then, is a driving principle underlying of youth court theory. Grounded in the logic and empirical saliency of *peer-norming,* the foremost assumption is that delinquent youth typically have an aversion toward adult authority and adult delivered dispositions. Youth-directed court proceedings feature assessment and judging of cases by peers, reiterating the belief that offenders will be more remorseful and inclined to desist from further delinquency when faced with negative labeling by peers (Bazemore & Schiff, 2005; Braithwaite, 1989; Braithwaite & Mugford, 1994).

Restorative justice (Braithwaite, 1999, 2002; Johnstone, 2002; Strang & Braithwaite, 2001), a relatively new philosophy impacting crime and delinquency practices perhaps more so than any rival perspective, is founded on four core principles that focus on repairing harm and rebuilding relationships damaged from criminal or delinquent behavior. Restorative justice practices seek to: (1) enable offenders to understand the harm and consequences of their action, (2) build and increase offender competencies, (3) provide victims an opportunity to voice concerns, and (4) emphasize that victims, offenders, and the community are all mutually interested stakeholders in the justice process (Godwin, 2001; Office of Juvenile Justice and Delinquency Prevention (OJJDP), 1998, 2004). Primarily based on Braithwaite's reintegrative shaming (1989), which contends societies better capable of exerting informal control will also be those experiencing lower rates of crime and delinquency, youth court offenders face constructive disapproval of their actions. Through positively oriented sanctioning tailored toward bringing a person back into the mainstream, it is contended that the community can reestablish severed social bonds and deter future offenses.

Law-Related Education (LRE) is another prominent youth court concept, first introduced by the Law-Related Education Act of 1978 which provided resources enabling students to acquire knowledge and skills pertaining to the guiding principles and processes of the law, the legal process, and the legal system. Drawing from this focal curriculum, LRE has become an integral course of study providing students with a variety of opportunities, including participation in youth court, to learn about abstract legal concepts and their function in a pluralistic, democratic society governed by the rule of law.

Youth court participants typically volunteer for participation in law-related educational seminars which serve the dual purposes of training youth to adequately conduct the youth court and provide exposure and empowerment through democratic voice in the justice process. LRE also fosters community cohesion. The youth court programs strive to provide a well-structured program environment that encourages community and court interaction through promoting volunteerism among both youth and adults to generate respect and appreciation for the community and the legal system, which, in effect, enhances social bonding. The degree of appreciation within the community is expressed in terms of volunteerism, which is vital for role modeling and, especially, operational costs. In fact, a key concept behind the creation of youth courts is cost benefit compared to traditional family court. Youth courts depend heavily on both youth and adult volunteerism, which particularly lowers personnel expenditures. Youth courts have the prospects of significantly reducing family court caseloads by handling a substantial number of offenders at relatively little cost to the community and offer long-term benefits by way of lessened costs associated with future offenses.

Youth Court Models

The youth court process, in theory, is intended to operate along the general lines of traditional family court. Defendants undergo an initial intake process that includes a formal interview with an adult program worker that frequently requires parental attendance. The youth court process is explained and both voluntary and confidential participation emphasized. Adults are responsible for an assortment of tasks and managerial functions including fundraising, staffing, budgeting, and supervising proceedings, whereas youth involvement varies in accordance to the four basic youth court models: (1) youth judge, (2) adult judge, (3) youth tribunal, and (4) peer jury.

The youth tribunal model is fundamentally similar to both the youth and adult judge models in that youth perform the duties of the clerk, bailiff, and attorneys, but the main difference is that this model removes jury involvement. A presiding youth judge and a panel of usually two other youth judges deliberate and decide relevant dispositions. In South Carolina, the youth judge and youth tribunal models are most utilized.

The peer jury model is relatively distinct and is the most participatory of the models. Because this format enables facilitation of multiple youth court objectives, in both number of participants and level of involvement, it is a frequently utilized youth court approach, more so nationally than in South Carolina. The proceedings in this model are absent of bailiffs, judges, or attorney representation. Instead, there is one presiding juror and a panel of jury members that directly question the defendant, parents, and witnesses and then determine an acceptable disposition. Recent youth courts using this model have begun to include community and defense advocates for making opening and closing arguments and ensure the fairness of the proceedings. Peer jury models can be particularly useful for offender reintegration in that youth may be invited or instructed to participate in future court sessions as jury members.

Youth Courts in South Carolina

The youth court movement in South Carolina emerged from a forged partnership between the South Carolina State Department of Education's *Project CHANCE* and the South Carolina State Bar's *Law Related Education*

(LRE). Project CHANCE is a truancy abatement and delinquency prevention initiative. It primarily focuses on youth development and skill enhancement in its six core elements: Character, Honor, Accountability, Nobility, Commitment, and Education. Project CHANCE originates from the conception that youthful offenders are less likely to commit more offenses when judged delinquent by their peers. This philosophy is derived from the extant literature praising the process known as "peer-reinforced norming."

The Law-Related Education Act of 1978 was endorsed with the intention of providing students with knowledge and skills pertaining to the guiding principles of legal process and the legal system. Drawing from this focal curriculum, LRE in South Carolina provides students with a variety of opportunities to learn about abstract legal concepts and issues including citizenship, governmental history, and their function in a multi-faceted society. Each year all members of South Carolina's Youth Court Association are invited to biannual training seminars conducted by the SC Bar's LRE division.

Youth court programs throughout the state are funded at the local, state, and federal level. While Project CHANCE and LRE characterize the brief history of South Carolina's youth court movement, the various programs differ and do not necessarily emphasize a uniform strategic approach to delinquency and related social problems. The Mt. Pleasant Youth Court Program in Charleston County is the oldest in the state and dates to 1995, followed by highly individualized others until the South Carolina's Department of Education-funded Project CHANCE initiative more than doubled the state's operative youth court programs to the current total of 21.

Despite the recent hype surrounding the movement, few comprehensive evaluations of youth court programs currently exist. Reichel and Seyfrit (1984), in one of the earliest assessments of youth courts, found that offenders, volunteers, and parents reported positive experiences with a Georgia teen court program. Other studies examining effectiveness outcomes suggest that that youth courts, compared to traditional adjudication, may reduce recidivism while improving sentence completion rates (Forgays & DiMilio, 2005; Harrison, Maupin, & Mays, 2001; Hissong, 1991; Rothstein, 1987; Minor, Wells, Soderstrom, Bingham, & Williamson, 1999; Shiff & Wexler, 1996; Zehner, 1997). A recent inventory of the nation's youth courts conducted by the American Youth Policy Forum (Pearson & Jurich, 2005) revealed an 89% sanction completion rate although the study failed to address offender recidivism.

METHODOLOGY

Evaluation Strategy

Evaluation of the South Carolina Youth Courts utilized a mixed-methodological approach in order to ascertain an accurate measure of both court effectiveness and efficiency relative to the traditional family court process. Both quantitative and qualitative research methods were employed in assessing the relative value and success of the youth court process. Following the initial acquisition of quantitative information for each of the youth courts during the first six months of the project, site visits were conducted in order to supplement and validate existing data. This qualitative element of the evaluation process allowed for internal validity checks in terms of confirmation and clarification of survey responses.

An informational letter and survey instrument was constructed and mailed to all active youth courts in the state ($N = 21$). Youth court coordinators were asked to complete the questionnaire and return it to the research team. Structured in four sections, the questionnaire inquired about descriptive characteristics of the courts, case information, performance indicators, and cost benefits.

Information solicited through the survey questionnaire included the location of the youth court program (school versus courthouse), the youth court model (adult judge, youth judge, youth tribunal, or peer jury), offense adjudication (time from offense to hearing) and disposition (sanction) length, the type and length of training provided for youth court members, and the demographics of youth court participants, both volunteers and respondents. Part II of the survey inquired as to how many cases the court heard during the past year, the number of cases referred by offense category, the sanctions given by the court, the use of mediation in proceedings, and the utilization of LRE. The aggregate recidivism rate of the court along with the percentage of sanctions completed served as performance indicators and cost benefit measures included the total budget expenditures and expenditures per program participant.

In addition to the questionnaires, the research team undertook site visits of each of the participating courts. During these visits, in-depth interviews lasting approximately 1 h were conducted with youth court coordinators and any other relevant staff available for questioning. In some cases, youth court student volunteers were available for focus group interviews consisting of three or more individuals. Further, direct observation of the actual youth court proceedings was utilized whenever possible. The inclusion of these

qualitative research techniques allowed for a more comprehensive evaluation of both the youth court process and measures of program outcome
success. The in-depth interviews conducted during the visits offered a "hands-
on" account of the operational effectiveness of the courts and allowed for
coordinators and support staff to identify areas for improvement.

The site visits also served the invaluable function of ensuring the validity
of reported quantitative data. Not only was the research team able to verify
and confirm responses given by coordinators, the interviews allowed the
validation of such information. Additionally, the visits allowed the
researchers to properly ascertain any information missing from the survey
questionnaires. Moreover, questions regarding the application of restorative
justice principles to the youth court implementation and process were posed
to coordinators and participants at this time.

In-depth interviews followed a systematic interview questionnaire, or a
youth court "profile sheet" containing additional questions for coordinators. Data solicited from coordinators included the specific location of
proceedings, the frequency of proceeding in terms of meeting days and
times, the sanctioning authority of the youth court, the funding source, the
number of cases since inception, and the inception date. Respondents were
also asked if they were familiar with restorative justice and if they believed
the theory's principles were achieved through the youth court process. The
interviews also allowed both staff and participants to identify any flaws with
the process or issues that had risen over the duration of the court.

Whenever possible, the research team utilized direct observation of
youth court proceedings. Although this was not uniform throughout the
evaluation due to scheduling conflicts, a concerted effort was made to gather
as much data as possible during observation sessions. During this time
research team members witnessed youth court hearings and recorded
detailed field notes describing the process. Observations made served as a
qualitative supplement to the quantitative measures of program success
derived from the survey questionnaire.

Variables

On the basis of data collected through both the survey and the youth court
site visit profile sheet, 18 variables were operationalized. Two outcome
measures were constructed to ascertain program effectiveness. *Accountability* indicates the percentage of sentences disposed that had been
successfully completed by youth court respondents and is a measure of

the accountability of respondents. *Recidivism* represents the aggregate percentage of re-offense by program respondents. Regression models were estimated for each of the outcome measures.

Independent variables included categorical measurements of *youth court site* (school versus courthouse), *youth court model*[1] (adult judge, youth judge/tribunal, peer jury), and *sanctioning authority* (school versus solicitor). Additional measures of *adjudication celerity* (average number of days from offense to adjudication), *disposition severity* (average length in days of disposition length), *respondent age* (average age of offenders), *budget expenditures* (total dollar amount of youth court budget), *cases since inception* (total number of cases heard since youth court inception), *cases in past year* (total number of cases heard during the past year), and *volunteer training* (total number of days for volunteer training) were included in model estimation.

The models also controlled for *respondent gender* (percent male), *volunteer gender* (percent male), *respondent race* (percent non-white), and *volunteer race* (percent non-white). Three-point ordinal severity scales were developed for *offense severity* (types of offenses adjudicated) and *sanction severity* (types of dispositions). Both scales ranked offenses and sanctions according to a minor, moderate, or severe score. Minor offenses included possession of tobacco, ID card violation, disrespectful behavior, traffic violations, and inappropriate behavior; moderate offenses included disorderly conduct, vandalism, and excessive tardiness; theft, minor or simple assault, possession of marijuana, alcohol offense, and disturbing schools constituted the severe offense category. Minor sanctions were victim apology and written essay; youth court jury duty and community service comprised the moderate sanction category; severe sanctions included restitution, mandatory treatment (e.g., drug/alcohol classes, anger management classes), and temporary lock-up in a correctional facility.

Analyses

Crosstabulations using Pearson chi-square tests of statistical significance were calculated for several sets of variables in order to assess possible relationships between individual measures. Chi-square tests were computed for *youth court model* and *sanction severity* as a means of determining a relationship between the type of youth court model (adult judge, youth judge or tribunal, peer jury) and severity of sanctions imposed, *youth court model* and *offense severity* to determine the existence of a similar relationship between the model and offenses adjudicated (minor, moderate, severe), and *offense* and *sanction severity*. Analyses utilized ordinary least squares (OLS) regression to determine the relative effects of independent variables upon outcome measures of recidivism and accountability. Two models were estimated (one for each of the dependent variables) which included all independent variables constructed.[2]

Additionally, a third OLS model was developed which censored the data set and computed the effects of youth court model, adjudication celerity, disposition severity, accountability (sanctions completed), volunteer training, and cases since inception on recidivism. Data censoring entails omitting certain cases whose values are grossly above or below the sample mean on several measures. In this instance, the youth court at Ridge View High School in Columbia had seen an overwhelming number of cases since inception (approximately 5,000) and had an unusually high recidivism rate (approximately 33%). This was due to the logistics of the youth court and the nature of the cases heard which deviated significantly from the norm. Model 3 was also estimated in order to test the effects of *implementation-specific* concepts which may reveal more about the value of youth courts in terms of reducing recidivism.

FINDINGS

Univariate statistics (see Table 1) and frequency distributions offered a description of the 21 youth courts comprising the population. One-third (33.3%) of all youth courts held proceedings at a school, while 57.1% were located in an actual courthouse. Only two youth courts did not fit either classification, instead located in county community centers. Adult judge models accounted for 28.6% of all youth courts surveyed, while youth judge or tribunal (47.6%) and peer jury (23.8%) comprised the remaining court models. Of all youth courts 81% received sanctioning authority from the county solicitor, the remaining 19% was derived from the school within which the court operated.

Approximately two-thirds (66.7%) of all courts had adjudication periods of one month or less, with an average length of 43.7 days. Disposition lengths ranged from 1 to 365 days, with an average of 60 days and a median score of 30 days. In terms of offense severity, an overwhelming majority (85.7%) of youth courts heard severe offenses, while 57.1% mandated punishments which ranked as "severe" according to the three-point ordinal

Table 1. Descriptive Statistics ($N = 21$).

	Mean	Median	Mode	SD	Variance	Range
Youth court site	1.76	2.00	2.00	.62	.39	2.00
Youth court model	1.95	2.00	2.00	.74	.55	2.00
Volunteer training	11.20	5.00	5.00	14.70	216.17	59.00
Adjudication celerity	43.76	14.00	14.00	71.54	5177.29	314.50
Disposition severity	59.99	30.00	30.00	75.72	5734.27	364.00
Respondent age	14.57	14.50	14.00	1.16	1.16	4.00
Respondent gender	56.48	50.00	50.00	20.57	423.18	67.00
Volunteer gender	43.52	41.37	30.00	23.52	553.29	95.00
Respondent race	62.58	65.00	100.00	30.46	927.74	100.00
Volunteer race	58.69	60.00	70.00	29.04	843.10	100.00
Cases in past year	81.95	24.00	2.00	201.10	40404.65	938.00
Offense severity	2.81	3.00	3.00	.51	.26	2.00
Sanction severity	2.57	3.00	3.00	.51	.26	1.00
Accountability	89.78	96.00	100.00	18.34	336.46	72.00
Budget expenditures	22262.00	18000.00	18000.00	28886.49	834429084.00	111111.00
Sanctioning authority	1.81	2.00	2.00	.40	.16	1.00
Cases since inception	336.29	72.00	8.00	1075.13	1155898.31	4998.00
Recidivism	5.50	3.00	.00	7.68	58.94	33.00

scale. The majority of youth courts (81.1%) also reported a completed sanctions rate of 90% or greater, with an average completion rate of 89.8%.

South Carolina's youth courts heard an average of 90 cases in the past year, and an average of 336 since inception. Cases heard in the past year ranged from a low of 2 to a high of 940.[3] In terms of youth court volunteer training, most programs (75%) required less than 10 days of training, with a range from 1 to 60 days. Youth courts that required more than 10 days of training were typically those housed in schools wherein the youth court was actually a component of the elective curriculum (i.e., students were allowed to take "Youth Court" as a course).

Budget expenditures varied greatly over the sample, as many courts were funded by "Project CHANCE" while others were a component of much larger funding streams, such as "Weed and Seed." Of youth courts 28.6% reported funding from Project CHANCE in the amount of $18,000, while the vast majority (85.7%) indicated funding levels below $30,000 annually. One youth court (Ridge View High School) reported an annual operating budget of $0.

South Carolina youth courts reported an average recidivism rate of 5.5%, well below the state and national averages for traditional family courts. South Carolina Department of Juvenile Justice (DJJ) (2005) has calculated

Table 2.   Results of Chi-Square Analysis.

Variable	χ^2
Youth court model by sanction severity	5.075*
Youth court model by offense severity	4.900
Sanction severity by offense severity	4.667*

*$p<.10$.

recidivism rates for previously incarcerated juveniles at 46.6% after 12 months and 68.1% after 24 months. Rates for the 21 courts ranged from 0% (no recidivism) to 33% (one out of every three respondents re-offended). Recidivism was calculated as an aggregate measure for each youth court and represents the overall rate of re-offense by youth court respondents. Recidivism measures were not uniform in terms of follow-up periods, specifically, not all youth courts have identical inception dates. Thus, while some courts reported recidivism trends for a year or longer, others had only recently begun to hear cases and could only report re-offense for a relatively short period of time. Moreover, several youth courts failed to adequately follow-up on cases after the end of the disposition period rendering the validity of their estimations questionable.

Results from chi-square tests (see Table 2 for all chi-square results) indicated a marginally significant relationship between youth court model and sanctions given ($p<.10$). Youth judge and youth tribunal models were more likely to impose severe sanctions than were adult judges or peer juries. However, no relationship existed between youth court model and offenses adjudicated. Chi-square tests were also employed to discern the relationship between offense severity and sanction severity. Theoretically, those youth courts hearing the most severe infractions will similarly be those who met out the harshest sentences. Findings suggest that such a relationship does in fact exist at a marginally statistically significant level ($p<.10$).

Two OLS models revealed the effects of all independent variables on sanctions completed (accountability) and recidivism, and a third implementation-specific model which estimated the influence of several selected independent variables on the outcome measure of recidivism. Results from the two models that included all predictor variables were inconclusive, with findings indicating no significant relationship between independent variables and outcomes measures (Tables 3 and 4). Only *cases since inception* exerted a significant, positive effect on recidivism ($\beta = .880$, $p<.05$) suggesting that youth courts that had been in operation for longer periods of time tended to

Table 3. Model 1 OLS Regression (y = accountability).

	β	SE	t
Youth court site	.188	16.144	.340
Youth court model	.384	11.887	.830
Volunteer training	.094	1.124	.106
Adjudication celerity	.612	.380	.852
Disposition severity	−.897	.675	−.829
Respondent age	1.168	12.967	1.431
Respondent gender	−.192	.571	−.321
Volunteer gender	−.549	.792	−.642
Respondent race	1.867	.629	1.903
Volunteer race	−1.018	.482	−1.492
Offense severity	−1.269	34.061	−1.329
Sanction severity	.339	18.723	.663
Budget expenditures	.357	.000	.690
Sanctioning authority	.888	46.505	.877
Cases since inception	−.551	.007	−1.330
N	21		
d.f.	19		
Adjusted R^2	−.312		

Table 4. Model 2 OLS Regression (y = recidivism).

	β	SE	t
Youth court site	.317	3.488	1.088
Youth court model	−.363	2.710	−1.396
Volunteer training	.341	.237	.738
Adjudication celerity	−.401	.087	−.986
Disposition severity	.591	.154	.970
Respondent age	.032	3.357	.061
Respondent gender	.027	.122	.086
Volunteer gender	−.311	.175	−.667
Respondent race	.050	.183	.071
Volunteer race	−.099	.127	−.225
Offense severity	.213	8.612	.357
Sanction severity	−.160	4.153	−.571
Budget expenditures	−.258	.000	−.906
Sanctioning authority	−.461	10.587	−.801
Cases since inception	.880*	.002	3.401
Accountability	.066	.105	.253
N	21		
d.f.	19		
Adjusted R^2	.645		

*$p < .05$.

Table 5. Model 3 OLS Regression Censored Sample (y = recidivism).

	β	SE	t
Youth court model	-.546*	1.309	-2.131
Volunteer training	.066	.068	.250
Adjudication celerity	-.111	.040	-.295
Disposition severity	-.020	.053	-.049
Cases since inception	.014	.008	.053
Accountability	.032	.059	.124
N	20		
d.f.	18		
Adjusted R^2	-.066		

*p = .05.

report higher average recidivism rates. Findings offered by the evaluation's qualitative dimension indicate that this may be the result of better follow-up practices among older youth courts and not necessarily indicative of a negative outcome.

Model 3 (Table 5) utilized a censored data set eliminating values from Ridge View High School. As mentioned above, data reported by Ridge View High School skewed the sample and thus rendered findings that may not have been representative of actual effects. Model 3 also attempted to isolate factors related to implementation and the logistics of the youth court. Results suggest only use of the peer jury model (as compared to either an adult judge or youth judge/tribunal model) exerted a statistically significant effect on recidivism ($\beta = -.546, p = .05$). Additionally, this model produced an adjusted R^2 of -.066, accounting for only 6.6% of variance in the dependent variable.

CONCLUSIONS

The current study evaluated South Carolina's youth courts ($N = 21$) in order to establish the relative worth and success of the program comparative to traditional family court adjudication. Courts were assessed using a mixed-methodological approach involving survey research, interviewing, and direct observation of the youth court process. Data were collected to ascertain levels of recidivism and accountability and to identify factors associated with favorable outcomes (i.e., low recidivism and high accountability).

Unfortunately, findings drawn from quantitative analyses were inconclusive. None of the variables identified exerted a significant effect on accountability while cases since inception served as the sole significant influence on recidivism. We hypothesized courts existing for longer periods of time would have lower recidivism as well as greater accountability, however, the opposite effect was found. Older courts, in fact, experienced significantly higher rates of recidivism than newer courts, although this may be attributable to more thorough follow-up of offenders. Interviews and observation conducted did suggest that older courts exhibited greater professionalism in terms of staff training and record keeping. Thus, responses provided by older courts, particularly regarding recidivism, may be more accurate (i.e., a result of under-reporting by newer courts).

Results from the third regression model, which incorporated only implementation-specific variables, indicate courts utilizing a peer jury model (compared to adult judge or youth judge/tribunal models) experience significantly lower rates of recidivism ($p = .05$). It is unclear at this juncture *what* it is about the peer jury model that lends itself to lower recidivism, although we suspect greater offender reintegration may be the key element. Peer juries tend to incorporate youth court service as a component of sanctioning (i.e., offenders are assigned to youth court duty) thereby mandating participation in the justice process. Theoretically, youth who view themselves as part of the process will most likely view sanctioning as fair and thus less likely to reoffend.

Although this evaluation failed to provide strong empirical support either for or against youth courts, findings did suggest a more fiscally conservative approach to delinquency disposition compared to traditional family court adjudication. While youth courts do feature slightly better recidivism outcomes for low-level delinquency, their value is clearer in terms of efficiency. In effect, youth courts offer slightly better deterrence for significantly less expenditure.

Theoretically speaking, youth courts serve as natural application for testing both reintegrative shaming and restorative justice. Future research and evaluation should operate within this theoretical framework, although researchers should be careful in making sweeping generalizations and assumptions about the roles reintegration and restoration play in achieving deterrence. All too often the specific components of these approaches are ignored as traditional outcome indicators, including recidivism, are reported as proxies for complicated ideas such as reintegration or restoration. We emphasize the need for mixed-methodologies when examining realization of complex concepts like restorative justice and reintegrative shaming.

204   HOLLY VENTURA MILLER

Although not adequately addressed in quantitative analyses, program implementation clearly impacts the success of individual youth courts. Based on findings from the qualitative dimension of the evaluation, we found the implementation intensity of key youth court concepts, particularly restorative justice principles, may provide a more useful basis upon which to evaluate programs. Specifically, variability in youth court outcomes may be the result of how well programs implements key features of the theoretical framework, rather than previously identified factors, such as court or offender characteristics. The validity of restorative justice and/or reintegrative shaming should not be overstated without thorough examination of the intensity and integrity of implementation intensity.

NOTES

1. The youth judge and youth tribunal models were collapsed into one category due to limited number of tribunal models.
2. Cases in the past year were omitted from the models due to an almost perfect correlation between this variables and cases since inception ($r = .96$).
3. This high score of 940 was attributable to Ridge View High School and not representative of a normal number of cases heard by a youth court.

REFERENCES

Bazemore, G., & Schiff, M. (2005). *Juvenile justice reform and restorative justice: Building theory and policy from practice*. Portland, OR: Willan Publishing.
Braithwaite, J. (1989). *Crime, shame, and reintegration*. Cambridge, UK: Cambridge University Press.
Braithwaite, J. (1999). Restorative justice: Assessing optimistic and pessimistic accounts. In: M. Tonry (Ed.), *Crime and justice, a review of research* (25, pp. 1–127). Chicago: University of Chicago Press.
Braithwaite, J. (2002). *Restorative justice and responsive regulation*. New York: Oxford University Press.
Braithwaite, J., & Mugford, S. (1994). Conditions of successful reintegration ceremonies: Dealing with juvenile offenders. *British Journal of Criminology, 34*(2), 139–171.
Bush, D. (2002). Findings from the OJJDP evaluation of teen courts to be released at national youth court conference. *Newsletter of the National Youth Court Center, 2*(2), 1–8.
Crawford, A., & Newburn, T. (2002). Recent developments in restorative justice for young people in England and Wales. *British Journal of Criminology, 42*, 476–495.
Forgays, D. K., & DiMilio, L. (2005). Is teen court effective for repeat offenders? A test of the restorative justice approach. *International Journal of Offender Therapy and Comparative Criminology, 49*(1), 107–118.

Godwin, T. M. (2001). Restorative justice and teen courts: Where should programs start? *The Newsletter of the National Youth Court Center, 1*(1), 1–8.

Harrison, P., Maupin, J. R., & Mays, L. G. (2001). Teen court: An examination of processes and outcomes. *Crime and Delinquency, 47*(2), 243–264.

Hissong, R. (1991). Teen court: Is it an effective alternative to traditional sanctions? *Journal for Juvenile Justice and Detention Services, 6*, 14–23.

Johnstone, G. (2002). *Restorative justice: Ideas, values, debates.* Portland, OR: Willan Publishing.

MacKenzie, D. L. (2000). Evidence-based corrections: Identifying what works. *Crime and Delinquency, 46*(4), 457–472.

Miller, J. M., Shutt, J. E., & Ventura, H. E. (2005). *Addressing delinquency through restorative justice and law related education: An evaluation of youth courts in South Carolina.* Columbia, SC: SC Bar.

Minor, K. I., Wells, J. B., Soderstrom, I. R., Bingham, R., & Williamson, D. (1999). Sentence completion and recidivism among juveniles referred to teen courts. *Crime and Delinquency, 45*(4), 467–480.

National Youth Court Center. (2002). Youth court stats. Available at www.youthcourt.net

Office of Juvenile Justice and Delinquency Prevention. (1998). *Guide for implementing the balanced and restorative justice model.* Washington, DC: Office of Juvenile Justice and Delinquency Prevention.

Office of Juvenile Justice and Delinquency Prevention. (2004). *The balanced and restorative justice project.* Washington, DC: Office of Juvenile Justice and Delinquency Prevention.

Pearson, S. S., & Jurich, S. (2005). *Youth court: A community solution for embracing crime.* Washington, DC: American Youth Policy Forum.

Petersilia, J., Lurigio, A. J., & Byrne, J. M. (1992). Introduction. In: J. M. Byrne, A. J. Lurigio & J. Petersilia (Eds), *Smart sentencing: The emergence of intermediate sanctions* (pp. ix–x). Newbury Park, CA: Sage.

Petersilia, J., & Turner, S. (1993). *Evaluating intensive supervision probation/parole: Results from a nationwide experiment.* Washington, DC: National Institute of Justice.

Puzzanchera, C., Stahl, A. L., Finnegan, T. A., Tierney, N., & Snyder, H. N. (2004). *Juvenile court statistics 2000.* Washington, DC: US Department of Justice, Office of Justice Programs, Office of Juvenile Justice and Delinquency Prevention.

Reichel, P., & Seyfrit, C. (1984). A peer jury in juvenile court. *Crime and Delinquency, 43*, 328–344.

Rothstein, R. (1987). Teen court: A way to combat teenage crime and chemical abuse. *Juvenile and Family Court Journal, 38*, 1–4.

Shiff, A. R., & Wexler, D. B. (1996). Teen court: A therapeutic jurisprudence perspective. *Criminal Law Bulletin, 32*, 342–357.

Strang, H., & Braithwaite, J. (Eds). (2001). *Restorative justice and civil society.* Cambridge, UK: Cambridge University Press.

Tonry, M. (1998). Intermediate sanctions in sentencing guidelines. In: M. Tonry (Ed.), *Crime and justice: A review of research* (Vol. 20, pp. 199–253). Chicago: University of Chicago Press.

Zehner, S. J. (1997). Teen court. *FBI Law Enforcement Bulletin, 66*(3), 1–7.

PART III:
NEW DIRECTIONS FOR
RESTORATIVE JUSTICE

POWER, PROFIT, AND PLURALISM: NEW AVENUES FOR RESEARCH ON RESTORATIVE JUSTICE AND WHITE-COLLAR CRIME

Nicole Leeper Piquero, Stephen K. Rice and
Alex R. Piquero

ABSTRACT

This chapter considers and highlights a different approach to dealing with the white-collar and/or corporate offender that departs from the more commonly used punitive approach utilized by the American criminal justice system. Currently, terms of incarceration for individual offenders and the use of hefty fines and strict regulations against organizational defendants are commonly used draconian punishments. Therefore, this article is designed to remind readers of another viable approach to dealing with white-collar and/or corporate crime, one which utilizes a compliance or cooperative strategy of social control; that is the use of a system of restorative justice.

Restorative Justice: From Theory to Practice
Sociology of Crime, Law and Deviance, Volume 11, 209–229
Copyright © 2008 by Emerald Group Publishing Limited
All rights of reproduction in any form reserved
ISSN: 1521-6136/doi:10.1016/S1521-6136(08)00409-0

INTRODUCTION

Historically, criminologists have been primarily concerned with street crimes, especially those sorts of violent crimes that generate fear and the risk of injury (e.g., assault and homicide). Thus, it should come as no surprise that the primary theoretical and empirical focus of criminologists has been on understanding and dealing primarily with street crimes. Because of this, much less is known regarding white-collar and corporate crime.[1] This is not to suggest, however, that scholars working in this area have not made advances to understand how the criminal justice system deals with and handles these "elite" offenders (see e.g., Benson & Cullen, 1998; Weisburd, Waring, & Chayet, 2001; Weisburd, Wheeler, Waring, & Bode, 1991) or on the etiology of such offending; but rather, much of what is known has mimicked or tracked more general forms of criminality despite the warnings from scholars working in the area that white-collar and street offenders are "drawn from distinctly different sectors of the American population" (Weisburd et al., 1991, p. 73).

Perhaps because of the tracking research agendas or the lack of empirical understanding on issues related to crimes of the elite, many policies and policy changes put into place for white-collar and corporate offenders follow from the more general criminological literature.[2] One such area is in sentencing policies. Since the late 1970s, the sentencing philosophy of the American criminal justice system has become more and more punitive with the ideals of rehabilitation giving way to the goals of deterrence and just desserts. This more punitive approach to sentencing has been enacted by tougher sentencing laws such as mandatory sentences and through the use of sentencing guidelines. White-collar and corporate crimes were not immune from this more punitive approach to sentencing but rather were held to the same standard as street offenses. In essence, the "get tough" approach was favored because of the lack of dropping (street) crime rates and an overall conclusion that "nothing works" in terms of offender rehabilitation programs (Martinson, 1974; Cullen, 2005). Whether this same punitive approach was necessary or relevant for "suite" crimes was never addressed or even asked. Rather, the assumption was made that the same tough approach was appropriate regardless of the offense type.

The purpose of this article is to consider and highlight a different approach to dealing with the white-collar and/or corporate offender that departs from the more commonly used punitive approach utilized by the American criminal justice system. Currently, terms of incarceration for individual offenders and the use of hefty fines and strict regulations against organizational defendants are commonly used draconian punishments. Therefore, this article is designed to remind readers of another viable approach to dealing with white-collar and/or corporate crime, one which utilizes a compliance or cooperative strategy of social control; that is the use of a system of restorative justice.

While the predominant method of social control utilized in the American criminal justice system relies upon an optimal penalty or deterrence approach, other forms of social control are available but much less utilized. Reiss (1984) outlined two of the many generic forms of social control: deterrence and compliance. The deterrence approach is a punitive model in which the wrong-doer is severely sanctioned so that future criminal behavior will be prevented, while the compliance approach is a preventive model in which would-be violators are enticed or rewarded for complying with the law (Reiss, 1984). While the two approaches may be thought of as opposing or contradictory (Grabosky, 1995), it is possible for the two to work together (see Scholz, 1984) such as the case with the federal sentencing guidelines (Nagel & Swenson, 1993). While the deterrence model appears to be the preferred approach with street crimes, cooperative, or compliant options are more commonly found within corporate regulation (Levi, 2002). Therefore, the time may have come where the study of "elite" offenders may help shed light onto the possibilities of other forms of social control which can be used for controlling general criminality.

The article proceeds with a review of the larger, more general restorative justice issue which is then followed by a specific discussion of reintegrative shaming which has become the premier example of "doing restorative justice." Then, focus turns to a review of the application of social control mechanisms applied to white-collar and corporate crimes. A series of potentially interesting theoretical and empirical research projects aimed at further developing and evaluating the application of restorative justice to white-collar crime are outlined. Finally, the article closes by highlighting the lessons learned from a cooperative control strategy of white-collar and corporate crime and then speculations are made as to how this can be incorporated into the existing system of American justice.

Restorative Justice

Restorative justice is an alternative to the current view that justice is best served by meting out harsh punishments for wrongdoings (i.e., just desserts). Instead, restorative justice "is about hurt begetting healing as an alternative to hurt begetting hurt" (Braithwaite & Braithwaite, 2001, pp. 4–5). Restorative justice, which complements efforts that invert assumptions regarding punitiveness (e.g., defiance theory), proffers that prevention is best obtained through truth-seeking grounded in mercy (Braithwaite, 2005). By emphasizing the restoration of harm to victims and the reintegration of offenders back into the community, restorative justice has established its voice in areas to include criminal justice (Braithwaite & Mugford, 1994; Umbreit, 1994; Bazemore, 2001; Karp, 2001; Strang, 2002; White, 2003; Rodriguez, 2007), problem behaviors in educational institutions and families (Moore & O'Connell, 1994; Lowry, 1997; Ahmed, 2001; Karp & Breslin, 2001; Morrison, 2001; Braithwaite & Strang, 2002; Nancarrow, 2006), and governance and human rights (Braithwaite, 1999; Cunneen, 2001; Shearing, 2001; Braithwaite, 2002a; McEvoy & Mika, 2002; Braithwaite, 2005). Research has also attended to restoration among minority populations (LePrairie, 1995; Cunneen, 1997; Behrendt, 2002; Blagg, 2002; Kelly, 2002; Daly & Stubbs, 2006).

Rather than viewing justice retributively – that of crime as violation of law and an act against the state – restorative justice presumes that crime is also a violation of one person by another. In short, crime causes harm and suffering to victims, offenders, and the larger community, and the onus should be on the criminal justice system to justify its intrusion into the lives of citizens (Braithwaite & Pettit, 1990, p. 9). With retribution, crime is believed to increase suffering, to alienate parties from one another, and to decrease the strength of social capital and informal social control (Christie, 1977; Zehr, 1990; Bazemore, 2001; Tosouni, 2004). To the contrary, restorative approaches focus on problem solving, obligations, dialogue, negotiation, restitution, and reconciliation (Zehr, 1990). Interventions include legal and lay actors (e.g., offenders, victims, and members of the community) in an informal, consensually based problem-solving process, and offenders are held accountable for repairing victims' physical and/or emotional losses without being stigmatized as a criminal (Daly, 2000; Kurki, 2000).

Restorative justice presumes a "common humanity" (Tutu, 1999) among offenders and victims. South Africa's Truth and Reconciliation Commission, for example, worked to name parties responsible for human rights violations, provided victims with a public forum, codified recommendations to prevent future abuse, facilitated reparations, and granted amnesty to those who fully disclosed their involvement in past abuses (Cunneen, 2001, p. 86). Standards appropriate for this horizontal deliberative model, or justice "created by persons with considerable equality brought about by closeness" (Christie, 2004, p. 75), include non-domination, respectful listening, restoration of personal property, dignity, freedom and, ultimately, the prevention of future injustice (Braithwaite, 2002a, p. 569). As such, consensually based problem solving frequently requires an investment of time: testimonials are encouraged from all attendees, whatever their level of emotion, as the model "is all about the people present (rather than legal formalities), people who come only once, prepared to stay until the case is resolved" (Sherman, 2001, p. 49). A post-project assessment of the Canberra Reintegrative Shaming Experiments (RISE) (Sherman, Braithwaite, Strang, & Barnes, 2001), for example, indicated that restorative group conferences took far longer than court proceedings, with conferences lasting approximately 90 min compared to 10 min for court processing (Harris, 2001). Other studies also indicate sizable time demands for participants (e.g., Coates, Umbreit, & Vos, 2003).

The restorative justice ideal is driven by dominion or that social systems ensure full, complete, and commonly understood freedoms to enjoy fundamental rights as a victim, accused, witness, or taxpayer (Braithwaite & Pettit, 1990). Through dominion, restorative justice:

> supports a codification of rights ...; opposes the notions of crimes of offense or consensual crimes but accommodates certain types of strict liability crimes; supports a right to protection from punishments against the person (capital, corporal punishment) and a presumption in favor of punishments against the property of offenders (fines, restitution) over punishments against province (imprisonment); supports some principles about how to distribute resources between different parts of the system (police, courts, prisons, etc.), and some principles for rendering police surveillance of suspects more accountable and for targeting investigations and prosecutions; supports a right to a fair trial and principles of sentencing that give prominence to denunciation and moral reasoning; and promises, finally, to support parole, work release, and remission of sentence for good behavior. (Braithwaite & Pettit, 1990, p. 10)

At its core, restorative justice requires a "web of productive social relationships" built on mutual understanding: a system which works to maximize the dominion of individual lives within a system of social justice (Morrison, 2001, p. 202). Consistent with this web, scholars argue that restorative rehabilitation differs from traditional rehabilitation through its emphasis on rebuilding social relationships between offenders and their communities (e.g., victim, offender's family, school teachers) (Bazemore, 1999; Karp & Breslin, 2001).

Reintegrative Shaming

Restorative justice's "explanatory dynamic" (Braithwaite, 2002a, p. 571) is reintegrative shaming, a practice which takes the accused through a process of understanding the consequences of his or her behavior, facilitates relational thinking, and moves understanding to a collective level (Morrison, 2001). Rather than label the accused as deviant (e.g., Lemert, 1967), reintegrative shaming focuses on labeling the harmful (criminal) act as evil, treating the offender with respect, while at the same time criticizing his or her behavior (Braithwaite, 1989). Scholarship suggests that procedural justice, satisfaction, and crime reduction are inextricably linked: that strategies of regulation based on the way members of the public are treated by legal authorities can enhance their willingness to cooperate and defer (Tyler, 1990).

In essence, reintegrative shaming is the medium through which apology, forgiveness, remorse, and censure of the offender's act takes shape. Emotions such as remorse are thought to be powerful forms of censure as they are articulated by the very person who has the most compelling reason to refuse to vindicate the victim (Braithwaite, 2002a, p. 571). As opposed to passive responsibility underpinning retribution, reintegrative shaming emphasizes active responsibility – a shift in orientation that is thought to change an offender's attitude toward the law and to facilitate conformity through emotional motivation (Kurki, 2000; Rice, 2006).

The more traditional stigmatizing criminal justice processes are thought to increase re-offending through their disrespect and humiliation of the individual; that is, she/he is cast as pariah instead of recipient of just and right punishment (Braithwaite, 1989). Through reintegration, both offenders and victims find a restoration of dominion (Braithwaite & Pettit, 1990). Similarities have been drawn to interaction rituals (Collins, 2004), or encounters where parties are influenced by one another's presence, interaction membership is clearly defined, participants are focused on a common purpose, and participants realize "entrainment," or a common emotional mood (Sherman et al., 2005). To date, desires for entrainment and reintegration have been sought through victim-offender mediation, peacemaking circles, restorative community service, financial restitution, victim impact panels, victim empathy classes, and family group conferencing (Bazemore & Umbreit, 2001), while also school anti-bullying programs, Chinese *bang jiao* programs, and exit conferences following business regulatory inspections (Braithwaite, 2002b).

It is important to note that there are some who reject a strict contrast between retributive and restorative justice. Daly (2000), for example, argues that parallels exist insomuch as restorative justice presumes a change in future behavior on the part of the offender, sanctions that "make things right" in individual cases, and a morally and mentally competent actor who is capable of taking responsibility for his or her action(s). Nonetheless, although retributive principles are still dominant in public opinion, there is evidence of a burgeoning interest in punishment that is less vindictive and more concerned with strengthening social bonds and empowering families (Umbreit, 1994). In some ways, public sentiments are punitive and progressive at once, wishing the correctional system to do justice, protect the public, and reform the wayward (Cullen, Fisher, & Applegate, 2000).

White-Collar and Corporate Regulation

Restorative justice proponents have argued that a complementary relationship exists between restorative justice principles and the regulation of corporate malfeasance. In fact, some contend that white-collar offenders may be most amendable to the effects of shaming, a process which requires that individuals be deeply embedded in a social network, because they are already well integrated into law-abiding groups (Levi, 2002, p. 148) and thus have much to lose. However, similar types of arguments have been levied to support the use of a deterrence strategy for controlling white-collar crime.

Chambliss (1967) argued that since white-collar offenders are not committed to a criminal lifestyle and that their crimes are instrumental rather than expressive (also see Braithwaite & Geis, 1982) they are most deterrable. Empirical research, however, has revealed that the use of criminal sanctions have had little, if any, effect on deterring white-collar criminality (Braithwaite & Makkai, 1991; Makkai & Braithwaite, 1994; Simpson, 1992, 2002; Simpson & Koper, 1992; Weisburd, Waring, & Chayet, 1995). The lack of support for the deterrence strategy led some scholars (Braithwaite, 1982, 1985; Braithwaite & Fisse, 1983; Scholz, 1984) to consider and develop alternative forms of crime control that are derived from a cooperative or compliance strategy; however, these alternative methods of regulatory enforcement are not completely devoid of a deterrence or punitive component.

Before proceeding to a discussion of the mixed or interrelated approaches of crime control it is important to note that most of the enforcement of corporate crime falls under the purview of regulatory agencies (and regulatory laws) and not within the traditional crime enforcement agencies (e.g., police departments).[3] The relevance of this point is that regulatory agencies prefer to utilize a compliant or cooperative strategy of social control rather than a punitive model, such as is preferred by the American criminal justice system. As Snider (1990, p. 376) notes, "regulatory law is different from traditional criminal law because its goal is not punishment, but to secure compliance and educate." The differing strategies of social control utilized by regulatory agencies and the criminal justice system sets up parallel but also overlapping models of justice.

The dual approach to crime control (i.e., deterrence and compliance) is much more commonly discussed in the corporate crime literature (see Braithwaite, 1982, 1985; Braithwaite & Fisse, 1983; Scholz, 1984) in large part due to the varying enforcement agencies and routes of prosecution that may be followed. While deterrence and cooperative approaches to social control may be thought of as opposing or contradictory systems (see Grabosky, 1995), they are best regarded as complementary or viewed as ends of a continuum where there is some shared or common middle ground. In most cases, social control systems are comprised of a mixture of deterrence and compliance models of enforcement (Reiss, 1984, p. 24). Advances toward the development of alternative methods of regulatory enforcement have been articulated by Braithwaite and his colleagues (1982, 1985) (Braithwaite & Fisse, 1983) as well as by the research of Scholz (1984).

Braithwaite and his colleagues often argue for an approach in which a combination of punishment and persuasion are utilized in order to achieve compliance with the law. The components of this proposed cooperative model have accrued over the years but include enforced self-regulation, informal social control, and a pyramid of enforcement.

The idea behind self-regulation is to allow organizations to police themselves. Although self-regulation has numerous advantages,[4] Braithwaite (1982) acknowledges that not all organizations will voluntarily self-regulate. As a result, he introduced the "enforced" element of external governmental pressure, along with the concept of self-regulation. The central component to this approach is the presence of an effective internal compliance program. In this situation, corporations would be required to draft a set of rules to cover a certain problem area and then send their proposal for approval by the regulatory agency (Braithwaite, 1985, p. 125). The enforced self-regulation approach can be generally viewed as a combination of elements from both the deterrence and compliance strategies of social control. Firms are encouraged, rather than required, to have compliance programs in place, and those that do tend to benefit from the reward by increasing their chances of receiving more lenient sentences (Simpson, 2002).

Braithwaite and Fisse (1983), building off the general criminality research (Williams & Hawkins, 1986), argue that informal social controls can play an important role in influencing would-be corporate violators to comply with the law. They define informal social control as "behavioral restraint by means other than those formally directed by a court or administrative agency" (p. 1). Specifically, they relate informal social controls to apply by means of stigma and adverse publicity. Both individuals and organizations may suffer from the consequences of negative publicity and the stigma associated with it. Because "reputation represents an expected stream of profits from performing a given activity or selling a given product," the loss of a good reputation represents a social cost to either the individual or the organization (Walt & Laufer, 1992, p. 326). An individual corporate offender has valued possession, such as social status, respectability, money, a job, and a comfortable home and family life that could easily be lost and hard to regain because of a tainted image (Braithwaite, 1985, p. 87). Similarly, a corporation that suffers from a loss of reputation may result in consumers or other corporations paying less for the tainted company's products or boycotting those products all together (Walt & Laufer, 1992). Therefore, the fear of consequences from these two layers of informal controls pressure would-be violators to conform to the law.

The final element, the enforcement pyramid, is based on the notion of a hierarchy of penalties (Snider, 1990) and is perhaps the best example of how the two social control systems operate together. Persuasion is viewed as a less intrusive form of social control and as such these types of sanctions should be attempted first and often. Therefore, persuasive sanctions comprise the bottom of the pyramid while more punitive sanctions, which are to be used less frequently, form the top of the pyramid. For effective social control, this approach should be attempted first and often in order to attain compliance with the law; formal legal interventions, the more formal and punitive forms of social control, should make up the top peak of the pyramid and only be used as a last resort (Braithwaite, 1985).

Ayres and Braithwaite (1992) recommend a pyramid strategy of responsive regulation, one where regulated firms are subject to escalating levels of intervention based on histories of non-compliance. Within the context of environmental or occupational health, for example, tiers of an enforcement pyramid might include persuasion (at the base of the pyramid) progressively moving to the use of a warning letter, civil penalty, criminal penalty, license suspension, and finally a license revocation (p. 35).

Scholz's (1984) approach to corporate regulation relies upon techniques of game theory.[5] In other words, the key to choosing an effective enforcement strategy is to identify when and with whom each approach is most appropriate. Thus, the "tit for tat" strategy helps to identify which approach would be most effective. The "tit for tat" rule is simply to "cooperate until the other player defects and then do in the next round what your opponent did last" (Scholz, 1984, p. 189). For example, enforcement agencies should approach business regulation in a cooperative rather than a punitive model until a firm deviates from compliance. Once one party has defected from compliance, the "tit for tat" strategy suggests that in the next round to treat the opponent the way you were treated. In other words, in the next round the regulatory agencies would take a more punitive approach in order to have the firm comply with the law. It is theorized that this strategy can be effective in the long run because of the dynamic and ongoing relationship between businesses and regulatory agencies (Simpson, 2002).

In sum, regulatory agencies have a preference for cooperative or compliant techniques of crime control over deterrent or punitive approaches. For example, a combination of persuasion, education, and civil or administrative remedies are preferred methods for regulatory agencies to secure compliance over the laying of formal criminal charges (Snider, 1990, p. 373). However, regulatory agencies can only secure compliance by finding a balance between persuasion and punishment. Scholars working in the arena of corporate regulation articulated separate models of combining persuasion and punishment that differ on the "premises about human motivation and different intervening processes" but that they agree that regulatory enforcement needs to be both "tough and forgiving" (Braithwaite, 1990–1991, p. 60).

Complementarity of Restorative Justice and Responsive Corporate Regulation

Parallels and similarities between restorative justice and enforcement of white-collar crimes are apparent, primarily, in the underlying strategy of crime control; that is a reliance on both punishment and persuasion. Restorative justice scholars call for regulation grounded in openness and similarly regulatory enforcement prefers to operate in an environment where business and industry stakeholders are consulted on the design of regulatory laws. In this regard the regulated are willing (or at least non-adversarial) partners with the regulators. Braithwaite (1990–1991) warns that a strategy of pure punishment from regulatory agencies can generate a backlash from businesses. The consequence of this backlash is the development of a business subculture that is resistance to regulation and whose members are likely to employ techniques of neutralization (Benson, 1985; Piquero, Tibbetts, & Blankenship, 2005) to justify their illegal acts. Just as fairness and motive-based trust have been found to yield dividends in street crime enforcement (e.g., Tyler & Huo, 2002), consumers, shareholders, and taxpayers benefit from a landscape where corporations are motivated to engage in self-regulatory behavior rather than simply respond to top-down incentives or sanctions (e.g., as in efforts to facilitate the self-policing of environmental violations) (Stretesky, 2006).

As Tyler (2006, p. 309) asserts, restorative justice is a viable model of proactive social regulation that does not generate the negative consequences associated with adversarial approaches to rule breaking. In other words, it is "not about picking good apples for reconciliation and bad apples for deterrence; it is about treating everyone as a good apple as the preferred first approach" (Braithwaite, 1999, p. 64). By framing one's response to white-collar offenses through the lens of mercy and truth-seeking, one learns how to prevent crime and misconduct nodally (e.g., malefactions within corporate work group/department) or nationally (e.g., Enron-style corporate collapse) (Braithwaite, 2005, p. 299).

As a result, opportunities abound for restorative justice to inform scholarship on the etiology of white-collar crime and the criminal justice system's response to such behavior. For example, Ritchie and O'Connell (2001) argue that restorative reform benefits formal organizations through its apt attention to individual and collective denial, self-centeredness, belief in resource scarcity, confusion, lack of reflection, and desire-for-control, characteristics which are common to many organizations and resemble those of addicted individuals (Schaef & Fassell, 1997). Desire-for-control, for example, is associated with rational choice considerations and corporate criminality (Piquero, Exum, & Simpson, 2005), with control surpluses (i.e., when the amount of control exercised is greater than the amount of control experienced) relating to exploitative acts (Piquero & Piquero, 2006). Consistent with Schaef and Fassell (1997), normative belief about the rightness of corporate social responsibility is associated with one's personality traits, values, attitudes, and thinking patterns (Mudrack, 2007).

Restorative justice's historic focus on common or street criminals (Kurki, 2000) should not dissuade its application to white-collar crimes. On the contrary, white-collar offenders may be the best "American" test sample. While most of the literature of corporate regulation has focused on the behaviors of organizational offenders (Levi, 2002), there is little reason to believe that the same underlying model of justice cannot and will not apply to individual white-collar actors. Levi (2002, p. 158) examined the use of shaming and stigma on financial criminals and found that it may be possible to induce "conscience by making offenders aware of the effects that behaviour has on others." However, he goes on to note that those with limited social and geographic mobility are more susceptible to the impact of shaming than are the "super-rich or professional confidence tricksters" (Levi, 2002, p. 158). In other words, it appears that those in the middle classes of society are more susceptible to the crime-controlling effects of shame than are the upper classes. This finding has direct import for white-collar crime in America.

Empirically very little was known about American white-collar offenders prior to the 1980s. The little that was known was derived from case studies. As such, many of the images of white-collar offenders conformed to Sutherland's earliest depiction – that of powerful upper-class business executives. However, two data collection efforts in the 1980s changed the portrait of white-collar offenders by providing information that detailed the characteristics of both offenders and offenses.[6] The samples from both data collection efforts were based upon individual offenders who were convicted in U.S. federal courts of a white-collar crime. Two notable findings emerged: (1) most of those convicted of white-collar crimes came from the middle class of society; that is, they were average citizens with moderate incomes, and (2) a substantial proportion of convicted white-collar offenders had at least one prior arrest (Piquero & Benson, 2004). Thus, it became clear that white-collar defendants were not as elite or law abiding as originally thought but what was confirmed is that they were substantially different from street offenders.

Given that white-collar offenders are different from street offenders and that they are largely comprised of average citizens from the middle classes coupled with perceptions that white-collar crimes are "inadvertent by-products of market competition rather than as crimes" (Russell & Gilbert, 1999, pp. 62–63) restorative justice seems like an applicable approach to white-collar crime control within the American criminal justice system. Previous findings, suggesting that those from the middle classes are more susceptible to shaming (Levi, 2002) and the relatively low importance, at least in terms of fear of crime, given to economic crimes lays the foundation for this approach of crime control to take hold and become entwined in the American view of justice.

Further, as classic explications of economic sociology assert that struggle, competition, and selection drive and sustain corporate relationships, restorative justice is well suited to restore balance "both backstage and frontstage" when power asymmetry among impacted parties is acute (Braithwaite, 2002a, p. 566). To Weber (1978), throughout the economy exists "the battle of man with man" (pp. 93, 108) – of domination by economic power and by authority. As he explains, "the great majority of all economic organizations, among them the most important and the most modern ones, reveal a structure of dominancy ... Domination in the quite general sense of power, i.e., of the possibility of imposing one's own will upon the behavior of other persons, can emerge in the most diverse forms" (p. 941).

Research on the etiology of white-collar crime has argued that appropriate motivation and opportunity, a confluence that has received considerable attention in criminological thought (e.g., with violent and property crime) (Cantor & Land, 1985), is conditioned by the political economy of industrial capitalism: a culture where competition defines character, competition is an indication of personal worth, and where fear of failure (and pressure for profitability, e.g., see Jenkins & Braithwaite, 2005) provides a "powerful symbolic structure" for white-collar offending (Coleman, 1987, pp. 417–418). As such, opportunities abound for scholarship to examine the intersections of power, profit, and pluralism. Just as restorative justice theory has been framed as being borne of social movement politics (Braithwaite, 1999, p. 9), so too has interest in white-collar crime stemming from the Watergate scandal (Katz, 1980, p. 178).

DISCUSSION

This chapter has considered the application of restorative justice as a model of justice that may be applicable to white-collar and corporate offending. In so doing, it is argued that restorative justice offers another viable approach to the American system of justice. By invoking the restorative justice ideal, and the notion of reintegrative shaming in particular, it is hoped that this provides a conduit that may help stem more compliance among white-collar and corporate actors with respect to their decision making, stemming it away from illegality, and toward legality.

But simply articulating how restorative justice is potentially applicable to white-collar and corporate punishment is not enough. As such, the article closes by highlighting several promising areas of theoretical and empirical research inquiry. Consider this simple question: Can restorative justice really work for suite crimes? The question posed above is a difficult one, primarily because the research and evaluation literature with respect to restorative justice in general is scant. It is the case that, in the experimental studies, restorative justice appears to be an effective (deterrent) punishment for primarily first-time and/or offenders who engage in relatively minor offenses. But such offenders may actually resemble a subset of some (but not all) types of white-collar offenders, especially those who are situationally induced to commit suite crimes because of temporary or situational factors (Piquero & Benson, 2004). These offenders are typically bonded to the communities they live in, but due to cultural and situational factors feel the pressure to engage in white-collar crime. By reminding them of the harm they caused to the broader community, restorative justice may be especially salient for such individuals. Consider the Enron scandal.[7] A restorative justice-oriented punishment here for those individuals guilty of committing the offenses would consider the broader, affected community including all those persons affected who lost their retirement funds. Punishment in the restorative justice sense for such an offender could consist not only of repaying the monies lost, but also meeting in a series of individual forum with people so that the victims can share their stories of loss and misfortune, and then attempt to reintegrate the offender back into the community. In this sense, restorative justice may not be a sole replacement for incapacitation efforts, but could also be used as a supplement to more traditional punishments. Thus, restorative justice could help spur organiza- tions – and more so individuals within organizations – to be more sensitive to their actions not only the individual victims but to the larger community of victims who may be by-products of the original victimization.

How might the application of restorative justice to white-collar crime be implemented and evaluated, and what sorts of information would we be interested in collecting to assess its effectiveness? First, there needs to be some determination about what sorts of white-collar crimes would fall under the purview of being applicable under a restorative justice approach. Issues here deal with the range of dollar loss, victim injury, and numerous other situational factors. Restorative justice may be more or less applicable for certain suite crimes compared to others. Questions remain as to whether restorative justice may be an effective way to control for price fixing, collusion, or even environmental waste illegalities. Second, there has to be an intense data collection protocol developed. Following the RISE experimental evaluations of restorative justice in Australia (Sherman et al., 2001), it is important that data be collected from both the offender and the victim, and to include both short-term and long-term follow-ups with respect to continued/curtailed involvement in crime as well as how restorative justice and shaming in particular has influenced other non- crime domains. Such domains certainly include measures of fairness and satisfaction with the criminal justice system. Tyler, Sherman, Strang, Barnes, and Woods (2007) argue, for example, that the social psychological processes of reintegrative shaming and procedural justice condition lower recidivism through increased legitimacy of the law. Third, there needs to be a serious buy-in from the criminal justice system – especially in the United States where white-collar crimes have come under intense scrutiny and the system has tended to respond with more severe punishments; that is, the restorative justice approach must be viewed as a potentially viable option, one that would be used in increasing and large numbers. Fourth, the citizenry needs to recognize that when punishment via restorative justice for white-collar crimes is employed that this is not just some simple "slap-on-the-wrist"; but rather must agree that other non-punitive approaches are a legitimate means for dealing with these kinds of offenders. Therefore, in applying the restorative justice model to white-collar offenders the sanctions utilized to entice compliance need to employ strategies that include both punishment and persuasion; otherwise a cry from the public-at-large will subject criminal justice and policy officials to criticism and likely eliminate restorative justice as a viable option. And above all else, the application of restorative justice to the study of white-collar crime should be implemented as an experimental design where individual offenders are randomly assigned to the restorative justice option, compared to others who undergo the existing system of justice. It must be recognized that there certainly will be difficulty associated with this proposed research study, especially given what will likely be relatively small sample sizes, but it is important to experimentally evaluate restorative justice in this regard.

In general restorative justice holds promise as a way to sustain relationships while still appropriately sanctioning offenders. It provides an exemplar for which white-collar offenders provide an interesting and appropriate test case for using this system in the United States. As such, this article has attempted to make this case that restorative justice can be considered a viable option for handling white-collar offenders while at the same time not completely removing the punitive nature of penalties desired by the American justice system. Additionally, some important questions and directions for future research have been outlined – all of which seek to provide fairness to business practices as well as with an eye toward reducing white-collar crime. Whether restorative justice has any chance of taking hold in the American system of justice is ultimately an empirical question, one that is believed to be worth addressing and one in which may be best suited for study within the context of white-collar offenders. If success may be found with this population of relatively "harmless" offenders, then may be for once the study of elite crimes may be able to help shape policy that can influence the control of general forms of criminality.

NOTES

1. White-collar crimes include those acts committed for the benefit of the individual while corporate crimes are those acts committed on behalf of an organization (Clinard & Quinney, 1973). Following Snider (1990, p. 374), this article views corporate crimes as "white-collar crimes committed with the encouragement and support of a formal organization, and intended at least in part to advance the goals of that organization." While organizations (as corporate actors) legally can be held accountable for the actions of its employees, the focus of this article is on individual actors who engage in criminal activities whether they are acting in their own self-interest or on behalf of the organization.

2. This is not to suggest that overlap does not exist between general criminality and white-collar criminality but rather it is much too early to definitively say that what is best for dealing with street offenders is the best approach taken with the more "elite" offenders (though see Braithwaite & Geis, 1982).

3. Regulatory agencies rely upon a combination of civil, administration, and criminal procedures to ensure compliance with their regulatory laws. In the United States, regulatory agencies do not have criminal jurisdiction over cases and therefore must refer a case to the Department of Justice for criminal prosecution. Whether or not the case gets criminally prosecuted is left to the discretion of federal prosecutors. Snider (1990) notes that criminal prosecution of cases is associated with regulatory failure.

4. See Braithwaite (1982) for a review of advantages derived from a strategy of self-regulation.

5. See Axelrod (1984) for a discussion of game theory.

6. The first study was lead by Stanton Wheeler and the second conducted by Brian Forst and William Rhodes.

7. However, cases such as Enron raise intractable challenges. Through its central focus on matters of law over matters of trust, this case illustrates how juridification (i.e., the widespread proliferation of law) has replaced the concept of justice with one of efficiency divorced from a common story (vision) for society (Foltz & Foltz, 2006, pp. 463, 466).

REFERENCES

Ahmed, E. (2001). Shame management: Regulating bullying. In: E. Ahmed, N. Harris, J. Braithwaite & V. Braithwaite (Eds), *Shame management through reintegration* (pp. 3–72). Cambridge, UK: Cambridge University Press.

Axelrod, R. (1984). *The evolution of cooperation*. New York: Basic Books.

Ayres, I., & Braithwaite, J. (1992). *Responsive regulation: Transcending the deregulation debate*. New York: Oxford University Press.

Bazemore, G. (1999). After shaming, whither reintegration? Restorative justice and relational rehabilitation. In: G. Bazemore & L. Walgrave (Eds), *Restorative juvenile justice: Repairing the harm of youth crime*. Monsey, NY: Criminal Justice Press.

Bazemore, G. (2001). Young people, trouble, and crime. *Youth and Society, 33*, 199–226.

Bazemore, G., & Umbreit, M. (2001). A comparison of four restorative conferencing models. *OJJDP Juvenile Justice Bulletin* (February).

Behrendt, L. (2002). Lessons from the mediation obsession: Ensuring that sentencing 'alternatives' focus on indigenous self-determination. In: H. Strang & J. Braithwaite (Eds), *Restorative justice and family violence* (pp. 178–190). Cambridge, UK: Cambridge University Press.

Benson, M. L. (1985). Denying the guilty mind: Accounting for involvement in a white-collar crime. *Criminology, 23*, 583–607.

Benson, M. L., & Cullen, F. T. (1998). *Combating corporate crime: Local prosecutors at work.* Boston: Northeastern University Press.

Blagg, H. (2002). Restorative justice and aboriginal family violence: Opening a space for healing. In: H. Strang & J. Braithwaite (Eds), *Restorative justice and family violence* (pp. 191–205). Cambridge, UK: Cambridge University Press.

Braithwaite, J. (1982). Enforced self-regulation: A new strategy for corporate crime control. *Michigan Law Review, 80*, 1466–1507.

Braithwaite, J. (1985). *To punish or persuade.* Albany, NY: State University of New York Press.

Braithwaite, J. (1989). *Crime, shame, and reintegration.* Cambridge: Cambridge University Press.

Braithwaite, J. (1990–1991). Convergence in models of regulatory strategy. *Current Issues in Criminal Justice, 60*, 59–65.

Braithwaite, J. (1999). Restorative justice: Assessing optimistic and pessimistic accounts. In: M. Tonry (Ed.), *Crime and justice: A review of research* (pp. 1–127). Chicago: The University of Chicago Press.

Braithwaite, J. (2002a). Setting standards for restorative justice. *British Journal of Criminology, 42*, 563–577.

Braithwaite, J. (2002b). *Restorative justice and responsive regulation.* New York: Oxford University Press.

Braithwaite, J. (2005). Between proportionality and impunity: Confrontation–truth–prevention. *Criminology, 43*, 283–305.

Braithwaite, J., & Braithwaite, V. (2001). Shame, shame management and regulation. In: E. Ahmed, N. Harris, J. Braithwaite & V. Braithwaite (Eds), *Shame management through reintegration* (pp. 3–72). Cambridge, UK: Cambridge University Press.

Braithwaite, J., & Fisse, B. (1983). Asbetos and health: A case of informal social control. *Australian–New Zealand Journal of Criminology, 16*, 67–80.

Braithwaite, J., & Geis, G. (1982). On theory and action for corporate crime control. *Crime and Delinquency, 31*, 292–314.

Braithwaite, J., & Makkai, T. (1991). Testing an expected utility model of corporate deterrence. *Law and Society Review, 25*, 7–39.

Braithwaite, J., & Mugford, S. (1994). Conditions for a successful reintegration ceremony. *British Journal of Criminology, 34*, 139–171.

Braithwaite, J., & Pettit, P. (1990). *Not just deserts: A republican theory of criminal justice.* New York: Oxford University Press.

Braithwaite, J., & Strang, H. (2002). Restorative justice and family violence. In: H. Strang & J. Braithwaite (Eds), *Restorative justice and family violence* (pp. 1–22). Cambridge, UK: Cambridge University Press.

Cantor, D., & Land, K. C. (1985). Unemployment and crime rates in the post–World War II United States: A theoretical and empirical analysis. *American Sociological Review, 50*, 317–332.

Chambliss, W. J. (1967). Types of deviance and the effectiveness of legal sanctions. *Wisconsin Law Review* (Summer), 703–719.

Christie, N. (1977). Conflicts as property. *British Journal of Criminology, 17*, 1–15.

Christie, N. (2004). *A suitable amount of crime*. London: Routlege.

Clinard, M. B., & Quinney, R. (1973). *Criminal behavior systems: A typology*. New York: Holt, Rinehart & Winston.

Coates, R., Umbreit, M., & Vos, B. (2003). Restorative justice circles: An exploratory study. *Contemporary Justice Review, 6*, 265–278.

Coleman, J. W. (1987). Toward an integrated theory of white-collar crime. *American Journal of Sociology, 93*, 406–439.

Collins, R. (2004). *Interaction ritual chains*. Princeton, NJ: Princeton University Press.

Cullen, F. T. (2005). The twelve people who save rehabilitation: How the science of criminology made a difference. *Criminology, 43*, 1–42.

Cullen, F. T., Fisher, B. S., & Applegate, B. K. (2000). Public opinion about punishment and corrections. In: M. Tonry (Ed.), *Crime and justice: A review of research* (Vol. 27, pp. 1–79). Chicago: University of Chicago Press.

Cunneen, C. (1997). Community conferencing and the fiction of indigenous control. *Australian and New Zealand Journal of Criminology, 30*, 292–311.

Cunneen, C. (2001). Reparations and restorative justice: Responding to the gross violation of human rights. In: H. Strang & J. Braithwaite (Eds), *Restorative justice and civil society* (pp. 83–98). New York: Cambridge University Press.

Daly, K. (2000). Revisiting the relationship between retributive and restorative justice. In: H. Strang & J. Braithwaite (Eds), *Restorative justice: Philosophy to practice* (pp. 33–54). Aldershot, England: Dartmouth/Ashgate.

Daly, K., & Stubbs, J. (2006). Feminist engagement with restorative justice. *Theoretical Criminology, 10*, 9–28.

Foltz, F. A., & Foltz, F. A. (2006). Technology, religion, and justice: The problems of disembedded and disembodied law. *Bulletin of Science, Technology and Society, 26*, 463–471.

Grabosky, P. N. (1995). Counterproductive regulation. *International Journal of the Sociology of Law, 23*, 347–369.

Harris, N. (2001). Part II. Shaming and shame: Regulating drink-driving. In: E. Ahmed, N. Harris, J. Braithwaite & V. Braithwaite (Eds), *Shame management through reintegration* (pp. 71–207). Melbourne: Cambridge University Press.

Jenkins, A., & Braithwaite, J. (2005). Profits, pressure and corporate lawbreaking. *Crime, Law and Social Change, 20*, 221–232.

Karp, D. R. (2001). Harm and repair: Observing restorative justice in Vermont. *Justice Quarterly, 18*, 727–757.

Karp, D. R., & Breslin, B. (2001). Restorative justice in school communities. *Youth and Society, 33*, 249–272.

Katz, J. (1980). The social movement against white-collar crime. In: E. Bittner & S. Messinger (Eds), *Criminology review yearbook* (p. 178). Beverly Hills, CA: Sage.

Kelly, L. (2002). Using restorative justice principles to address family violence in aboriginal communities. In: H. Strang & J. Braithwaite (Eds), *Restorative justice and family violence* (pp. 206–222). Cambridge, UK: Cambridge University Press.

Kurki, L. (2000). Restorative and community Justice. In: M. Tonry (Ed.), *Crime and justice: A review of research* (pp. 235–303). Chicago: The University of Chicago Press.

Lemert, E. M. (1967). *Human deviance, social problems, and social control*. Englewood Cliffs, NJ: Prentice Hall.

LePrairie, C. (1995). Community justice or just community? Aboriginal communities in search of justice. *Canadian Journal of Criminology, 37*, 521–545.

Levi, M. (2002). Suite justice or sweet charity? Some explorations of shaming and incapacitating business fraudsters. *Punishment and Society, 4*, 147–163.

Lowry, J. M. (1997). Family group conferences as a form of court-approved alternative dispute resolution in child abuse and neglect cases. *University of Michigan Journal of Law Reform, 31*, 57–92.

Makkai, T., & Braithwaite, J. (1994). The dialectics of corporate deterrence. *Journal of Research in Crime and Delinquency, 31*, 347–373.

Martinson, R. (1974). What works: Questions and answers about prison reform. *Public Interest, 35*, 22–54.

McEvoy, K., & Mika, H. (2002). Restorative justice and the critique of informalism in Northern Ireland. *The British Journal of Criminology, 42*, 534–562.

Moore, D. B., & O'Connell, T. (1994). Family conferencing in Wagga Wagga: A communitarian model of justice. In: C. Alder & J. Wundersitz (Eds), *Family conferencing and juvenile justice*. Canberra, Australia: Australian Studies in Law, Crime, and Justice, Australian Institute of Criminology.

Morrison, B. (2001). The school system: Developing its capacity in the regulation of a civil society. In: H. Strang & J. Braithwaite (Eds), *Restorative justice and civil society* (pp. 195–210). New York: Cambridge University Press.

Mudrack, P. (2007). Individual personality factors that affect normative beliefs about the rightness of corporate social responsibility. *Business and Society, 46*, 33–62.

Nagel, I. H., & Swenson, W. M. (1993). The federal sentencing guidelines for corporations: Their development, theoretical underpinnings, and some thoughts about their future. *Washington University Law Quarterly, 71*, 205–259.

Nancarrow, H. (2006). In search of justice for domestic and family violence. *Theoretical Criminology, 10*, 87–106.

Piquero, N. L., & Benson, M. L. (2004). White-collar crime and criminal careers: Specifying a trajectory of punctuated situational offending. *Journal of Contemporary Criminal Justice, 20*, 148–165.

Piquero, N. L., Exum, M. L., & Simpson, S. S. (2005). Integrating the desire-for-control and rational choice in a corporate crime context. *Justice Quarterly, 22*, 252–280.

Piquero, N. L., & Piquero, A. R. (2006). Control balance and exploitative corporate crime. *Criminology, 44*, 397–430.

Piquero, N. L., Tibbetts, S. G., & Blankenship, M. B. (2005). Examining the role of differential association and techniques of neutralization in explaining corporate crime. *Deviant Behavior, 26*, 159–188.

Reiss, A. J., Jr. (1984). Selection strategies of social control over organizational life. In: K. Hawkins & J. M. Thomas (Eds), *Enforcing regulation* (pp. 23–35). Boston: Kluwer-Nijoff Publishing.

Rice, S. K. (2006). *General strain amid restoration: An examination of instrumental and expressive offenses*. Gainesville, FL: University of Florida.

Ritchie, J., & O'Connell, T. (2001). Restorative justice and the need for restorative environments in bureaucracies and corporations. In: H. Strang & J. Braithwaite (Eds), *Restorative justice and civil society* (pp. 149–164). New York: Cambridge University Press.

Rodriguez, N. (2007). Restorative justice at work: Examining the impact of restorative justice resolutions on juvenile recidivism. *Crime and Delinquency, 53*, 355–379.

Russell, S., & Gilbert, M. J. (1999). Truman's revenge: Social control and corporate crime. *Crime, Law, and Social Change, 32*, 59–82.

Schaef, A. W., & Fassell, D. (1997). *Addictive organizations*. San Francisco: Harper & Row.

Scholz, J. T. (1984). Deterrence, cooperation and the ecology of regulatory enforcement. *Law and Society Review, 18*, 179–224.

Shearing, C. (2001). Transforming security: A South African experiment. In: H. Strang & J. Braithwaite (Eds), *Restorative justice and civil society* (pp. 14–34). New York: Cambridge University Press.

Sherman, L. W. (2001). Two Protestant ethics and the spirit of restoration. In: H. Strang & J. Braithwaite (Eds), *Restorative justice and civil society* (pp. 35–55). New York: Cambridge University Press.

Sherman, L. W., Braithwaite, J., Strang, H., & Barnes, G. C. (2001). *Reintegrative shaming experiments (RISE) in Australia, 1995–1999*. Ann Arbor, MI: Inter-University Consortium for Political and Social Research (ICPSR 2993).

Sherman, L. W., Strang, H., Angel, C., Woods, D., Barnes, G. C., Bennett, S., Inkpen, N., & Rossner, M. (2005). Effects of face-to-face restorative justice on victims of crime in four randomized, controlled trials. *Journal of Experimental Criminology, 1*, 367–395.

Simpson, S. S. (1992). Corporate-crime deterrence and corporate-control policies. In: K. Schlegel & D. Weisburd (Eds), *White collar crime reconsidered* (pp. 289–308). Boston: Northeastern University Press.

Simpson, S. S. (2002). *Corporate crime, law, and social change*. New York: Cambridge University Press.

Simpson, S. S., & Koper, C. S. (1992). Deterring corporate crime. *Criminology, 30*, 347–375.

Snider, L. (1990). Cooperative models and corporate crime: Panacea or cop-out. *Crime and Delinquency, 36*, 373–390.

Strang, H. (2002). *Repair or revenge: Victims and restorative justice*. New York: Oxford University Press.

Stretesky, P. B. (2006). Corporate self-policing and the environment. *Criminology, 44*, 671–708.

Tosouni, A. (2004). *Reintegrative shaming among youthful offenders: Testing the theory through a secondary data analysis*. Long Beach: California State University.

Tutu, D. (1999). *No future without forgiveness*. New York: Doubleday.

Tyler, T. (1990). *Why people obey the law*. New Haven, CT: Yale University Press.

Tyler, T. (2006). Restorative justice and procedural justice: Dealing with rule-breaking. *Journal of Social Issues, 62*, 307–326.

Tyler, T., & Huo, Y. J. (2002). *Trust in the law: Encouraging public cooperation with the police and courts*. New York: Russell-Sage.

Tyler, T. R., Sherman, L., Strang, H., Barnes, G. C., & Woods, D. (2007). Reintegrative shaming, procedural justice, and recidivism: The engagement of offenders' psychological mechanisms in the Canberra RISE drinking-and-driving experiment. *Law and Society Review, 41*, 553–586.

Umbreit, M. (1994). *Victim meets offender: The impact of restorative justice and mediation*. Monsey, NY: Criminal Justice Press.

Walt, S., & Laufer, W. S. (1992). Corporate criminal liability and the comparative mix of sanctions. In: K. Schlegel & D. Weisburd (Eds), *White collar crime reconsidered* (pp. 309–331). Boston: Northeastern University Press.

Weber, M. (1978). *Economy and society.* Los Angeles: University of California Press.

Weisburd, D., Waring, E., & Chayet, E. (1995). Specific deterrence in a sample of offenders convicted of white-collar crimes. *Criminology, 33,* 587–607.

Weisburd, D., Waring, E., & Chayet, E. F. (2001). *White-collar crime and criminal careers.* New York: Cambridge University Press.

Weisburd, D., Wheeler, S., Waring, E., & Bode, N. (1991). *Crimes of the middle classes: White-collar offenders in the federal courts.* New Haven, CT: Yale University Press.

White, R. (2003). Communities, conferences and restorative social justice. *Criminal Justice, 3,* 139–160.

Williams, K. R., & Hawkins, R. (1986). Perceptual research on general deterrence: A critical review. *Law and Society Review, 20,* 545–572.

Zehr, H. (1990). *Changing lenses: A new focus for crime and justice.* Scottdale, PA: Herald Press.

CHALLENGING CULTURES OF VIOLENCE THROUGH COMMUNITY RESTORATIVE JUSTICE IN NORTHERN IRELAND

Anna Eriksson

ABSTRACT

This chapter focuses on aspects of community restorative justice practices in Northern Ireland that have been central in challenging embedded cultures of violence within the current transitional context. It is argued that a strict adherence to restorative justice values, in combination with a flexible approach to the process used, are two core strengths of practice that have facilitated such a possibility. Moreover, these grassroots initiatives work well with organised, structured, and hierarchical communities, which in the Northern Irish context translate to paramilitary organisations. They are arguably less effective in relation to looser community structures, such as vigilante groups and individual violent responses to crime and conflict.

Restorative Justice: From Theory to Practice
Sociology of Crime, Law and Deviance, Volume 11, 231–260
Copyright © 2008 by Emerald Group Publishing Limited
All rights of reproduction in any form reserved
ISSN: 1521-6136/doi:10.1016/S1521-6136(08)00410-7

INTRODUCTION

The community-based restorative justice projects that are the focus of this chapter are some of the most high-profile developments of restorative justice in the last decade. The projects were established in some Republican and Loyalist communities in Northern Ireland in 1998 with the explicit aim of providing non-violent alternatives to practices of paramilitary punishment violence. In the Republican areas in which they operate (14 altogether) they are called Community Restorative Justice Ireland (CRJI); and in the four Loyalist areas, Northern Ireland Alternatives (Alternatives). They are led by former combatants and political ex-prisoners of the Provisional Irish Republican Army (IRA) and the Ulster Volunteer Force (UVF), respectively, and the presence of these individuals have caused much controversy within Northern Ireland and elsewhere. Indeed, these projects have been a key feature of a high-profile contest between state and community over the ownership of justice and in debates around the management and prevention of crime and antisocial behaviour within the period of transition which Northern Ireland is currently undergoing (McEvoy & Eriksson, 2008).[1]

It has been argued that a period of protracted violent conflict gives rise to 'a culture of violence' which creates a socially permissive environment within which violence continues to be used to resolve interpersonal conflict and respond to communal problems of crime and disorder even after peace accords have been signed and the violent political conflict ended (Steenkamp, 2005). This chapter will discuss how the day-to-day practice of community restorative justice projects in Northern Ireland can contribute to challenging and perhaps even changing such embedded cultures of violence at the individual and communal levels.

I will argue that these restorative justice projects are characterised by three key features which makes such an endeavour possible. Firstly, the presence of former combatants and political ex-prisoners is crucial in providing moral, political, and military leadership during such transformations (McEvoy & Eriksson, 2006). Secondly, in combination with the first point, the strong grassroots ethos and the emphasis on local community members as volunteers provides a moral authority and legitimacy to challenge and educate both paramilitary organisations and the wider community in non-violent approaches to conflict resolution. This is especially important in contexts where the legitimacy of the state and the criminal justice system has been severely questioned (McEvoy & Newburn, 2003; Roberts & McMillan, 2003; Shearing, Cartwright, & Jenneker, 2006).

Thirdly, the firm adherence to certain key restorative justice *values* in combination with a flexible approach to the *process* has resulted in the projects being able to respond to a wide range of communal and interpersonal conflicts. This feature has also allowed the projects to adopt a needs-based approach, where the process of restorative justice practice is adapted based on the particular needs of participants, be they disputing neighbours, young people involved in drugs, alcohol and antisocial behaviour, victims, statutory agencies, or representatives of the various paramilitary organisations.[2]

Such flexibility, and a focus on participant needs, positions CRJI and Alternatives to better address the underlying causes and correlations of conflict, crime, and antisocial behaviour within their local communities. Moreover, one of the most important roles of the projects within the transitional phase and beyond is the contribution they are making, not necessarily in relation to specific incidents, but on how such incidents are normally responded to at the individual and communal levels. By affecting these wider modes of conflict resolution, modes that reflect existing violence-supportive values and norms, CRJI and Alternatives can arguably contribute to challenging and even changing an embedded culture of violence within local communities in Northern Ireland. It is important to note that I am not arguing that community restorative justice will provide a complete solution to the complex issues experienced at the community level, during a transition or otherwise. I am however arguing that a well-run restorative justice project may act as a vehicle, or facilitator, for some of the trans-formative practices that are taking place in this particular societal context.

The third key feature mentioned above, the flexible needs-based practice of the projects, will be the focus of the arguments to follow. The discussion will firstly locate the use of restorative justice within transitional societies more generally, and then define a culture of violence and outline how it has manifested itself within the jurisdiction. Secondly, I will provide examples based on fieldwork and interviews undertaken between 2004 and 2007, to illustrate how such a culture of violence can arguably be challenged and even changed through restorative justice practice. Obviously, there are many wide-ranging changes taking place in Northern Ireland at present, and the practice of community restorative justice is only one of those. Hence, any results need to be interpreted with caution due to a lack of reliable base-line data and an inability to account for every aspect of this time of transition. However, the aim of this chapter is to contribute to three areas of research and debate. Firstly, it aims to explore the contribution that grassroots, informal justice initiatives can make in challenging a culture of violence within the framework of restorative justice. Secondly, the arguments here speak to broader debates within restorative justice by exploring the extent to which the framework may be applied to much more serious incidents of violence and criminality, rather than its traditional focus on juvenile and minor crimes. Thirdly, and perhaps somewhat ambitiously, it aims to contribute to the emerging literature on a criminological approach to peace-building, both within post-conflict societies and high-crime communities elsewhere.

RESTORATIVE JUSTICE IN TRANSITION

Restorative justice in transitional societies faces a number of additional difficulties to those traditionally associated with more stable jurisdictions. State-based initiatives may be regarded with some cynicism by affected communities where the state justice system has been contorted during the conflict (e.g. through emergency legislation) or where the police or state security forces have been guilty of human rights abuses in their war against the non-state forces (Roche, 2002; Nowrojee, 2005). Adherence to legal formalism, due process, proportionality and related benchmarks for ensuring good restorative justice practice in state-based programmes are not easily divorced from such violent histories when government and politics have been so closely related (Chayes & Chayes, 1998; Ruth-Heffelbower, 2000). Indeed, as has been the case in Northern Ireland, restorative justice programmes which are led by police or other criminal justice agencies (O'Mahony, Chapman, & Doak, 2002; Campbell et al., 2005), may struggle to develop partnerships with precisely those local communities most directly effected by the conflict, thus severely limit the transformative potential of restorative justice in the areas where it is most needed.

   In such a context, it makes sense that communities themselves should take primary ownership over the establishment of programmes, deciding what type of intervention might be suitable, who is going to be involved, which values will guide their work and devise their own benchmarks of practice as part of a broader 'legitimation process' (Mika & McEvoy, 2001). Those with the greatest stake in justice reconstruction – often those who have been on the receiving end of violence and criminality from the state, paramilitary actors and indeed local 'ordinary' offenders – should themselves be direct participants in the process as innovators, planners, and implementers (Ratuva, 2003; Pankhurst, 1999).

It is a central tenet of this chapter that restorative justice has much to offer in the wider context of conflict resolution in transitional societies, when focusing on the dimensions of restoration that matter to victims, offenders, and communities (Neuffer, 2002; Nowrojee, 2005; Villa-Vicencio, 2006). The inherent flexibility of restorative processes makes it capable of being highly sensitive to the political, social, and cultural context in which it is applied, and consequently suitable for a wide range of situations. Within the transitional context, restorative processes can empower individuals, strengthen communities, and address legitimacy deficits (Llewellyn & Howse, 1999; Roche, 2002; Froestad & Shearing, 2007). It has the potential to deal with the relationship between traditionally excluded communities and the state through procedural justice measures. Moreover, I would argue that restorative justice in transitional societies can, through a bottom-up approach, challenge ingrained cultures of violence and facilitate bridge-building between communities and state by engaging in crime management and prevention at the local level. Community participation in decision-making processes regarding the rebuilding of a society adds transparency, accountability, legitimacy, and, importantly, minimises the risk of renewed conflict (Candio & Bleiker, 2001; Roche, 2003).

Restorative justice has recently been implemented as part of conflict resolution interventions in relation to broader political conflicts, such as in Northern Ireland (Auld, Gormally, McEvoy, & Ritchie, 1997; Winston, 1997; McEvoy & Mika, 2001). South Africa has also implemented different initiatives of restorative justice to address the legacy of the Apartheid regime (Hayner, 1994, 2001; Villa-Vincencio, 1999; Skelton, 2002; Llewellyn, 2007); and in relation to community-based Peace Committees (Shearing, 2001; Roche, 2002; Cartwright, Jenneker, & Shearing, 2004; Cartwright & Jenneker, 2005; Froestad & Shearing, 2007). In Rwanda, the *gacaca* system was implemented to deal with the aftermath of genocide, which arguably mirrors the values and processes of restorative justice (Waldorf, 2006). These newer and extended uses of restorative justice indicate a shift in thinking regarding the possible applications of the framework, even though far from all proponents of the discipline agree on the appropriateness of such new directions. Nonetheless, some writers argue that this is the direction we must take if we wish to address social and political injustice:

> Until its proponents have made profound shifts in thinking, restorative justice will remain trapped within Western rational thought, constrained by unexamined assumptions. We must challenge our assumptions about human nature and our relationships, and contextualise restorative justice politically, socially, and economically in the larger

world. Only then can restorative justice become a force for positive social change. (Napoleon, 2004, p. 34)

The restorative justice work in local communities in Northern Ireland closely mirrors the initiatives in South Africa (Shearing, 2001; Roche, 2002; Cartwright et al., 2004; Cartwright & Jenneker, 2005; Froestad & Shearing, 2007), which build on local capacity, knowledge, and experience to devise appropriate solutions to crime and conflict within their own communities. The affirmation and development of new social norms through participatory practices such as restorative justice is an especially important feature in a transitional society, where systems of informal and formal justice, and the relationship between them, are in a process of renegotiation (Dzur & Olson, 2004). One major difference between the South African version of grassroots justice initiatives and that of Northern Ireland is that the former developed in partnership with the state and relevant statutory agencies. Such a dynamic was lacking during the first 10 years of practice of community restorative justice in Northern Ireland, and is only now emerging. The next section will explore a 'culture of violence' in more detail, before moving on to ways of challenging such a culture through grassroots initiatives in local communities in the Northern Irish context.

CULTURES OF VIOLENCE

In general, the expression 'cultures of violence' is used as a shorthand for the assertion that there is a direct link between exposure to violence over a long period of time and an acceptance of violence as a means of resolving interpersonal conflict or deal with frustrations in everyday life (Hayes & McAllister, 2001; Steenkamp, 2005). Hence, the experience of prolonged violent conflict in areas such as Northern Ireland, South Africa, and Sierra Leone has arguably resulted in the use of violence as a means of conflict resolution becoming embedded in the broader values and norms which guide behaviour in any one community, e.g. the local culture (Vogelman & Lewis, 1993; Du Toit, 2001; Ferme, 2001; Knox & Monaghan, 2002; MacGinty & Darby, 2002; Kynoch, 2005). When such violence continues after a conflict is over, a culture of violence is said to exist within the transitional society. According to Steenkamp, violence thus 'loses its political meaning and becomes a way of dealing with everyday issues ... a socially accepted mechanism to achieve power and status in society' (2005, p. 254).

There are some studies that consider the *emergence* of a culture of violence (see Rupesinghe & Rubio, 1994; Curle, 1999; Hamber, 1999; Bourgois, 2001), but they pay little attention to how such violent cultures are *maintained* in the transitional society and beyond. For example, Ervin Staub has covered, in a series of publications, the creation of cultures of violence from a psychological perspective, arguing that the frustration of basic human needs – such as the needs for security, a positive identity, a sense of effectiveness, belonging, autonomy, and justice – create an inclination towards violence and aggression (see Staub, 1989, 1996, 1999, 2003). The frustration of basic human needs does not only stem from micro-interactions within the family and peer groups, but can result from rapid social change, economic marginalisation, and living in a conflict zone where there is a continuous risk of attack by other groups (Staub, 1989; also see Kelman, 1990). Staub has explored the effects of such frustration and its consequence in terms of violence within the family context, youth violence, terrorism, and genocide. He asserts that we need to create conditions where these basic needs can be fulfilled, especially in relation to children, as to contribute to the development of peaceful relations.

The communal level of a culture of violence has been covered more comprehensively than the individual. For example, in relation to what some argue is a culture of violence in the American south (Gastil, 1971; Cohen & Nesbitt, 1994). It has also been explored in relation to practices of the Sicilian Mafia (Cottino, 1999). This literature is, however, exploratory and descriptive, and again focuses on the original formation of such violent cultures, not their maintenance. The avoidance of a more in-depth analysis is a missed opportunity, in that such an omission prevents an exploration of the factors and processes which not only maintain such cultures, but which can challenge them as part of broader peace-building and crime prevention efforts in the transitional context. Arguably, such an analysis can also be an important component of crime prevention efforts in high-crime communities in more 'settled' societies.

A culture of violence and its maintaining factors can exist on several levels: international, state, collective, and individual (Steenkamp, 2005). The last two are the focal points of discussion here, and it is argued that it is at these two levels where community restorative justice can have the greatest impact. It is important to note, however, that the different levels are interconnected, in that micro-processes take place within and are affected by larger macro-processes, i.e. violence committed by an individual takes place within a broader social, political, and economic context.

The key to understanding a culture of violence is that culture is not something one is born with but rather it is learned through socialisation, using the symbols and behavioural codes available to members of any one society. It is also passed down from one generation to the next (Groff & Smoker, 1996). It has been argued that in the Northern Irish context, such a transfer of knowledge and values forms part of a

> socialisation which is restricted almost exclusively to a reproduction of the values of one's own respective political community. (McAuley, 2004, p. 545)

In Northern Ireland, this has resulted in sharply defined borders between Republican and Loyalist communities (Shirlow & Murtagh, 2006), communities which are not just physically created but rely on a prominent symbolic language (evident in murals, songs, language, and annual parades) which play a central role in the construction of community (Cohen, 1985). Importantly, culture is strongly tied into questions about national identity and one's community's relationship with the state (Groff & Smoker, 1996).

In Northern Ireland, words such as the Catholic/Protestant, Nationalist/ Unionist, and Republican/Loyalist community, are terms that can be deployed in an exclusionary and sectarian fashion. The lived reality for many working-class urban communities in particular is highly segregated. Local community identity in these areas is symbolised in the construction of community borders by means of painted curb stones, flags, murals, and so-called peace walls as part of an ingrained communal segregation (Shirlow & Murtagh, 2006).[3] As Crawford and Clear (2001) have noted:

> In order to consider the genuine potential of restorative and community justice, we need to shed the rose-tinted glasses worn by many advocates and confront the empirical realities of most communities. The ideal of unrestricted entry to, and exit from, communities needs to be reconciled with the existence of relations of dominance, exclusion, and differential power. The reality is that many stable communities tend to resist innovations, creativity, and experimentation, as well as informal social control, and the way these processes play out lacks inclusive qualities and offender-sensitive styles. They can be coercive and tolerant of bigotry and discriminatory behaviour. Weaker parties within such communities often experience them not as a home of connectedness and mutuality but as a mainspring of inequalities that sustain and reinforce relations of dependence. They are often hostile to minorities, dissenters, and outsiders. (p. 137)

It is against this larger backdrop of a divided society and strained relationships between communities, and between communities and the state, that the values and norms which maintain a culture of violence in Northern Ireland exist. When considering utilising restorative justice initiatives to address communal conflict within such areas, such features must be explicitly recognised.

A CULTURE OF VIOLENCE IN NORTHERN IRELAND

The existence of a culture of violence in Northern Ireland has been noted by several writers (MacGinty & Darby, 2002; Knox & Monaghan, 2002; Jarman, 2004), even though the actual expression 'culture of violence' has been used sparingly and with little attempt of analyse as to why such a culture is maintained in the transitional phase and beyond. There is research which highlights the impact of violence on the people of Northern Ireland more generally (Feldman, 1991), and the frequent incidents of security force harassment experienced by young people in Northern Ireland before the Good Friday Agreement of 1998 more specifically (Bell, 1990; Amnesty International, 1991). For example, a report by the human rights organisation Helsinki Watch (1992) concluded that the harassment of children under 18 from both communities was endemic. Such experiences contribute to mistrust and a decrease in the legitimacy and credibility of the criminal justice system and, by extension, the state (McAuley, 2004). Importantly, such experiences contribute to the maintenance of a culture of violence that is intergenerational in its nature (Steenkamp, 2005).[4]

One of the most visible signs of an embedded culture of violence in Northern Ireland is the use of punishment violence by paramilitary organisations (Feenan, 2002; Monaghan, 2002, 2004; McEvoy & Mika, 2001, 2002). Such punishment violence was part of informal systems of 'justice' which involved shootings (in arms, legs, joints, or a combination) and/or beatings (using baseball bats which are sometimes studded with nails, iron bars, cudgels, hurley sticks, etc.) for the purpose of punishing offenders of crime and antisocial behaviour or as a means of ensuring discipline within paramilitary organisations. Measures like warnings, curfews, and exclusions from the community were also common (Bell, 1996; Feenan, 2002; Hamill, 2002; Monaghan, 2002; Jarman, 2004). As persuasively argued by McEvoy (2003), such informal systems of 'policing' are best viewed as

A complex interplay between the contested legitimacy of state policing (particularly in Republican areas); a reliance upon and demand for paramilitary retribution by local communities; the organisational capacity and self-image of the paramilitary groups as 'protectors' of their communities; and the emergence of groups of alienated young

> antisocial men who viewed punishment violence as an occupational hazard of their
> lifestyles and in some instances, as a badge of honour. (p. 322)

Paramilitary organisations were largely responsible for informal social control within their communities, in the absence of a legitimate and/or effective formal social control mechanism, e.g. the police. One result of such reliance on paramilitary organisations to manage conflict at the community level was, according to interviewees, an abdication of responsibility for one's own conflicts, by individuals, families, and in extension, the community. Moreover, an ineffective criminal justice system and weak state control over informal alternatives (McEvoy & Newburn, 2003; Roberts & McMillan, 2003; Cartwright et al., 2004; Shearing et al., 2006) are two important sustaining factors of a culture of violence in transitional societies (Steenkamp, 2005). Hence, where the state is unable to consolidate its monopoly over violence through effective sanctioning, the norms and values legitimising the personal use of violence are likely to linger (Darby & MacGinty, 2000).

Moreover, young people can emerge from protracted periods of conflict as one of the most marginalised groups in society (Higgins & Martin, 2003). They are likely to have limited, if any, experience of institutional civil life and participation, and a mistrust of the political system and its actors (Simpson, 1993). They are socially isolated because of the break-up of family networks, economically vulnerable with (at best) an interrupted education and have direct experience of violence. Consequently, they are at risk of becoming involved in violent actions as a means of acquiring a sense of belonging and status which results in a situation where violence and social rewards become interlinked (du Toit, 2001; Steenkamp, 2005). As was mentioned by Jarman (2004) in relation to Northern Ireland,

> These types of activities, whether it's rioting, antisocial behaviour, low-level crime, or just hanging around on street corners, also bring many young people into frequent contact with the police and here too a relationship based on mutual suspicion and hostility and a lack of mutual respect serves to increase the marginalisation of many young people. For many young people, there is little expectation of anything outside the boundaries of their local estate; they have low educational attainments, few job prospects outside the black economy, and in such a situation, drugs, crime and violence provide the parameters of their expectations. (p. 434)

For some young people in such situations, joining paramilitaries or drug gangs for status, respect, and financial gain provide a viable option, further embedding a culture of violence.

This issue was frequently mentioned during the research, and it was said that the continuing presence of paramilitary groups, particularly in Loyalist areas, play a central and detrimental part in the lives of many young people in these areas, who are still joining different paramilitary groups, even though the 'war' is over.[5] This arguably occurs for a number of reasons. Firstly, Loyalist paramilitary organisations held considerable degrees of power in their communities during the Troubles, and even though efforts are being made by several organisations and individuals, the process of reversing this power relationship is a difficult and slow one. As noted by Winston (1997),

> With the considerable social, political and symbolic significance attached to these organisations, it is a quite natural progression for young men to join one of the paramilitary groups in their late teens. Membership is high, and the organisations have tended to represent an important locus of power in the area. (p 124)

Secondly, paramilitary organisations, particularly Loyalist ones, have been linked to the drug trade in Northern Ireland (Silke, 2000; Monaghan, 2002). The distribution of illegal drugs is one part of a wider network of organised crime (Higgins & McElrath, 2000). This particularly affects young people who are vulnerable to such influences. The manager of east Belfast Alternatives, in an interview in June 2005, was only too aware of the effects of such communal influences. The following quote is somewhat lengthy, but clearly illustrates the effects of a culture of violence in transitional Belfast and the work faced by community organisations trying to challenge and change the situation:

> The young ones, they are what we would call 'ceasefire soldiers' who join for various reasons. We would say, in our analysis, from talking to them, that peer pressure is incredible in these areas. And for protection, they are joining. It is hard to stand on your own two feet and say 'no, I am not joining', when all your friends are telling you to. And you have people coming to you, pressurising you, and 'I am going to hit you', they have a whole team behind them. And a lot of kids would join just to get that team behind them. This is one of the main reasons, we are finding. And once they are in they are getting sucked into drugs etc. Drugs is a massive problem in east Belfast, massive. Thankfully we have, in this area, a leadership that are trying to stomp it out.[6] The young people are leaving school without any qualifications, they have no jobs to go to. Their role-models within the community are the ones driving the BMWs wearing gold chains etc. And where are they getting their money? Drugs ... We had one young lad, 11 years old, sitting in this office telling us that his only goal in life was to become a drug dealer, because he sees them as role models. And it is about breaking that vicious cycle, and it is gong to be a long, slow, process. It is not going to change over night.[7]

Violence as a means of acquiring social benefits such as honour and prestige can also be seen, for example, in relation to many of the 'victims' of punishment violence, that they carry it as a badge of honour within their community (McEvoy, 2003), and that one is not taken seriously until one has been punished. A punishment beating or shooting becomes a measure that the young person is having an impact in the community, that he is acknowledged as someone to be reckoned with, even if this only holds true within the peer group's subculture (Hamill, 2002). Violence equips them with power that they would not normally have if they had to compete with the rest of the community on an equal footing, because of their limited educational or wealth resources. While these violent peer groups, such as gangs or the youth wing of paramilitaries, are not unique to transitional societies, these violence-supporting values and norms are reinforced by the political acceptance of the use of violence during the war by both the state and community (du Toit, 2001). The challenge is to integrate these youths into civil society and to find alternatives to street life.

By way of summary of this point, it can be argued that peer pressure, social rewards for violence, limited sanctioning for attacks on the 'other' community, and a communal glorification of violence are all important factors in maintaining a culture of violence in the post-conflict society. So are a punitive community, rapid social change, a not fully legitimate police force and the marginalisation and disadvantage of many youths in the transitional context. Arguably, restorative justice, with its focus on the (re)integration of young people, of addressing underlying reasons for offending, a future looking philosophy, and emphasis on participation, inclusiveness, and responsibilisation, can be a well-placed vehicle to address such complex issues within the transitional society.

Importantly, several of these maintaining factors of a culture of violence exist at the grassroots level. Hence, any initiatives that could be effective in addressing such issues, should ideally be grassroots, bottom-up ones, indigenous to the local communities in which they work. As mentioned in the introduction, community restorative justice in Northern Ireland can clearly be characterised to be such local grassroots initiatives, a unique feature that positions them well to address these complex and interdependent issues.

CHALLENGING A CULTURE OF VIOLENCE AND ITS MAINTAINING FACTORS THROUGH COMMUNITY RESTORATIVE JUSTICE

If restorative justice projects can foster greater involvement in and ownership over crime management ... then they may become a tool for greater community tolerance, cohesion and non-violence. (McEvoy & Mika, 2001, p. 375)

CRJI and Alternatives were, as mentioned above, established to provide a non-violent alternative to paramilitary punishment violence (Auld et al., 1997; Winston, 1997; McEvoy & Mika, 2001, 2002), practices which can be seen belonging firmly within a framework of a culture of violence. As was argued by Knox and Monaghan (2002),

> In Northern Ireland, there is still a strong support for summary justice, a legacy of years of violent struggle ... there is an obvious time lag in moving away from transitional status where the formal justice system remains ineffectual and politically tainted, to one which can command the credibility and trust of the communities ... This has resulted in a hiatus. The transition to acceptable and effective policing and criminal justice systems inevitably is taking longer than envisaged which provide justification for paramilitaries and vigilantes to tackle violent crime. (p. 139–140)

To effectively address the complex issues surrounding punishment violence, it was clear for CRJI and Alternatives from the outset that a multifaceted approach was needed (Auld et al., 1997; Winston, 1997). As such, different targets of intervention were taken into consideration. The restorative justice work could not have a narrow focus of dealing with individuals under threat by paramilitary groups, but also the very people who carried out such attacks. Moreover, as mentioned earlier, the projects made the assumption that they needed to address the underlying causes of crime and antisocial behaviour in relation to the people who came into contact with them, and include victims and extended family networks in the discussions. Wider community practices and expectations in relation to conflict resolution in the community also formed part of the focus of their practice.

Hence, the aim of practice in relation to punishment violence can be said to be four-fold: mediating directly for people under threat by paramilitaries; addressing underlying causes of why people came to the attention of paramilitaries in the first place; engaging with paramilitary groups themselves in terms of modes of conflict resolution; and involving the wider community. All four targets of intervention can challenge an embedded culture of violence within the community in different ways which will be discussed below. The values and processes of restorative justice are arguably central to this endeavour.

The principles and practices of restorative justice can provide a useful organising framework through which communities can themselves take a lead in the transformations required. At the individual level, this can arguably be achieved by involving individuals and their families in processes defined by restorative justice values such as non-violence, inclusiveness, respect, reparation, integration, and empowerment. Importantly, it is the opportunity to actually *experience* the use of such values in interpersonal interaction, which for some people may be for the first time, which is the powerful change agent at this level. At the communal level, restorative justice can potentially challenge cultures of violence by affecting conflict resolution practices in both paramilitary organisations and wider community networks, both of which will be explored later in the chapter.

CRJI and Alternatives utilise somewhat different restorative processes which reflects the restorative justice background of the key individuals who were instrumental in setting them up (see Auld et al., 1997; Winston, 1997), and also their more specific aims of practice. CRJI uses shuttle mediation, family group conferencing, and victim-offender mediation. The precise model at any one time is adapted to suit the particular case at hand, its circumstances and participants. Alternatives has largely adhered to a model they call Intensive Youth Programme, which is specifically aimed at young people under threat by paramilitaries. During this programme, the young person works one-on-one with a key worker and aims to address the reasons why he (and on occasion, she) came to the attention of the paramilitaries. Different types of community work, the possibility of victim-offender mediation, re-engagement with education or work usually form part of the contract agreed to by the participant. Alternatives also has an active section working exclusively with victims in the community. This does not only relate to people who have been victims of the young people in the project, but anyone who asks for assistance.

Neither CRJI nor Alternatives have a set time limit for cases, they generally stay open and active for as long as the participants need them to be. However, many cases are resolved within hours, particularly in relation to mediation between neighbours or negotiating with a paramilitary organisation to lift the threat against someone. Below is an example of a successful case, taken from CRJI records in 2001. It demonstrates CRJI's use of shuttle mediation between a young person under threat and the Provisional IRA. The mediations took place after a beating and hence did not prevent the punishment attack, but arguably prevented the situation from rapidly escalating:

> The case concerned a punishment attack on a 13-year-old boy who had been taken from his home and severely beaten with sewer rods. The IRA referred the case to CRJI after the mother of the boy had brought a complaint to their office. The IRA initially denied involvement. CRJI made a visit to the boy's home and spoke to him and his mother to clarify what had happened. The IRA was then contacted to find out

who had carried out the beating. Support was given to the family by CRJI during this time. It emerged that it was the IRA who had carried out the beating. CRJI and a member from the IRA went to the family's home where the IRA member apologised for this 'unforgivable behaviour'. Members of the IRA also apologised to CRJI for lying about their involvement in the first place. CRJI kept in contact with the family and helped secure a place in school for the young boy. A total of 18 hours were spent working on the case.

In relation to similar cases, a practitioner at CRJI said that he and other senior staff met on a regular basis with members of the Republican movement in a type of workshop where they talked about what they do, educating the IRA in restorative justice practices:

> The work we do ... it gives CRJI an opportunity to create awareness among the armed groups in the area about community needs. Like when you talk to the armed groups about a particular person, then there is a better understanding by the armed groups about where the person is coming from. Whereas before, none of that would have been taken into consideration, there was just a person who was causing problems and 'let's deal with him'. But they, just as our volunteers, would now have a better understanding of what the issues are that need to be taken into consideration.[8]

This quote and the case study above, illustrate the point made previously, that CRJI and Alternatives have adopted a multifaced approach when working with punishment violence cases, involving the young person in question, the individual paramilitary members involved, and the wider organisational structures of the various paramilitary organisations in the area. This allows them to challenge embedded cultures of violence from several directions, both individual and collective, arguably increasing their potential effectiveness in this regard.

The evidence available so far in relation to effectiveness in challenging punishment violence indicates that it is indeed possible. Obviously there are several factors which affect levels of punishment violence, but based on a recent evaluation undertaken by Professor Harry Mika (2006), CRJI and Alternatives have been successful in minimising the use of paramilitary punishment attacks within the geographical areas in which they work. Between 2003 and 2005, 327 cases were handled by CRJI and Alternatives together, which involved confirmed paramilitary threats or someone at risk to be placed under such threats in the very near future (Mika, 2006).[9] Moreover, as emerged clearly from my own field research, there were numerous informal contacts and negotiations with paramilitary organisations in both communities, both in relation to young people and other community matters. Mika (2006) estimated such informal contacts to range between 7 and 10 for every case of punishment violence dealt with formally.

Mika (2006) reports that between 2003 and 2005, intervention by CRJI stopped 82 per cent and Alternatives 71 per cent of potential paramilitary attacks within their respective geographical remit areas.[10] The number of cases successfully prevented increased each year. For example, in 2003, Alternatives successfully prevented an estimated 40 per cent of possible punishment attacks; at the end of 2005, the figure was 90 per cent. The comparable figures for CRJI were 78 per cent and 94 per cent, respectively (Mika, 2006).

The effects of community restorative justice do not only extend to ending individual punishment attacks. As mentioned above, field research also indicates that the practice of CRJI and Alternatives can be a catalyst for change for both the Provisional IRA and the UVF respectively. The work undertaken by community restorative justice in these areas informs and questions the role of the armed groups, now and for the future, in relation to methods of conflict resolution (McEvoy & Mika, 2002; Mika, 2006) and, moreover, partnerships with the police and other statutory agencies (McEvoy & Eriksson, 2008). Such practice can arguably challenge ingrained cultures of violence within paramilitary organisations. This, in turn, can permeate wider community structures in relation to violent responses to conflict, crime, and antisocial behaviour in the larger community. It is to such effects of community restorative justice that I now turn.

It is important to note that the cases dealing explicitly with threats of punishment violence only made up 4 per cent of the caseload for CRJI and 3 per cent for Alternatives between 2003 and 2005. During this period, it was also reported that CRJI handled 4,849 cases *not* related to punishment beatings, and Alternatives reported formal contact with 2,139 young people and 1,719 engagements with victims, also *not* related to paramilitary threat (Mika, 2006). Among the non-punishment violence cases, CRJI in particular deals with a wide range of issues. As by way of illustration, Fig. 1 summarises all the cases dealt with by the four main CRJI offices in Belfast in 2006 according to type of case.

Moreover, in the 1,005 cases dealt with in 2006, 4,412 people were directly involved as participants, with the average number of participants per case being 4.4. Volunteers and practitioners spent 4,150 h working on these cases. What is arguably striking with this data is the high number of cases and people who have been directly involved in a restorative justice process

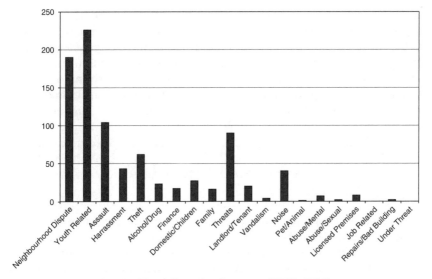

Fig. 1. Total Cases by Category (CRJI, 2006).

within geographically quite small areas of Northern Ireland. Considering that the four offices in question are staffed by a total of four full-time coordinators and approximately 30 volunteers, the numbers are impressive.

On the Loyalist side where the projects are considerably smaller, targeted more exclusively at young people under paramilitary threat, and involve intensive youth work (McEvoy & Mika, 2001), a total of 132 cases were processed between 1999 and 2004 (Mika, 2004). Moreover, formal contact is made with a wide range of people, even though far from all are involved in an Intensive Youth Programme. As reported by Mika (2006), the casework at Alternatives between 2003 and 2005 included formal contact with 2,139 young people and 1,719 engagements with victims. This work was supported through a network of 268 community volunteers (p. 23). Such high numbers are also, I would argue, an indicator of, not only the local legitimacy of the projects, but an indication of the need for these types of community-based conflict resolution services, and arguably, of an underlying culture of violence which contributes to the high case load.

Today, when paramilitary groups have largely relinquished their responsibility in relation to informal social control, and the police have still to gain full legitimacy and effective practice within these working-class communities, a void exists. The managers of both CRJI and Alternatives have argued that their organisation is vital in filling this void. This gap in social control, or in effective approaches to the prevention, management, and resolution of conflict at the individual and communal levels, is evident in the changing remit and focus of practice for both projects in recent years. It is arguably these changes in practice, changes which are a response to shifts in individual and communal needs, which allow them to address several other maintaining factors of a culture of violence, apart from 'just' paramilitary punishment violence.

AFFECTING WIDER COMMUNITY PRACTICES OF CONFLICT RESOLUTION

This punitive community is a very good reason for the continuing need for CRJI.[11]

A common theme mentioned in all interviews conducted with practitioners of Alternatives and CRJI was a focus on wider practices and expectations in relation to conflict resolution in the community. Such a focus of practice was, and still is, an integral part of their work. Ending practices of punishment violence, and by extension, challenging an embedded culture of violence, cannot be achieved by a singular focus on paramilitary groups (Mika, 2006). As was mentioned by the project manager of Alternatives, there are still some people in the community who put active pressure on the different paramilitary groups to continue their tradition of 'policing'. He states:

> I think that the biggest problem ... if people come to us and say 'aye, the paramilitaries have to stop shooting kids this way', then we would have been a hell of a lot further on. It's the appetite within these communities where people go to the paramilitaries and say 'what do you mean you are not going to shoot them? I want them shot'. And trying to convince people that punishment violence is not the answer, we had it for 30 years and it did not solve anything. We don't say we have a magic wand but we feel that in the long term it is far more valid for our community to address these issues by having residents taking responsibility, to have young people address and own up to the damage they have done within their communities, and to do that in a restorative way, as opposed to beating them.[12]

Several interviewees within both CRJI and Alternatives mentioned that they could see a change in communal attitudes towards violence. In particular, there is a change in how young people are viewed, both by paramilitary groups as argued above, and by the 'ordinary' community. A practitioner at Shankill Alternatives said,

> I think there is an acceptance by most people that things need to change. I do understand that there is a dilemma and that some people believe, especially with serious repeat

offenders, that things need to be handled in a punitive way. However, there are genuine people within paramilitary groups who do not want to have to do these sorts of things. It is a case where people go 'shopping' – they go to one [paramilitary] group and if that group does not do what they want to do, then they will go to another, maybe from a different area. It is so complex, but I do think that there a shift gradually ... and I believe Alternatives has been part of that. And there is also things going on within paramilitary groups themselves ... they are moving on like. And people have come here and said that they would normally go to the paramilitaries but that they don't want anyone shot, they just want it to stop. I think that slowly but surely it is a trickle towards that. There is still an appetite among people towards a punitive way, but there is a shift, there is a change.[13]

Such a change is, however, slow. Knox and Monaghan (2002) pointed out the difficulty that communities, which had for 30 years demanded and witnessed 'rough justice', would have in accepting an alternative which was centred around apologies, reparation, and community service. Such a mind-shift, they argued, would necessarily take time. As an interviewee in relation to community restorative justice practice mentioned,

We do have to combat the attitudes of some people out there who do go to the paramilitaries, who don't go to the police, who don't want another alternative but who go to the paramilitaries for justice. Because it is seen as a swift and immediate type of justice ... it is very visual if a young person has been shot you know.[14]

There is no grand plan to achieve such a change in the transitional society. Instead, as was mentioned by CRJI volunteers in Derry, a city on the north coast of the province, the way they view the potential of community restorative justice to challenge cultures of violence is 'case by case, by offering alternatives to the traditional methods of dealing with crime and antisocial behaviour'.[15] As a practitioner at an Alternatives project mentioned,

People in this area would say that the police are proving ineffective ... So people go to people like us, or the paramilitaries, or local churches – people within their local community who they can trust. So we have to change that, you know, the community mind-set. And hopefully through the paramilitaries we can do that. Because if they say 'no, we won't do that, we will send him to Alternatives', *that* will make people think. Again, it is going to be a long, slow, process and I am making no apologies for that.[16]

Viewed in such a way, practices of restorative justice at the micro-level, working directly with individuals and their families, can have an impact on the macro-community, which includes both paramilitary organisations and the wider community, a dynamic generally referred to by practitioners as the 'ripple effect'. Such a ripple effect of practice can have wide-ranging positive corollaries within punitive communities. The manager of CRJI in Derry who said, that one of the major contributions the practices of restorative justice have provided in the areas where they work is to raise the threshold of when people ask to have someone shot or beaten, highlighted this. This is a major change for communities that for many years have relied on paramilitaries for conflict resolution.

Attitudes supportive of violence in the resolution of local problems with crime and disorder clearly emerged in research undertaken by Hamill (2002) in relation to practices of punishment violence in Nationalist west Belfast. As part of her research, she attended several public meetings where the problem of high levels of antisocial behaviour by young people in the area was discussed. The meetings were attended by local residents and representatives from youth and community projects, but also by people from statutory agencies and political parties. The dominant mood during these meetings was anger and frustration, and one local resident said:

> We have fought long and hard for everything in this area, for traffic lights, the health centre, the schools, and then the hoods[17] come along and break into them and ruin them. The joy-riders ram into pensioners' housing terrifying these old people. As a community what are we supposed to do? We have to draw the line and say something is no longer acceptable and can no longer be tolerated. (Hamill, 2002, p. 61)

Hamill also noted that the demands for harsher intervention against hoods all came from local residents, 'They can't stab other people and get away with it; they need to be taught a lesson they'll never forget' (2002: p. 61). The people involved in the efforts to persuade local communities regarding the potential of restorative justice during the *Blue Book* consultation (e.g. Auld et al., 1997) reported similar harsh community attitudes.[18]

Another example of such an existing culture of violence surfaced during interviews with a group of CRJI volunteers from one part of west Belfast in 2004. They stated that this particular community was a very punitive one, and using violence to solve interpersonal conflict was not new to people in this area. On several occasions, mothers had come into a CRJI office with their son, asking to have him beaten up, since they simply could not handle him anymore. Such requests were explained by practitioners to be due to the longstanding practices of punishment violence in the community. It was mentioned that some people in the area had become used to solutions which were punitive, quick, and very visible. Hence, the argument went, when people asked for someone to be beaten or shot, they were basically doing what they knew.

By extension, people's fear of victimisation, combined with inadequate protection from the state, can lead them to use violence to restore order and security. This was obviously seen more clearly during the Troubles, especially in Republican communities. One interviewee in a Loyalist area commented on such punitive tendencies in the community:

> From the victims' perspective, they say that 'I hold off going to the paramilitaries and you have 8 weeks to fix the problem', and then they see the kid out and about every weekend misbehaving ... 'where is the evidence then that your approach is working, whereas if I went to the club and say that this kid is bothering me, and then I see him hobbling around, that would be much more satisfying'. And that view is not to be discounted, you know. I find the case persuasive, that [going to the paramilitaries] does not resolve the case on a community level, and it might not resolve the problem on an individual level either in terms of re-offending, but I don't think that you can deny that there is something immensely satisfying with someone who has injured you, getting injured himself, you know. You see that they have been punished for what they have done.[19]

Similar community opinions were displayed in an area in north Belfast in 2004, where a new CRJI project was being established at the time.[20] When conducting a local survey and asking for community feedback via the Community Charter which was distributed to people's houses, many people wrote on the back of the Charter what they would like to do to the 'hoods', for example, 'don't shoot them six times, once should be enough', 'tarring and feathering and tie them to a lamp post', 'throw them out, they don't deserve anymore chances', and 'bring back public flogging'.[21]

A related expression of what is arguably a punitive community is vigilante type groups and/or individual community members who are acting without any type of group membership. In relation to vigilante groups, Foster's (1995) work on informal social control in high-crime areas notes that residents often prefer to deal with low- and medium-level crime and disorder informally, through existing social networks, rather than reporting them to the police. Her conclusions resonate closely to the experiences in Northern Ireland. The vigilante groups under consideration here exist in both Republican and Loyalist communities, but, based on primary research, seem to be more frequent in the former. They tend to operate under semi-legitimate names such as Community Watch and Safer Neighbourhood Projects. The problem is not the presence of such groups (after all they are a common feature across the UK) (Bolton, 2006; Crawford, 2006; Farrow & Prior, 2006), but the *quality and nature* of such a presence in Northern Ireland. Some people participate in ad hoc vigilante groups, often following a particular incident which angers the community, such as a murder or sexual assault when the perpetrator is known. Others join Community

Watch on a more permanent basis. As noted by one interviewee in west Belfast:

> I think people just have decided that they want to live in a better place, and that they want to make their own community safer. A lot of people who are out on the streets would themselves have been victims at some point of crime and antisocial behaviour. For instance people would have tried to steal their cars or whatever, so people feel that they need to be out there and protect theirs and their neighbour's property.[22]

Importantly, however, these violent responses to crime and conflict by the wider community are qualitatively different from that of paramilitary organisations. I have used the term 'disorganised community', to describe these type of groups. It is 'disorganised' because they stem from a situation where these groupings *lack* the organised military structures, permanent membership and leadership which signify paramilitary groups such as the IRA and the UVF. Considering that CRJI and Alternatives were established to work with the organised structures of paramilitary organisations, they arguably lack the tools necessary to effectively challenge all of the violent practices of disorganised vigilante groups. As one Republican activist mentioned: 'there are not enough of our fucking people in there', a statement that signifies the unique features of CRJI (and Alternatives), in that they were established to work with organised paramilitary structures, where the ripple effect of practice can have an impact through effective leadership and hierarchical structures. This is arguably a unique feature of restorative justice practice in the transitional context.

It is important to note, however, that not all people within these areas are supportive of punishment violence in particular or of paramilitary groups in general. It has been argued that such variation in community support for paramilitary punishment makes it a site of struggle over crime management and informal social control within communities (Brewer, Lockhart, & Rodgers, 1998). Brewer et al. (1998) have argued that certain community dynamics can be added to the list as sustaining systems of informal social control such as 'the survival of community structures, extended family kinship patterns, neighbourliness, and legitimate authority accorded to community representatives' (p. 570). When such systems of informal social control are characterised by *values* which support the use of violence, they help to sustain a culture of violence in the transitional period (Steenkamp, 2005). This does not necessarily mean that crime levels have to be abnormally high, but rather that violence is then readily used as an approach to conflict resolution and as a means of addressing local problems with crime and antisocial behaviour when they do occur.

CONCLUSION

Sullivan and Tifft (1998) state that injustices are incurred, not just as a result of interpersonal violence, but as a result of 'societal structural violence, that is violence done to people through the exercise of power, and hierarchical social arrangements that support the maintenance of this power' (p. 43). Hence, they argue, if restorative justice is to be achieved, efforts cannot be confined to restorative approaches to conventionally defined acts of harm and injustice, i.e. 'ordinary crimes'. Rather, it is necessary to address the social structural conditions that reproduce harm, inequality and violence. This, I would argue, is what community restorative justice in Northern Ireland is trying to achieve, by not only addressing the offending and victimisation of individuals, but actively working to deal with the underlying causes of such outcomes. They challenge longstanding structural hierarchies by providing non-violent alternatives to paramilitary systems of punishment violence and by educating individuals and the larger community in non-violent and inclusive conflict management and resolution.

Contributing to ending practices of punishment violence in Loyalist and Republican communities has to be seen as a considerable achievement by community restorative justice projects in the transitional context of Northern Ireland. Previous publications have certainly highlighted its centrality to the overall peace process (McEvoy & Mika, 2001; Mika & McEvoy, 2001; Knox & Monaghan, 2002; McEvoy & Mika, 2002). Importantly, both projects have noted that even though levels of crime and antisocial behaviour in their communities are not decreasing, this has not resulted in a renewed increase in punishment attacks. Instead, the caseloads of both projects, especially CRJI, have increased in relation to crime and antisocial behaviour in recent years. This arguably indicates four interrelated things. Firstly, a reduced community reliance on paramilitaries to deal with such issues; a reduced willingness by paramilitary groups themselves to engage in such practices; high or even increasing levels of offending and antisocial behaviour in the transitional context; and finally, but importantly, a lingering reluctance to report even serious incidents to the Police Service of Northern Ireland (PSNI). What can be clearly stated, however, is that the practice of community restorative justice has decreased the number of punishment attacks and exclusions occurring in the areas in which they work.

Moreover, the practice of restorative justice can raise the threshold of punitive attitudes in the community, consequently lessening calls for punishment violence and vigilante type actions. The effects are seen in relation to other participants in a restorative justice process, the views of volunteers, and wider community structures. Furthermore, by addressing the situation that many youths find themselves in, a situation characterised by disadvantage and marginalisation, another maintaining factor of a culture of violence is affected. Hence, the values embedded in social networks that help to sustain a culture of violence in the transitional phase (Steenkamp, 2005), can arguably be challenged and even changed, through grassroots, bottom-up restorative justice initiatives. At least that is the experience from the Northern Ireland context.

Based on such conclusions, I would again assert that restorative justice can be a useful framework around which to construct indigenous initiatives of conflict resolution. This is because good restorative justice practice has the potential of taking into account political, social, and economic factors that underlie and sustain criminal and antisocial behaviour in the transitional society. Moreover, the forward-looking philosophy and practice of restorative justice provides a useful focal point of intervention. Such a forward-looking approach can allow for the focus of conflict resolution practices in the transitional society to be on the maintaining factors of a culture of violence and subsequent criminality and antisocial behaviour, instead of the causes of the violent conflict per se. Such a focus arguably contributes to an emerging criminology within post-conflict societies by stretching the criminological imagination beyond much current application towards real contribution to the many challenges faced by transitional societies around the world.

NOTES

1. The arguments and tensions surrounding community restorative justice and the potential impact of the projects were investigated during a four-year period (2004–2007), through a combination of qualitative and quantitative methods. These included unique access to interviews with all practitioners of restorative justice projects in Republican and Loyalist communities, and samples of volunteers, victims, offenders, and families who had participated in the projects. This style of embedded ethnography with former combatants from both Loyalist and Republican backgrounds is rare (see Sluka, 1989) and provides a useful insight into the role that such individuals can play in post-conflict contexts. A total of 32 interviews and focus groups were conducted in direct relation to the projects, totalling 62 individuals. Included in that number are interviews with statutory agencies and local politicians, e.g. the PSNI, the Probation Board, the Housing Executive (NIHE), the Social and Democratic Labour Party (SDLP), Sinn Féin, the Democratic Unionist Party (DUP),

and the Progressive Unionist Party (PUP). The quantitative data collected covers over 1,000 cases from four offices of CRJI in west Belfast. The cases cover the period between 2002 and 2006 and were entered into an Access database that was constructed for the purpose. Variables which were analysed were: number and nature of participants in cases; number of hours spent dealing with each case; what processes and outcomes each case entailed; who had referred the case to the organisation; which outside agencies were involved, both as a point of referral and as part of outcome agreements; and any follow-up information that was included. The same unrestricted access to case data was not granted in relation to Alternatives, but no restrictions were placed in interviews and I was provided unfettered access to all of their projects.

2. Alternatives work mainly with the UVF and the Red Hand Commando. The other large Loyalist paramilitary organisation, the UDA, does not engage with community restorative justice. CRJI works primarily with the Provisional IRA but also engages in negotiations with the dissident Republican groups (the Real IRA, Continuity IRA, and the INLA) with the aim of persuading them to forego their reliance on violence to achieve their aims.

3. The number of the so-called peace walls has actually increased since 1998. In the cease-fire year of 1994, there were a reported 15 such walls in Belfast, in 2000 there were 27, and in 2003 they had increased to a number of 37. The most well-known wall is the one dividing west Belfast into the Falls and the Shankill. The highest number of walls, however, are to be found in north Belfast, indicating higher levels of segregation between communities which are geographically smaller, and where feeling of being under threat from the 'other' are still prominent (Jarman, 2004; Shirlow & Murtagh, 2006).

4. It is important to note, however, that the impact of such experiences may very well differ between communities, with such experiences being mediated by social structures and one's relationship with the state.

5. This was the situation during the field research in Loyalist areas in the summer of 2005. The situation, however, is bound to change rapidly, after the UVF issued a statement on 3 May 2007, announcing that the organisation is transforming into a non-military one and that they were putting their weapons beyond use. In the statement, the UVF also pledged their support for community restorative justice in Loyalist areas (*BBC News Northern Ireland*, 'UVF calls an end to terror campaign', 3 May 2007).

6. This statement also reflects the ambivalent relationship within and between different paramilitary groups, where some groups would be involved in importing and distributing drugs in the community, and another working hard to stop it. Feuds between different factions, especially within Loyalism, are not unusual outcomes to these tensions.

7. Interview 2 June 2005.

8. Interview with CRJI practitioner, 2 December 2004.

9. Mika (2006) listed five limitations with data collection, namely: PSNI reports include 'paramilitary styled' assaults and shootings, which may be unrelated to paramilitary activity; data refers to 'Republican' and 'Loyalist' groups which include several paramilitary organisations. CRJI cases include IRA exclusively, and Alternatives' cases include UVF and RHC exclusively; PSNI data refers to shootings

and assaults that have occurred, and does not include threats or exclusions, whereas CRJI and Alternatives' case data does include these two categories as well; PSNI reports refer to 'shootings and assaults', which include different types of violence – Alternatives and CRJI cases include only threats related to crime and antisocial behaviour, and do not include matters related to paramilitary internal disciplinary violence or personal vendettas; and finally, aggregated police data is based upon geographic District Command Units which do not correspond (and are often much larger) than the service catchments of Alternatives and CRJI (p. 22). It is vital to be aware of such limitations of data if the impact of community restorative justice is to be measured with as much accuracy as possible.

    10. See Mika (2006) for the exact procedure of calculating these numbers. The report can be found at: http://www.law.qub.ac.uk/schools/SchoolofLaw/Research/InstituteofCriminologyandCriminalJustice/Research/Publications

    11. Interview with CRJI manager, 9 November 2004.
    12. Interview with Alternatives manager, 19 May 2005.
    13. Interview with Project manager, 19 May 2005.
    14. Interview with Alternatives practitioner, 2 June 2005.
    15. Interview 31 March 2005.
    16. Interview with manager, east Belfast Alternatives, 2 June 2005.
    17. A local derogatory term for juvenile delinquent.
    18. Interview with Kieran McEvoy, 15 January 2006.
    19. Interview with victim support worker, Shankill Alternatives, 19 May 2005.
    20. This office has since closed due to a lack of funding.
    21. Interview with north Belfast CRJI coordinator, 14 February 2005.
    22. Interview with CRJI worker, 2 December 2004.

ACKNOWLEDGEMENT

The author wishes to thank her colleagues, new and old, for their helpful comments on various versions of this chapter: Dr Marie Segrave, Dr Dean Wilson, and Dr Louise Mallinder. Any mistakes that remain are my own. Moreover, my sincere appreciation to all the hardworking and committed individuals who work and volunteer for CRJI and Alternatives. They not only provided me with unprecedented access, but also were extraordinarily generous with their time and knowledge during the research period and beyond.

REFERENCES

Amnesty International. (1991). *United Kingdom: Allegations of ill-treatment in Northern Ireland.* London: Amnesty International.

Auld, J., Gormally, B., McEvoy, K., & Ritchie, M. (1997). *Designing a system of restorative justice in Northern Ireland*. Belfast: The Authors.

Bell, C. (1996). Alternative justice in Ireland. In: N. Dawson, D. Greer & P. Ingram (Eds), *One hundred and fifty years of Irish law*. Belfast: SLS Legal Publications.

Bell, D. (1990). *Acts of union: Youth culture and sectarianism in Northern Ireland*. Macmillan Education.

Bolton, S. (2006). Crime prevention in the community: The case of Neighbourhood Watch. *Criminal Justice Matters, 64*, 40–41.

Bourgois, P. (2001). The power of violence in war and peace: Post-cold war lessons from El Salvador. *Ethnography, 2*(1), 5–34.

Brewer, J. D., Lockhart, B., & Rodgers, P. (1998). Informal social control and crime management in Belfast. *The British Journal of Sociology, 49*(4), 570–585.

Campbell, C., Devlin, R., O'Mahony, D., Doak, J., Jackson, J., & Corrigan, T. (2005). *Evaluation of the Northern Ireland youth conference service* (No. 12). Belfast: Northern Ireland Office.

Candio, P., & Bleiker, R. (2001). Peace building in East Timor. *The Pacific Review, 14*(1), 63–84.

Cartwright, J., & Jenneker, M. (2005). Governing security: A working model in south Africa – the peace committee. Paper presented at the "A New Decade of Criminal Justice in South Africa – Consolidating Transformation?" Conference. Villa Via Hotel, Gordon's Bay, Western Cape, South Africa.

Cartwright, J., Jenneker, M., & Shearing, C. (2004). Local capacity governance in South Africa: A model for peaceful coexistence. Paper Originally Presented at the in Search for Security conference in Montreal Hosted by the Law Commission of Canada. Montreal, Canada.

Chayes, A. H., & Chayes, A. (1998). Mobilizing international and regional organizations for managing ethnic conflict. In: E. Weiner (Ed.), *The handbook of interethnic coexistence*. New York: The Continuum Publishing Co.

Cohen, A. P. (1985). *The symbolic construction of community*. UK: Routledge.

Cohen, D., & Nesbitt, R. (1994). Self-protection and the culture of honor: Explaining southern violence. *Personality and Social Psychology Bulletin, 20*(5), 551–567.

Cottino, A. (1999). Sicilian cultures of violence: The interconnections between organized crime and local society. *Crime, Law and Social Change, 32*(2), 103–113.

Crawford, A. (2006). 'Fixing broken promises?': Neighbourhood wardens and social capital. *Urban Studies, 43*(5/6), 957–976.

Crawford, A., & Clear, T. (2001). Community justice: Transforming communities through restorative justice? In: G. Bazemore & M. Schiff (Eds), *Restorative community justice: Repairing harm and transforming communities* (pp. 127–149). Cincinnati: Anderson Publishing Co.

Curle, A. (1999). *To tame the hydra: Undermining the culture of violence*. Charbury: John Carpenter.

Darby, J., MacGinty, R. (Eds). (2000). Northern Ireland: Long, cold peace. In: *The management of the peace process* (pp. 61–106). London: Macmillan.

Du Toit, P. (2001). *South Africa's brittle peace: The problem of post-settlement violence*. Basingstoke: Palgrave Macmillan.

Dzur, A. W., & Olson, S. M. (2004). The value of community participation in restorative justice. *Journal of Social Philosophy, 35*(1), 91–107.

Farrow, K., & Prior, D. (2006). 'Togetherness'? Tackling anti-social behaviour through community engagement. *Criminal Justice Matters, 46*, 4–5.

Feenan, D. (2002). Justice in conflict: Paramilitary punishment in Ireland (north). *International Journal of the Sociology of Law, 30*, 151–172.

Feldman, A. (1991). *Formations of violence: The narrative of the body and political terror in Northern Ireland.* Chicago: Chicago University Press.

Ferme, M. C. (2001). *The underneath of things: Violence, history, and the everyday in Sierra Leone.* Berkeley: University of California Press.

Foster, J. (1995). Informal social control and community crime prevention. *British Journal of Criminology, 35*(4), 563–583.

Froestad, J., & Shearing, C. (2007). Conflict resolution in South Africa: A case study. In: G. Johnstone & D. Van Ness. (Eds), *Handbook of restorative justice* (pp. 534–556). UK: Willan Publishing.

Gastil, R. D. (1971). Homicide and a regional culture of violence. *American Sociological Review, 36*(3), 412–427.

Groff, L., & Smoker, P. (1996). Creating global/local cultures of peace. In: UNESCO (Ed.), *From a culture of violence to a culture of peace* (pp. 103–128). France: UNESCO Publishing.

Hamber, B. (1999). Have no doubt there is fear in the land: An exploration of continuing cycles of violence in South Africa. *South African Journal of Child and Adolescent Mental Health, 12*(1), 5–18.

Hamill, H. (2002). Victims of paramilitary punishments attacks in Belfast. In: C. Hoyle, R. Young & Centre for Criminological Research, University of Oxford (Eds), *New visions of crime victims* (pp. 49–70). Oxford and Portland, Oregon: Hart Publishing.

Hayes, B. C., & McAllister, I. (2001). Sowing dragon's teeth: Public support for political violence and paramilitarism in Northern Ireland. *Political Studies, 49*, 901–922.

Hayner, P. B. (1994). Fifteen truth commissions – 1974 to 1994: A comparative study. *Human Rights Quarterly, 16*(4), 597–655.

Hayner, P. B. (2001). *Unspeakable truths: Facing the challenge of truth commissions.* London: Routledge.

Helsinki Watch. (1992). *Children in Northern Ireland: Abused by security forces and paramilitaries.* US: Human Rights Watch.

Higgins, J., & Martin, O. (2003). *Violence and young people's security.* Hague Appeal for Peace: Partnership Organisation.

Higgins, K., & McElrath, K. (2000). The trouble with peace: The cease-fires and their impact on drug use among youth in Northern Ireland. *Youth and Society, 32*(1), 29–59.

Jarman, N. (2004). From war to peace? Changing patterns of violence in Northern Ireland, 1990–2003. *Terrorism and Political Violence, 16*(3), 420–438.

Kelman, H. C. (1990). Applying a human needs perspective to the practice of conflict resolution: The Israeli–Palestinian case. In: J. W. Burton (Ed.), *Conflict: Human needs theory.* New York: St. Martin's.

Knox, C., & Monaghan, R. (2002). *Informal justice in divided societies: Northern Ireland and South Africa.* New York: Palgrave Macmillan.

Kynoch, G. (2005). Crime, conflict and politics in transition-era South Africa. *African Affairs, 104*(416), 493–514.

Llewellyn, J. (2007). Truth commissions and restorative justice. In: G. Johnstone & D. Van Ness (Eds), *Handbook of restorative justice* (pp. 351–370). UK: Willan Publishing.

Llewellyn, J., & Howse, R. (1999). Institutions for restorative justice: The South African truth and reconciliation commission. *University of Toronto Law Review, 49*, 355–388.

MacGinty, R., & Darby, J. (2002). *Guns and government: The management of the Northern Ireland peace process*. London: Palgrave Macmillan.

McAuley, J. W. (2004). Peace and progress? Political and social change among young loyalists in Northern Ireland. *Journal of Social Issues, 60*(3), 541–562.

McEvoy, K. (2003). Beyond the metaphor: Political violence, human rights, and 'new' peacemaking criminology. *Theoretical Criminology, 7*(3), 319–346.

McEvoy, K., & Eriksson, A. (2006). Restorative justice in transition: Ownership, leadership and 'bottom-up' human rights. In: D. Sullivan & L. Tifft (Eds), *The handbook of restorative justice: Global perspectives* (pp. 321–336). London and New York: Routledge.

McEvoy, K., & Eriksson, A. (2008). Who owns justice? Community, state and the Northern Ireland transition. In: J. Shapland (Ed.), *Justice, community and civil society: A contested terrain*. Willan Publishing.

McEvoy, K., & Mika, H. (2001). Punishment, politics and praxis: Restorative justice and non-violent alternatives to paramilitary punishment. *Policing and Society, 11*(1), 359–382.

McEvoy, K., & Mika, H. (2002). Restorative justice and the critique of informalism in Northern Ireland. *British Journal of Criminology, 43*(3), 534–563.

McEvoy, K., & Newburn, T. (Eds). (2003). *Criminology, conflict resolution and restorative justice*. Basingstoke: Palgrave Macmillan.

Mika, H. (2006). *Community based restorative justice in Northern Ireland: An evaluation*. Belfast: Institute of Criminology and Criminal Justice, Queen's University.

Mika, H., & McEvoy, K. (2001). Restorative justice in conflict: Paramilitarism, community and the construction of legitimacy in Northern Ireland. *Contemporary Justice Review, 3*(4), 291–319.

Monaghan, R. (2002). The return of "captain moonlight": Informal justice in Northern Ireland. *Studies in Conflict and Terrorism, 25*, 41–56.

Monaghan, R. (2004). 'An imperfect peace': Paramilitary 'punishments' in Northern Ireland. *Terrorism and Political Violence, 16*(3), 439–461.

Napoleon, V. (2004). By whom, and by what processes, is restorative justice defined, and what bias might this introduce? In: H. Zehr & B. Toews (Eds), *Critical issues in restorative justice* (pp. 33–46). Monsey, New York, UK: Criminal Justice Press, Willan Publishing.

Neuffer, E. (2002). *The key to my neighbor: Seeking justice in Bosnia and Rwanda*. London: Bloomsbury.

Nowrojee, B. (2005). *"Your justice is too slow": Will the ICTR fail Rwanda's rape victims?* Geneva: United Nations Research Institute for Social Development.

O'Mahony, D., Chapman, T., & Doak, J. (2002). *Restorative cautioning: A study of police based restorative cautioning pilots in Northern Ireland* (No. 4). Belfast: Northern Ireland Statistics and Research Agency.

Pankhurst, D. (1999). Issues of justice and reconciliation in complex political emergencies: Conceptualising reconciliation, justice and peace. *Third World Quarterly, 20*(1), 239–255.

Ratuva, S. (2003). Re-inventing the cultural wheel: Reconceptualising restorative justice and peacebuilding in ethnically divided Fiji. In: S. Dinnen, A. Jowitt & T. Newton Cain (Eds), *A kind of mending: Restorative justice in the Pacific Islands* (pp. 149–163). Canberra, ACT: Pandanus Books.

Roberts, P., & McMillan, N. (2003). For criminology in international criminal justice. *Journal of International Criminal Justice, 1*(2), 315–338.

Roche, D. (2002). Restorative justice and the regulatory state in South African townships. *British Journal of Criminology, 42*(3), 514–533.

Roche, D. (2003). *Accountability in restorative justice*. Oxford: Oxford University Press.

Rupesinghe, K., & Rubio, M. (Eds). (1994). *The culture of violence*. New York: The United Nations University Press.

Ruth-Heffelbower, D. (2000). Indonesia: Restorative justice for healing a divided society. Paper Presented at the April 2000 "just Peace?" Conference in Auckland, New Zealand.

Shearing, C. (2001). Local capacity policing. In: J. Sarkin (Ed.), *Policing, crime and justice* (pp. 191–197). Brussels: Maklu.

Shearing, C., Cartwright, J., & Jenneker, M. (2006). A grass root governance model: South African peace committees. In: V. Luker, S. Dinnen & A. Patience (Eds), *Law, order and HIV/AIDS in Papua New Guinea*. Canberra: Pandanus.

Shirlow, P., & Murtagh, B. (2006). *Belfast: Segregation, violence and the city*. London: Pluto.

Silke, A. (2000). Drinks, drugs and rock 'n' roll: Financing loyalist terrorism in Northern Ireland – part two. *Studies in Conflict and Terrorism, 23*, 107–127.

Simpson, G. (1993). Women and children in violent South African townships. In: M. Motshekya & E. Delport (Eds), *Women and children's right in a violent South Africa* (pp. 3–13). Institute for Public Interest, Law and Research: Pretoria West.

Skelton, A. (2002). Restorative justice as a framework for juvenile justice reform: A South African perspective. *British Journal of Criminology, 42*, 496–513.

Sluka, J. (1989). *Hearts and minds, water and fish: Support for the IRA and the INLA in a Northern Irish Ghetto*. Greenwich, CT: Jai Press.

Staub, E. (1989). *The roots of evil: The origins of genocide and other group violence*. New York: Cambridge University Press.

Staub, E. (1996). The cultural-societal roots of violence: The examples of genocidal violence and of contemporary youth violence in the United States. *American Psychologist, 51*, 117–132.

Staub, E. (1999). The origins and prevention of genocide, mass killing and other collective violence. *Peace and Conflict: Journal of Peace Psychology, 5*, 303–337.

Staub, E. (2003). Notes on cultures of violence, cultures of caring and peace, and the fulfillment of basic human needs. *Political Psychology, 24*(1), 1–21.

Steenkamp, C. (2005). The legacy of war: Conceptualising a 'culture of violence' to explain violence after peace accords. *The Round Table, 94*(379), 253–267.

Sullivan, D., & Tifft, L. (1998). Criminology and peacemaking: A peace-orientated perspective on crime, punishment and justice that takes into account the needs of all. *The Justice Professional, 11*(1–2), 5–34.

Villa-Vincencio, C. (1999). A different kind of justice: The South African truth and reconciliation commission. *Contemporary Justice Review, 1*, 407–429.

Villa-Vicencio, C. (2006). Transitional justice, restoration, and prosecution. In: D. Sullivan & L. Tifft (Eds), *The handbook of restorative justice: A global perspective* (pp. 387–400). London and New York: Routledge.

Vogelman, L., & Lewis, S. (1993). Gang rape and the culture of violence in South Africa. *Der Uberblick, 2*, 39–42.

Waldorf, L. (2006). Rwanda's failing experiment in restorative justice. In: D. Sullivan & L. Tifft (Eds), *The handbook of restorative justice: A global perspective* (pp. 422–434). London and New York: Routledge.

Winston, T. (1997). Alternatives to punishment beatings and shootings in a loyalist community in Belfast. *Critical Criminology: An International Journal, 8*(1), 122–128.

GETTING BEYOND THE LIBERAL FEEL-GOOD: TOWARD AN ACCOUNTABILITY-BASED THEORETICAL RESEARCH PROGRAM FOR RESTORATIVE JUSTICE

J. Mitchell Miller, Christopher L. Gibson and John Byrd

ABSTRACT

Advocates of restorative justice have recently argued that this reform movement is ideologically diverse, perhaps because the potential for program expansion and the realization of funding support is largely dependent on mainstream normative criminal justice system processes. This chapter examines the ideological underpinnings that shape restorative programming to the conclusion that restorative justice is philosophically liberal. The liberal agenda of the restorative justice paradigm is assessed in terms of implications for societal benefit, traditional justice system goals, and the future of restorative justice. Unintended and counterproductive consequences of the left-leaning nature

Restorative Justice: From Theory to Practice
Sociology of Crime, Law and Deviance, Volume 11, 261–278
Copyright © 2008 by Emerald Group Publishing Limited
All rights of reproduction in any form reserved
ISSN: 1521-6136/doi:10.1016/S1521-6136(08)00411-9

of restorative justice are considered with particular emphasis on accountability. It is argued that the establishment of accountability-based theoretical research programs is necessary in order to further both theoretical and programmatic restorative justice initiatives.

INTRODUCTION

Restorative justice has emerged as a major international criminal justice movement over the last three decades, one that continues to gain momentum in multiple societal spheres. Restorative philosophy is evident throughout the juvenile and criminal justice systems in rehabilitative, punishment, victim services, and faith-based applications and certainly prominent in contemporary social science theory and philosophy. A literal plethora of books and articles generated in recent years give testimony to the bandwagon popularity of this "new" approach (Beck, Britto, & Andrews, 2007; Dorne, 2008; Zehr & Toews, 2004; Karp & Clear, 2002; Umbreit, Vos, Coates, & Brown, 2003; Johnstone, 2003; Weitekamp & Kerner, 2002; Sullivan & Tifft, 2001; Van Ness & Strong, 2006). While restorative justice, relative to other justice system strategies and directions, is still considered to be a fairly new orientation to addressing the problems of delinquency and crime, it is similar to the 1960s and 1970s American grassroots social movements in terms of desire for policy change. Often characterized as justice "reform", restorative justice is an alternative paradigm of justice that contrasts sharply with traditional retributive and "just deserts" models of justice (Bazemore & Schiff, 2005).

Whereas crime is normally defined in terms of legal violations that are deemed transgressions against the state, restorative justice emphasizes interpersonal violations and related injury. The focus of justice from the restorative perspective is thus on solving problems derived from crime, such as specifying liability so as to effect offender responsibility and the attachment of related obligations. Rather than establishing blame and guilt so as to affect the delivery of punishment per se, the restorative immediate, short-term end game is harm reparation. Dialogue, negotiation, and the harmonious resolution of cases are touted as an alternative to mainstream normative legal processes. Perhaps most importantly, restitution and the reconciliation of parties (victims and offenders) replaces punishment for either retributive or deterrence purposes as the primary basis by which to asses whether justice is realized. Reconciliation is viewed as a utilitarian mechanism for ending criminal careers and reducing the personal and social harms of crime. As such, it is not the goals, at least the objective of crime reduction, of restorative justice that is alternative to traditional justice system objectives as much as the process.

By emphasizing reconciliation, restorative justice seeks to repair social injury – an outcome often neglected if not ignored in formal legal processes where one social injury is typically replaced with another in an eye-for-an-eye manner. Such reconciliation is facilitated through community-based restorative processes that encourage holistic stakeholder involvement. In the conventional system, discourse is largely between the state and passive offenders with less attention to victims who assume a primary role in the restorative paradigm. Also, the normative interpretation of offender accountability (i.e., the delivery of punishment deemed proportionate to offense) is redefined in terms of desire for offenders to both understand the impact of their wrongful behavior and participate in decisions regarding the best course of action by which to make things right.

This chapter recognizes the conceptual and programmatic breadth and diversity of restorative justice programs, as well as its speedy ascent. Social policies, practices, and movements that realize fast popularity typically result in widespread program development that unfortunately yield unintended consequences, primarily because: (1) movements are ahead of scientific support and thus proceed without the benefit of a solid knowledge base (i.e., reliance on research-based best practices) and (2) rapid program proliferation invites a lack of implementation intensity. These two issues are often difficult to divorce for implementation intensity issues are assessed according to compliance with best-practices benchmarks that, if nonexistent, may not be discernable.

Although some restorative justice scholars have advocated for the development of theory and policy based on lessons learned from practice (e.g., Bazemore & Schiff, 2005), the bulk of the extant literature on restorative justice suggests that the issue of accountability is seldom prioritized. This is not to say that restorativists have ignored accountability as several works have been devoted to the topic (Roche, 2003; Sherman & Strang, 2004). These works, somewhat ironically, are primarily commentaries, literature reviews, and, at best, meta-analyses giving evidence to the lack of and need for accountability in the restorative justice movement more so than empirical work actually expanding the evaluation knowledge base on what works, why, and in what problem contexts. These efforts have been focused more on European than American restorative initiatives, perhaps because the movement is better rooted in the collective justice mindset outside of the United States which seems more reluctant to embrace policy platforms other than those on a rehabilitation–deterrence continuum (Gavrielides, 2007).

Restorative justice scholars and critics alike acknowledge that the general progression of the movement, especially in its early days, has transpired *sans* serious embracement of a research-based, best-practices orientation. Given the popularity of restorative justice and the widespread implementation of related juvenile and adult offender programming, knowing if and in what manner restorative tactics work is seemingly a basic focus and foremost concern for the future of the restorative justice movement. Rather than engage program evaluation and empirical scrutiny, restorative justice advocates have, by and large, focused on and settled for unchecked program growth, perhaps measuring success as greater presence, without demanding more science. This is understandable in practitioner-social activist contexts, which in restorative justice programming often means other than justice agency functionaries such as non-profit, faith-based, and private as well as state social service providers of wrap-around services, because doing so literally expands the market for their services. Academic restorative justicians, however, have been equally, and largely inexcusably, guilty of spirited social activism and advocacy – their guilt based in full knowledge that adequate science is lacking. Of course, this is a sweeping generalization that is more accurate in some areas than others for restorative justice is certainly not monolithic and, as many have observed, can and does mean different things across stakeholders. A recent United Nations funded study whose primary purpose was the measurement of the gap between restorative justice theory and practice, for example, found that more than 82% of practitioners surveyed believed that when "restorativists" refer to restorative justice, they do not use it in the same context (Gavrielides, 2007).

While variably defined and diverse in application, restorative justice is more or less ideologically singular. Below, after reviewing the philosophical basis and natural appeal of restorative justice, we consider how its ideological underpinnings are inconsistent with and unwelcoming of science and have stunted its potential to realize more meaningful and general justice system utilization. More meaningful utilization, defined as funding allocations, program development, implementation, and modifications derived from accountability, is arguably essential if restorative justice is to effect optimal social betterment and evolve as a mainstream rather than alternative justice paradigm. This means that restorative justice must embrace the goals of the system and work within its realities. Restorative justice advocates seem reluctant, and consistently critical, of major system agenda points. Professor Gordon Bazemore, for example, in touting one of many existing restorative justice textbooks lobbied for the development of future restorative justice programming based on other than recidivism indicators (the foremost outcome measure by which the vast majority of criminal justice program effectiveness are gauged), particularly intermediate outcomes presumably reflecting the levels of program activity and participation for offenders, victims, and the community (Van Ness & Strong, 2006).

The sheer number of programs and the breadth of their application, perhaps at first glance, might suggest that restorative justice has already become institutionally embedded. But recognition of the reasons for rapid expansion, such as fiscal expediency, quasi-formal service delivery, and localized community political simplicity, may well be undermined by scientific refutation in the near future. This certainly is not apt to happen overnight for the restorative justice movement has both so outdistanced and devalued scientific scrutiny that it will take several years for science to catch up. Moreover, the infusion of science into the restorative justice movement is likely to be sporadic and findings that limit or discourage restorative practices are likely to be in selective areas with positive scientific reinforcement in others. Relatedly, recommendations for a theoretical research program consistent with mainstream justice system functions are presented below as a course of action by which to both congeal and advance the restorative justice paradigm.

The Nature and Appeal of Restorative Justice

To some, restorative justice is but a synonym for transformative justice (Sullivan & Tifft, 2001). Given the inequities and shortcomings of the formal justice systems in the United States, particularly the concentration of state justice resources on the disenfranchised (what Marxists and other critical criminologists would consider state-production of crime and the perpetuation of a socio-economically disadvantaged criminal class) and the widespread failure of both rehabilitation and deterrence efforts as indicated by minimally responsive recidivism and relapse rates, it is easy to understand the general appeal of and attraction to restorative justice philosophy. Restorative justice, at a minimum, is a plausible alternative to addressing serious and persistent social problems seemingly resistant to other conventional policies and practices. Its rise, however, is far more than simple alternative. There are numerous additional reasons for the restorative justice surge. It is, for example, human nature to solve problem. In the United States, at least, such tendency is manifested in the pioneer spirit, participatory government, and a democratic ethos.

There are certain unifying themes which, collectively, are inherently indicative of the restorative justice paradigm despite the diversity of various individual restorative programs. While some view the increasing interest in restorative justice as a throwback to 1970s rehabilitative philosophy, it is important to recognize that the underlying philosophies and principles of restorative justice comprise a different and important evolution in society's response to crime. Van Ness and Strong (2006), for example, identify four "cornerpost values" that distinguish restorative justice and guide how restorative processes are managed:

- *Encounter*: Affected parties are given the opportunity to meet the other parties in a safe environment to discuss the offense, harms, and appropriate sanction responses.
- *Amends*: Those responsible for the harm resulting from the offense are also responsible for repairing it to the extent possible.
- *Reintegration*: The parties are given the means and opportunity to rejoin their communities as whole, contributing members.
- *Inclusion*: Affected parties are invited to directly shape and engage in restorative practices.

These values are observable in major types of restorative justice programs. Three key programs have influenced the development of restorative justice:

- *Victim–offender mediation* began as a program to impact offenders and help them understand the harm they caused to victims and as a community-based program rather than one carried out by the formal criminal justice system. In the Texas prison system, for example, it has evolved into such areas as allowing victims and survivors of serious violent crimes the opportunity to meet with their offender for the purpose of achieving some level of healing.
- *Conferencing* differs from victim-offender mediation notably by the inclusion of more people in the meeting, such as family members, supporters and government representatives.
- *Circles* have indigenous roots and are variously known as sentencing circles, community circles, and healing circles. They are the most inclusive of the three processes with interested members of the community allowed

to participate even if they have no relationship with the victim or offender.

The above values and program features combine for "a process whereby all the parties with a stake in a particular offense come together to resolve collectively how to deal with the aftermath of the offense and its implications for the future" (Marshall, 1999). Many have gone further in describing restorative justice and how it differs from a justice system based on the concept of retribution by identifying three principles that govern the implementation of restorative justice and necessary systemic reform (Weitekamp & Kerner, 2002; Umbreit et al., 2003). First, justice requires that we work to heal victims, offenders, and communities that have been injured by crime. Second, victim, offenders, and communities should have the opportunity for active involvement in the justice process as early and as fully as they wish. Third, we must rethink the relative roles and responsibilities of government and community in promoting justice. From the restorative perspective, government is responsible for preserving a just order and the community for establishing a just peace.

Restorative justice, then, is very much community justice. Communities feel they know what is best in terms of their justice needs and how to define and solve their own problems. This is fundamentally American, real political bearing at the local level, and evident in the definitional nature of many restorative justice programs and processes. Elements of conferencing and healing peacemaking circles, for example, are rooted in the problem-solving practices of Native Americans wherein stakeholders have voice in justice processes that simultaneously affirm the value of community self-regulation. Such participatory models are seldom the case in our formal justice system. In most restorative justice processes, stakeholders have the opportunity to participate, both direct or primary victims and community members who suffer collateral harm from crime. Such elements in regulatory process are clearly democratic – people have voice and thus feel valued and have real opportunities to impact the outcome of cases, perhaps in ways that leave them feeling like the system is a collective enterprise wherein their input and views actually matter. In a sense, this is democracy functioning informally at the most basic level.

The current Western criminal justice system's formal protocol of prosecution with defense attorneys, prosecutors, and subsequent impersonal sentencing processes suddenly becomes personal and victims are no longer ignored. So, the community-based and grassroots nature of conferencing between offenders and victims, the sanctioning of delinquents by peers rather than formal authorities in youth or teen courts, and a general goal of punishing so as to reintegrate instead of "scare straight" are, when compared to the more rigid and legalistic proceedings of the traditional system, inherently divergent from the status quo and thus liberal in nature.

Criminologists and sociologists of deviance have long acknowledged the saliency of informal social control mechanisms and have often deemed them to be as or more viable than formal justice system approaches (Miller, Tewksbury, & Schreck, 2008). Informal social control features celerity, the leverage of normative consensus (holistically, not just in strict legal terms), and is not dependent on a contingencies correlated with system proceedings and resource availability. Moreover, the need for social acceptance and approval, the avoidance of shame and ridicule, a general desire to belong, and the formation and perpetuation of social bonding are all powerful social forces that, according to restorative justice, can be utilized and leveraged to address crime in ways that reduce harm, serve the demands of restitution, and minimize future victimization by bringing offenders back into the fold of an embracing and forgiving societal mainstream. Such an approach is thought to be more effective than the depersonalizing warehousing of prisoners or the escalation of young criminal careers caught up in a justice juggernaut where meaningful rehabilitation either does not exist or is delivered in an image over substance fashion. That is, incarceration that serves only to incapacitate offenders from the larger society while intensifying criminal networks and knowledge in prison settings is, at best, a short-term non-solution.

If nothing else, less formal versions of social control typically feature efficiency. Most restorative justice programs rely heavily, if not primarily, on volunteers who endorse program philosophy and strive to make a difference – in lieu of paid professional criminal justice practitioners. Offenders channeled into restorative justice programs are not "passed off" entirely to citizen collectives, rather restorative justice programs typically utilize formal justice system functionaries in conjunction with volunteers and stakeholders and thus have, though variable, some degree of oversight. Nonetheless, considerable savings provide relief from federal and state budgets heavily rooted in justice expenditures and generate popular culture support among taxpayers to the extent that programs are not overly characterized as soft on crime. While this fiscal conservatism would seemingly appeal across the whole of society, restorative justice program-ming support can be all but lost if service delivery and case disposition is vested in social programming frequently equated with leniency for offenders.

Liberal, Conservative, or Other?

The American undergraduate is typically first exposed to the ideas of restorative justice in introductory criminal justice or criminology courses. As Peter B. Kraska (2004) has noted in arguing for the dichotomization of theories of crime and theories of justice, restorative justice, while clearly in the latter category, is almost always grouped with peacemaking criminology and other theories deemed "radical" or anti-system. In reality, the vast majority of restorative justice programs are not altogether at odds with the system, instead they attempt to augment it by delivering services where gaps may exist due to lack of resources or vision. Such labeling as a "conflict" perspective is curiously at odds with the goals and aspirations of a movement vested in the holistic repair of harm and the reintegration of offenders whose cognitive and value systems have somehow been reworked through the effects of restorative justice to more pro-social and non-criminal outcomes. Clearly, the aspects of restorative justice at odds with the system have been over-emphasized at the expense of the philosophy's other dimensions and attributes. Nonetheless, classification of restorative justice with conflict theories, though erroneous, serves to immediately characterize the philosophy and movement as far left liberal.

In these undergraduate classes where students first hear of restorative justice, Braithwaite's (1989) famous reintegrative shaming theory is a common point of departure into restorative philosophy. In short, focus is less on the original causes of criminal offending (as would be expected in a justice theory) and more on the nature of system processing. Offenders are made accountable through the very powerful force of social shaming for misbehavior by peer groups and the larger community. Shaming, effected through formal mechanisms like youth courts wherein delinquents are subjected to embarrassment (and sanctioning) by peers, communicates the social unacceptability of delinquent acts and constitutes an intangible form of punishment. Offenders may escape some or all sanctioning elements of the process of the formal system, but not the social ostracism of the restorative approach. This is ideally coupled with tangible forms of punishment as well, such as community service work, fiscal restitution, and victim apologies that further increase offender embarrassment and elevate cognizance of generated harm. Rather than seek additional punishment, it is presumed that offenders will be made aware of their crimes and related social harm (i.e., victimization). In contrast to the we versus them reality of the formal system's adversarial and impersonal nature (where offenders are assembly-line processed and avoid shame, embarrassment, and the guilt associated with victim confrontation) restorative justice contends that these practices, collectively, effect accountability.

More importantly, rather than ensuring deeper system involvement through penalizing and harsh sentencing, offenders receive mercy and forgiveness (rooted in a liberal outlook of presumed awareness, social reciprocity, and a harmonious society). In return for this mercy, forgiveness and a "second-chance", it is purported that offenders experience remorse, opt out of recidivism, and are reintegrated into mainstream society as productive citizens. In gross oversimplification, mercy is exchanged for future legal compliance with offenders ideally desisting from future offending.

Restorative justice programs assume a natural dichotomy of sorts based on where offenders are situated in the system. Shaming and reintegration-based programs, constituting one-half of this dichotomy, essentially aim to prevent future criminality (as well as repair harm and effect restitution) by repairing severed social bonds that are thought to be the focal cause of offending in the first place. In as much as these programs are effective, restorative justice has great potential to lower crime rates, minimize future victimization, and enhance the quality of community life at minimal costs to taxpayers. Shaming is not always an element in reintegration-oriented programming and focus may be as much on peacemaking and healing victims as on crime prevention. In fact, crime prevention itself is rarely a pronounced theme of restorative programs – it being a concept more reflective of traditional criminal justice goals – but rehabilitation and delivery of services to offenders are both principle features and desired primary outcomes.

The second half of this dichotomy involves restorative justice programs that are almost entirely victim and family focused. Though restorative justice advocates of mediation and peacemaking approaches typically claim broader benefits, efforts to help, for example, family members of homicide victims realize psychological relief if not closure. Such approaches are far more limited in terms of capacity for effecting general criminal justice system goals. While a calloused characterization, such mediation and conferencing efforts, though altruistic and no doubt helpful to those suffering from the loss of loved ones, have very limited potential for macro-level social betterment in terms of crime prevention, restitution, or rehabilitation. Typically situated in a faith-based context, such efforts involve face-to-face encounters between victims' families and their assailants. These conferences, whether in group circle or more private formats, almost always occur in correctional settings.

Restorative justice service providers seek, then, to address the needs of victims and their families and to generally instigate or further healing processes. Other goals include the assumption of responsibility by violent offenders for the harm they have caused that may or may not involve apologies. In a sense, this approach is a form of social work and talk therapy wherein offenders come to terms with their acts and, presumably, accept responsibility. Victims, in turn, have the opportunity to see, often for the first time or the first time out of court, offenders and pose questions of why crimes were committed and even solicit details about the crimes. While learning the details of terrible and often gruesome events seems better left alone, reports abound that the process does indeed facilitate healing. Many of these conferences are facilitated by faith-driven groups, if not various religions directly. These service providers view the restorative process as the right thing to do and applications of religious principles such as mercy, forgiveness, and the ease of the psychological suffering of victims. Such as advocates, like former Wisconsin Supreme Court Justice Janine Geske, teach law students these practices and unapologetically merge their own spiritual convictions with restorative justice to the extent that the practice of one is indistinguishable from expression of the other (Geske, 2006). Critics cannot help but wonder if the foremost beneficiaries of these efforts are the advocates themselves who clearly realize a sense of important accomplishment and a pronounced "liberal feel-good" stemming from a belief that they are doing the "right thing" as specified by Judean-Christian values. To the extent that such practices come to define perceptions of restorative justice, critical question arise. Should restorative justice focused on offender–victim reconciliation and healing be funded, in light of virtually no potential to reduce crime – either in the general public or even at the individual offender level as such offenders are serving lengthy sentences, if not life or even death sentences? What are the political ramifications for merging religion into the process? Should human and other resources expended on these activities be better allocated to address offenders likely to rejoin society in rehabilitative context?

While both of these restorative program types are seemingly inherently liberal, restorative justice has been argued to be ideologically neutral (Dorne, 2008). Consideration of differences between left/liberal and right/conservative views as they relate to justice help determination of whether restorative justice is right- or left-leaning and, more importantly, what implications result from ideological orientations for practice and programming. Liberalism entails antiauthoritarian views and sympathy for the economically and socially downtrodden, be they offenders or victims. From this perspective, the world is in many ways unfair so reform is generally welcomed and embraced. Restorative justice, to the extent that it is both alternative and reformist, ostensibly is liberal or left-leaning in nature. In contrast, conservativism involves maintenance of traditional practices and existing relations, the status quo, and respect for authority and rules.

In the context of criminal justice, it is fairly easy to delineate between liberal and conservative viewpoints. From the conservative perspective, criminals: (1) lack self-control, (2) consciously choose to commit the majority of their offenses, (3) use poverty as an excuse for crime, (4) respond to the certainty, swiftness, and severity of punishment, and (5) are fundamentally out to beat the system. On the other hand, liberals tend to view criminals as: (1) natural products of disadvantaged environments and negative social influences, (2) "salvageable" through rehabilitation, and (3) receptive to opportunities for pro-social change. Thus restorative justice, to the extent that it is a challenge to conventional practices and policies, is clearly apt to be defined, understood and supported differently based on ideological and political subscription. In that proponents of restorative justice believe that there is a need for alternatives to standard normative criminal justice practices, they are, presumably, liberally oriented.

The overwhelming humanitarian nature of restorative justice seemingly negates the need for discussion of its ideological basis. Virtually all of its characteristics and practices suggest a liberal orientation-forgiveness, mercy, social bonding, reintegration, mediation – none of these are conservative in nature. The crime prevention properties of reintegrative shaming theory are apparently ideologically neutral, but only at first glance and certainly not intentionally. John Braithwaite, the founder of reintegrative shaming theory, has stated that "viewing restorative justice as "crime control" only impoverishes its mission" (1989, p. 136). He instead lobbies for the broad application of restorative principles across virtually all life dimensions, including family, employment, politics, and, particularly liberal, the distribution of resources. Taking issue with the distribution of resources suggests that existing methods are inadequate and that macro-level change is needed. To the extent that such change is related to racism, sexism, and classism, a liberal agenda exists.

We are not interested in engaging a general debate here over the ideological values and goals of the criminal justice system as a benchmark by which to compare restorative justice. Such a comparison would certainly have utility for examination of levels of political support for restorative justice and related funding allocations. Advocates of restorative justice understand that in order to further the movement they must work within existing bureaucratic and legal realities of the juvenile and criminal justice systems. This means that restorative justice is more or less dependent on conservatives and liberals alike and in order to maintain operations and, especially, grow, it is vital that those in the movement assume ideological neutral postures. Below, we observe that such a posture is something of a false front; that is, restorative justice is predominantly ideologically liberal and that its liberalism is counterproductive to restorative justice in terms of hampering its ability to more widely impact the social problem of crime. Identification of false assumptions that unfortunately characterize restorative justice provides a basis for the establishment of an applied criminological theoretical research program useful for both confirming the empirical saliency of some restorative justice elements and realizing the limits of others.

Toward a Theoretical Research Program for Restorative Justice

Before considering specific elements and research questions comprising a theoretical research program for restorative justice, we briefly survey the general nature of theoretical research programs. A theoretical research program is an anatomic "set of related theories" (Wagner, 1984, p. 90) which is collectively engaged in by scientists. The theoretical research program's orienting strategy controls the types of issues and strategies employed by researchers. For example, restorative justice programs are concerned with crime prevention in some contexts, victim healing in others, and both in still other applications. Are these issues congruent or is utilitarian choice required in order to move forward, both in political and social scientific terms?

A theoretical research program is also composed of core and auxiliary formal theory sets, both of which may be falsifiable (Berger & Zelditch, 1993). Program growth occurs either through composition of the sets or in the organization, clarity, or refinement of elements already in the set. A theoretical research program also leads to theory growth in five possible ways: elaboration, variation, proliferation, integration, and competition. *Elaboration* occurs when a new theory assumes a structure similar to an old theory but is "more comprehensive, more precise, more rigorous, or has greater empirical support". *Variation* occurs when a new theory is a slight modification of a prior theory, typically conflicting over a small part of a domain. *Proliferation* occurs when a new theory adopts a structure similar to an old theory but the predictions apply to different explanatory domains.

Integration occurs when a new theory consolidates two other theories and subsumes many (though typically not all) of the predictions of the old theories. Finally, *competition* occurs when a new theory attempts to displace another by establishing its comparative inadequacy. Each aspect of theoretical growth has useful properties, but, of the five, competition has proven the least useful: Competing social scientific theories have rarely been resolved by direct competition, and sociologists and other social scientists will often cling to inadequate theories even under relatively clear demonstrations of inadequacy. These unfortunate reality means that popular perspectives are apt to be accepted without sufficient empirical confirmation and major or driving conceptual elements recycled and extended to additional topics. If faulty, the potential for greater harm through misinformation dissemination will result.

Therefore, unless the theory and testing processes are rigorous and the theoretical statements falsifiable, a theoretical research program can easily further complicate and confuse a general theoretical perspective or philosophy. The very fact that calls are made for a theoretical research program in a given area likely indicates either pure or applied theoretical stagnation. To the extent that restorative justice is an applied, utilitarian movement rather than a philosophy (although in fact, it is both), determination of a theoretical research program carries the potential to move a perspective beyond ideological deadlock. More theory without research, sound empirical support, has been abundant throughout the restorative justice movement and the time is past due for evaluative scrutiny of restorative programs toward the focused goal of establishing account-ability. Beyond simple quasi-experimental, before-after outcome assess-ments of whether various restorative models work or not, and to what extent, mixed-methodological research models are needed to determine the saliency of specific restorative concepts.

Engaging a theoretical research program for restorative justice will force choices – the emphasis of some restorative justice goals and programs over others. This will naturally result from the infusion of science. There will be winners and losers as some programs will be found effective and others will not. Funding implications and political choices will likely result. Ramifica-tions may be as myopic as ideal timeframes for mediation or healing processes or as broad as pitting the relative value over program types, such as those categorized in the aforementioned dichotomy. Assuming empirical confirmation for both, it is probable that policy makers, agency adminis-trators and the general public will favor crime prevention approaches that offer broad social benefit over victim service activities.

Regardless, restorative justice is in dire need of theoretical research programs that distance the movement away from its current limited, social work-like version of input over output and process over outcome style of social science. The new premium should be accountability. To the extent that accountability modifies restorative justice, programming toward the realization of conventional criminal justice goals (e.g., recidivism and relapse reductions, crime prevention factoring into enhanced quality of life), restorative justice has the potential to be less alternative and more mainstream. This does not mean wholesale ideological sellout, just removal of some liberal baggage that both actually hinders the growth of restorative justice due to ideological polarization and practices not based in or confirmed by sound research. In this manner, the movement can progress beyond the liberal "feel-good" and realize its true potential.

The call for the development of restorative justice theoretical research programs is not as simple or as limited as a call for program evaluation. The community and grassroots nature of the majority of restorative justice programs often means programs are funded from a variety of philanthropic, faith-based, private foundation and non-profit sources, as well as state and federal agencies. Accordingly, program evaluation is frequently neither a required program component nor an affordable luxury. A greater number of restorative justice programs should be evaluated across program type. However, more fundamental pure research has been largely by-passed in restorative justice relative to other leading justice paradigms and theoretical perspectives. Below, we focus briefly on Braithwaite's reintegrative shaming theory by way of exampling a series of research questions toward a theoretical research program. An important point here is that a theoretical research program for restorative justice will necessarily be pluralistic – that is, multiple programs will address various dimensions of restorative justice. Some will be pure research and others will be applied research oriented and specific research foci will vary across juvenile and adult programs. The type of theoretical research program we are advocating, then is a step-wise process involving the confirmation of basic theoretical assumptions prior to assessment of these concepts in action through program evaluation. Otherwise, researchers will struggle with determinations of whether observed program shortcomings or outright failure are attributable to theoretical or implementation failure.

A theoretical research program for reintegrative shaming theory, for illustrative and consideration purposes, should examine the viability of driving concepts assumed to be valid. First, are offenders responsive to shaming? Perhaps some are and others are not. Social learning and cultural transmission theories suggest otherwise. The social shame and related ostracism resulting from the same delinquent act, shoplifting for example, is likely to be viewed differently across the social strata. What is condemned and generates scorn in one neighborhood may be seen as little more than bad luck in another. Beyond pure sociological considerations germane to social shaming, perhaps individual and biosocial factors affect variable responses to shaming within similar social environments. At a more macro level of analysis, how does the homogeneity or heterogeneity of communities shape definitions of crime, deviance, and respect for authority and related determinations of what is taboo and thus subject to shaming. In terms of sanctioning, how does shaming vary by gender, race, and other social variables and with what results?

In addition to considering the nature of shaming, what about the equally central concept of social reintegration? Given the vast overrepresentation of the poor, undereducated, and otherwise disadvantaged among the criminal class, as well as the elements of the social bond (e.g., attachment, commitment, and belief in the conventional order), perhaps it is a false assumption that offenders were ever effectively socially bonded in the first place. The theory presumes that crime is, in part, a function of severed pro-social bonds. However, it may well be that such social bonds never truly existed in the first place. Efforts to repair nonexistent mental constructs are clearly in vain and likely better replaced with a more storative form of bonding intended to establish social bonds that were either not developed or underdeveloped during offenders socialization and maturation processes.

Last, do offenders, with their differentially associated social learning in criminal subcultural contexts, have the ability to define and internalize forgiveness and mercy? And, if so, do they genuinely see the value resulting from leniency and the opportunity for societal integration or do they play along so as to escape harsher punishment. Recidivism rates, though unpopular in restorative justice, would certainly be a strong indicator of effectiveness. In as much as minimizing social harm is a major objective of restorative programming, whether or not future crimes and related victimization occurs is seemingly a vital indicator. Here accountability becomes relevant for if offenders are not deterred and see restorative justice as a means of beating the system, it is likely that more crime will occur. Moreover, the absence of deterrence or rehabilitation may even be counterproductive as offenders perceive minimal consequences for behavior, thus making crime more worthwhile due to limited and non-threatening sanctioning.

The point here is not to exhaustively identify the questions specific to reintegrative shaming theory, nor to consider the answers to the above questions. Rather, these questions, collectively, establish a research protocol by which to assess both pure and applied research questions central to the testing of theoretical concepts and propositions. The answers are critical to both ascertaining specific overall theoretical accuracy and the value of utilizing concepts found within theories that might be used in more isolated fashion or utilized in integrated theoretical approaches. While the degree of pure and applied symmetry will no doubt vary across theoretical research programs in different areas and purposes throughout the restorative justice movement, the time is past due for the establishment of these research protocols. The future of the restorative justice paradigm may well depend on their development, for, in American society, to be scientific is to be highly valued.

REFERENCES

Bazemore, G., & Schiff, M. (2005). *Juvenile justice reform and restorative justice: Building theory and policy from practice*. Portland, OR: Willan Publishing.

Beck, E., Britto, S., & Andrews, A. (2007). *In the shadow of death: Restorative justice and death row families*. New York, NY: Oxford University Press.

Berger, J., & Zelditch, M., Jr. (Eds). (1993). *Theoretical research programs: Studies in the growth of theory*. Stanford, CA: Stanford University Press.

Braithwaite, J. (1989). *Crime, shame and reintegration*. Cambridge, UK: Cambridge University Press.

Dorne, C. K. (2008). *Restorative justice in the United States*. New Jersey: Pearson/Prentice Hall.

Gavrielides, T. (2007). *Restorative justice theory and practice: Addressing the discrepancy*. Monsey, NY: Criminal Justice Press.

Geske, J. (2006). Why do I teach restorative justice to law students? *Marquette Law Review, 89*(1), 327–334.

Johnstone, G. (2003). *A restorative justice reader: Texts, sources, context*. Cullompton, Devon, UK: Willan.

Karp, D. R., & Clear, T. R. (Eds). (2002). *What is community justice: Case studies of restorative justice and community supervision*. Thousand Oaks, CA: Sage.

Kraska, P. B. (2004). *Theorizing criminal justice: Eight essential orientations*. Prospect Heights, IL: Waveland Press.

Marshall, T. (1999). *Restorative justice: An overview*. London: Home Office Research Development and Statistics Directorate.

Miller, J. M., Tewksbury, R., & Schreck, C. J. (2008). *Criminological theory: A brief introduction* (2nd ed.). Boston, MA: Allyn and Bacon.

Roche, D. (2003). *Accountability in restorative justice*. New York: Oxford University Press.

Sherman, L. W., & Strang, H. (2004). Restorative justice: What we know and how we know it. Jerry Lee Program on Randomized Trials in Restorative Justice. Philadelphia, PA.

Sullivan, D., & Tifft, L. (2001). *Restorative justice: Healing the foundations of our everyday lives.* Monsey, NY: Criminal Justice Press.

Umbreit, M. S., Vos, B., Coates, R. B., & Brown, K. A. (2003). *Facing violence the path of restorative justice and dialogue.* Monsey, NY: Criminal Justice Press.

Van Ness, D. W., & Strong, K. H. (2006). *Restoring justice: An introduction to restorative justice* (3rd ed.). Florence, Kentucky: Lexis Nexis.

Wagner, D. G. (1984). *The growth of sociological theories.* Beverly Hills, CA: Sage.

Weitekamp, E. G. M., & Kerner, H.-J. (2002). *Restorative justice: Theoretical foundations.* Cullompton, Devon, UK: Willan.

Zehr, H., & Toews, B. (Eds). (2004). *Critical issues in restorative justice.* Monsey, NY: Criminal Justice Press.

SUBJECT INDEX

Accountability, 33, 169, 172, 178–180, 191, 194, 196–203, 235, 261–264, 270, 274–276

Anomie, 47

Cognitive-behavioral, 146, 150

Collective interest, 8, 19, 23

Collective justice, 263

Conferencing, 6, 61–62, 82, 86, 89, 101–102, 172–173, 175, 214, 244, 266–267, 270

Corporate crime, 209–211, 215–216, 224

Corporate regulation, 211, 215, 217–219

Counseling, 20, 143–144, 146

Cultures of violence, 231–233, 235–237, 239, 241, 243–247, 249, 251, 253, 255

Deterrence, 65, 94, 127, 147, 191, 203, 210–211, 215–216, 219, 262, 264–265, 276

Differential association, 142, 146

Discrimination, 7, 17

Diversion, 12, 43, 86, 90, 148, 189

Faith-based mentoring, 139, 141, 143, 145, 147, 149, 151, 153, 155, 157–160

Globalization, 89

Implementation intensity, 204, 263

Indigenous justice, 4–6, 9–13, 17–18, 20, 24–25

Inequality, 3–4, 9, 14, 16, 22, 85, 253

Irish Republican Army, (IRA), 32, 34, 36–41, 44–48, 50–51, 55, 232, 244–246, 252, 255

Loyalist, 33, 35–36, 41, 44–47, 49–53, 55, 232, 238, 240–241, 247, 251, 253–255

Maori, 63, 87, 93

Mediation, 5, 17, 40–43, 61, 63, 145, 172–174, 177, 179, 195, 214, 244, 266, 270, 272, 274

Milieu, 99, 101, 103, 105–109, 111, 113, 115, 117, 119, 121, 123, 125–130

Mortality, 101, 127

Organizational defendants, 209, 211

Paramilitary, 32–37, 39–41, 43, 47–48, 50, 52–55, 231–234, 239–241, 243–249, 252–253, 255–256

Peacemaking, 10, 43, 52, 63, 149, 214, 267, 269–270

Peer norming, 191

Pluralism, 209, 211, 213, 215, 217, 219, 221, 223

Prison ministries, 143

Profit, 177, 209, 211, 213, 215, 217, 219, 221, 223, 264, 275

Program evaluation, 100, 107–108, 127, 129–130, 151, 168, 264, 275

Punishment beatings, 35, 46, 246

Rational choice, 219

Realpolitik, 32, 53

Recidivism, 20, 99–101, 103, 108–112, 118–131, 140–141, 145, 149, 151, 154, 160, 174, 194–195, 197–203, 223, 265, 270, 275–276

Reconciliation, 12, 16, 59–61, 69–72, 76, 88, 94, 145, 148–149, 177, 212, 219, 262–263, 271

Regulatory agencies, 215–216, 218, 224

Rehabilitation, 25, 99, 144–151, 160, 210, 213, 264–265, 268, 270, 272, 276

Reintegration, 42, 81, 88, 93, 139–140, 144–145, 148, 150–151, 171, 185, 193, 203, 212, 214, 266, 269–270, 272, 276

Religiosity, 141–142

Reparation, 15–16, 67, 71–72, 169, 178, 243, 249, 262

Republican, 32, 35–36, 38–41, 44–47, 49–52, 54, 147, 232, 238–239, 245, 251–255

Restorative justice, 1, 3–6, 9–10, 12–18, 20, 22, 24–26, 31, 34–35, 40–44, 48–55, 59–61, 63, 65, 67–69, 71–73, 75–77, 81–82, 84, 86, 88, 90, 92, 94, 99–103, 105, 107, 130–131, 139, 141, 143–149, 151–153, 155, 157, 159–161, 167–178, 180–182, 184–185, 189, 191, 193, 195–197, 199, 201, 203–204, 207, 209, 211–215, 218–223, 231–239, 241–247, 249–256, 261–277

Retributive justice, 168

Selection bias, 101, 107, 109, 129

Self-regulation, 216, 224, 267

Shaming, 145, 191–192, 203–204, 211, 213–215, 219–223, 269–270, 272, 275–277

Sinn Fein, 32–33, 41, 48, 50, 51

Social bonding, 142, 146, 191–192, 268, 272

Social justice, 9, 48, 74–76, 213

Social learning, 130, 141–142, 146, 275–276

Techniques of neutralization, 218

Theoretical research program, 261–262, 265, 273–275, 277

Victim-offender mediation (VOM), 61–62, 172, 214, 244, 266

White-collar crime, 209, 211, 215, 218–224

Youth authority, 191

Youth courts, 12, 189–195, 197–204, 269